# Teaching Confucianism

## AAR
AMERICAN ACADEMY OF RELIGION

### TEACHING RELIGIOUS STUDIES SERIES

SERIES EDITOR
Susan Henking, Hobart and William Smith Colleges

A Publication Series of
The American Academy of Religion
and
Oxford University Press

TEACHING LEVI-STRAUSS
*Edited by Hans H. Penner*

TEACHING ISLAM
*Edited by Brannon M. Wheeler*

TEACHING FREUD
*Edited by Diane Jonte-Pace*

TEACHING DURKHEIM
*Edited by Terry F. Godlove Jr.*

TEACHING AFRICAN AMERICAN RELIGIONS
*Edited by Carolyn M. Jones and Theodore Louis Trost*

TEACHING RELIGION AND HEALING
*Edited by Linda L. Barnes and Inés Talamantez*

TEACHING NEW RELIGIOUS MOVEMENTS
*Edited by David G. Bromley*

TEACHING RITUAL
*Edited by Catherine Bell*

# Teaching Confucianism

EDITED BY
JEFFREY L. RICHEY

OXFORD
UNIVERSITY PRESS

2008

# OXFORD
UNIVERSITY PRESS

Oxford University Press, Inc., publishes works that further
Oxford University's objective of excellence
in research, scholarship, and education.

Oxford   New York
Auckland   Cape Town   Dar es Salaam   Hong Kong   Karachi
Kuala Lumpur   Madrid   Melbourne   Mexico City   Nairobi
New Delhi   Shanghai   Taipei   Toronto

With offices in
Argentina   Austria   Brazil   Chile   Czech Republic   France   Greece
Guatemala   Hungary   Italy   Japan   Poland   Portugal   Singapore
South Korea   Switzerland   Thailand   Turkey   Ukraine   Vietnam

Copyright © 2008 by The American Academy of Religion

Published by Oxford University Press, Inc.
198 Madison Avenue, New York, New York 10016

www.oup.com

Oxford is a registered trademark of Oxford University Press

All rights reserved. No part of this publication may be reproduced,
stored in a retrieval system, or transmitted, in any form or by any means,
electronic, mechanical, photocopying, recording, or otherwise,
without the prior permission of Oxford University Press.

Library of Congress Cataloging-in-Publication Data
Teaching Confucianism : edited by Jeffrey L. Richey.
  p. cm. — (Teaching religious studies series)
Includes bibliographical references and index.
ISBN 978-0-19-531160-0
1. Confucianism.   2. Philosophy, Confucian.
I. Richey, Jeffrey L.
BL1852.T43 2008
299.5'12071—dc22        2007010413

9 8 7 6 5 4 3 2 1

Printed in the United States of America
on acid-free paper

子曰: 性相近也, 習相遠也。

*The master said: By nature, people are pretty much alike; it is learning and practice that set them apart.*

Analects, 17:2

# Acknowledgments

I would like to express my gratitude to the following persons, without whose invaluable support the publication of this volume would not have been possible: Susan Henking, editor of the American Academy of Religion's Teaching Religious Studies series, who guided the project from proposal to acceptance; Phyllis Gabbard, administrator for the Department of Philosophy and Religion at Berea College, who initiated me into the mysteries of Microsoft Word's formatting functions and otherwise helped me in every way; Cynthia Read, Julia TerMaat, Linda Donnelly, and Daniel Gonzalez of Oxford University Press, who patiently dealt with the many questions asked by a novice author and editor; participants in the American Academy of Religion's Confucian Traditions and Chinese Religions Groups, the Southeast Early China Roundtable, and my students and colleagues at Berea College, the University of Findlay, and the Church Divinity School of the Pacific, all of whom offered valuable lessons about teaching Confucianism; the contributors to this volume, who endured a long wait, several deadline adjustments, and the indignities of subjecting one's work to another's editorial hand; those who taught me Confucian history, ideas, practices, and texts, including Charles D. Orzech, Michael J. Puett, Tu Wei-ming, David N. Keightley, Kwong-loi Shun, and Judith A. Berling; those who taught (and teach) me Confucian lessons about the past as a spiritual resource for the present and future, often unknowingly—my grandparents and parents, my mother-in-law, my wife, and my sons.

# Contents

Contributors, xi

Introduction: Teaching Confucianism as a Religious Tradition, 3
*John H. Berthrong and Jeffrey L. Richey*

Part I   Teaching Confucianism in Practice

The Social and Religious Context of Early Confucian Practice, 27
*Mark Csikszentmihalyi*

Learning Confucianism through Filial Sons, Loyal Retainers, and Chaste Wives, 39
*Keith N. Knapp*

Divination and Sacrifice in Song Neo-Confucianism, 55
*Joseph A. Adler*

Part II   Teaching Confucianism in History

The Mencius-Xunzi Debate in Early Confucian Ethics, 85
*Aaron Stalnaker*

Understanding the Ethical Universe of Neo-Confucianism, 107
*Robert W. Foster*

Problematizing Contemporary Confucianism in East Asia, 157
*Yiu-ming Fung*

Part III   Teaching Confucianism in Dialogue

Reenchanting Confucius: A Western-Trained Philosopher Teaches the *Analects*, 187
*John J. Furlong*

Teaching Confucianism in Christian Contexts, 203
*Judith A. Berling*

Index, 225

# Contributors

**Joseph A. Adler** is Professor of Religious Studies and Director of the Asian Studies Program at Kenyon College in Gambier, Ohio. He founded the American Academy of Religion's Confucian Traditions Group in 1992, is the author of *Chinese Religious Traditions* (2002) and (with Kidder Smith Jr., Peter K. Bol, and Don J. Wyatt) *Sung Dynasty Uses of the I Ching* (1990), and has contributed articles to several volumes devoted to the study of the Confucian tradition. His translation of Zhu Xi (Chu Hsi)'s *Introduction to the Study of the Classic of Change* was published in 2002.

**Judith A. Berling** is Professor of Chinese and Comparative Religions and Dean Emerita at the Graduate Theological Union in Berkeley, California. She is the author of *Understanding Other Religious Worlds: A Guide for Interreligious Education* (2004), *A Pilgrim in Chinese Culture: Negotiating Religious Diversity* (1997), and *The Syncretic Religion of Lin Chao-en* (1980). She has contributed to *Religion and Peacebuilding*, ed. Harold Coward and Gordon S. Smith (2004), *The Cambridge History of China, Volume 8: The Ming Dynasty, Part 2* (1998), and *Popular Culture in Late Imperial China*, eds. David Johnson, Andrew J. Nathan, and Evelyn S. Rawski (1985). A specialist on Ming dynasty Neo-Confucianism, Daoism, and Buddhism, she is interested in how learning about diverse religious traditions, especially the religious traditions of East Asia, can inform and influence the self-understanding of Christian students, whether in the theological school or the denominational college or university.

**John H. Berthrong** is Associate Dean for Academic and Administrative Affairs, Director of the Institute for Dialogue Among Religious Traditions, and Assistant Professor of Comparative Theology at Boston University. He is a founding member of the North American Interfaith Network and a member of the Interfaith Relations Commission of the National Council of Churches of Christ in the United States of America. His publications include *Confucianism: A Short Introduction* (2000, with Evelyn Nagai Berthrong), *The Divine Deli: Religious Identity in the North American Cultural Mosaic* (1999), *Transformations of the Confucian Way* (1998), and *All under Heaven: Transforming Paradigms in Confucian-Christian Dialogue* (1994), as well as numerous articles and book chapters on interfaith dialogue, Chinese religion and philosophy, and comparative theology and philosophy.

**Mark Csikszentmihalyi** is Associate Professor and Chair of East Asian Languages and Literature and Religious Studies at the University of Wisconsin at Madison. He is the author of *Material Virtue: Ethics and the Body in Early China* (2004), *Readings in Han Chinese Thought* (2006), a coeditor (with P. J. Ivanhoe) of *Religious and Philosophical Aspects of the Laozi* (1999), and a contributor to *Confucius and the Analects: New Essays* (2002). He also is editor of the *Journal of Chinese Religions* and an associate editor of the *Journal of the American Academy of Religion*.

**Robert W. Foster** is Associate Professor of History and Coordinator of the Asian Studies Program at Berea College in Berea, Kentucky. A specialist in Song dynasty Neo-Confucianism, he has translated and interpreted Song materials for numerous publications, including *The Human Tradition in Pre-Modern China* (2002) and *The Hawai'i Reader of Traditional Chinese Culture*, eds. Victor H. Mair, Nancy S. Steinhart, and Paul R. Goldin (2005).

**Yiu-ming Fung** is Professor of Humanities at the Hong Kong University of Science and Technology. An analytic philosopher with a special interest in Chinese philosophy and comparative philosophy, his publications include *The Myth of Transcendent Immanence: A Perspective of Analytic Philosophy on Contemporary New Confucianism* (2002) and "Three Dogmas of New Confucianism—A Perspective of Analytic Philosophy," in *Two Roads to Wisdom: Chinese and Analytic Philosophical Traditions* (2001).

**John J. Furlong** is Bingham Professor of Philosophy and Chair of the Humanities Division at Transylvania University in Lexington, Kentucky. He is a coeditor (with William J. Carroll) of *Greek and Medieval Studies in Honor of Leo Sweeney, S.J.* (1994), (with William J. Carroll and C. Stephen Mann) *The Search for the Individual: Roots of Western Civilization* (1990), and (with Leo Sweeney and William J. Carroll) *Authentic Metaphysics in an Age of Unreality* (1988). Trained in Western philosophy, he is concerned with how Western-trained scholars can be sensitive to hermeneutical contexts when introducing themselves and their students to Chinese thought. In 2002, he received the Kentucky Professor of the Year Award from the Carnegie Foundation for the Advancement of Teaching and the Council for Advancement and Support of Education.

**Keith N. Knapp** is the Westvaco Professor of National Security Studies at The Citadel, The Military College of South Carolina, in Charleston. He is the author of *Selfless Offspring: Filial Children and Social Order in Medieval China* (2005) and is a contributor to *The Encyclopedia of Religion*, 2nd ed., ed. Lindsay Jones (2005); *The Hawai'i Reader of Traditional Chinese Culture*, eds. Victor H. Mair, Nancy S. Steinhart, and Paul R. Goldin (2005); *Filial Piety in Chinese Thought and History*, eds. Alan K. L. Chan and Sor-hoon Tan (2004); and *The Encyclopaedia of Confucianism*, ed. Xinzhong Yao (2003). He has published widely on Confucianism and early medieval Chinese social and religious history.

**Jeffrey L. Richey** is Associate Professor of Religion at Berea College in Berea, Kentucky, where he also teaches in the Asian Studies Program. He is a contributor to *Confucius Now: Contemporary Encounters with the Analects*, ed. David Jones (forthcoming) and *Riding the Wind with Liezi: New Scholarship on the Daoist Classic*, eds. Jeffrey Dippmann and Ronnie Littlejohn (forthcoming), and is the author of numerous encyclopedia entries on early Chinese intellectual and religious history. His articles on early Chinese spirituality and thought have been published in the *International Review of Chinese Religion and Philosophy*, the *Journal of the Economic and Social History of the Orient*, and *Numen: International Review for the History of Religions*. He serves as the Chinese Philosophy Area editor for *The Internet Encyclopedia of Philosophy* (available online at www.utm.edu/research/iep).

**Aaron Stalnaker** is Assistant Professor in the Department of Religious Studies at Indiana University at Bloomington. He is the author of *Overcoming Our Evil: Human Nature and Spiritual Exercises in Xunzi and Augustine* (2006) as well as articles on early Chinese thought and Christian ethics in the *Journal of Religious Ethics*, the *Journal of the Society of Christian Ethics*, *International Philosophical Quarterly*, and *Philosophy East and West*. His entry on Xunzi appears in *The Encyclopedia of Religion*, 2nd ed., ed. Lindsay Jones (2005).

# Teaching Confucianism

# Introduction: Teaching Confucianism as a Religious Tradition

*John H. Berthrong and Jeffrey L. Richey*

"*Is* Confucianism a religious tradition?" Each component of this question could be unpacked to reveal reasons why Confucianism *is not* a religious tradition.[1] Yet as this chapter and the volume it introduces are intended to demonstrate, reasons to regard and teach Confucianism as an authentic East Asian religious tradition are both abundant and sound.

Problematizing Confucianism as a Religious Tradition

In the words of Wilfred Cantwell Smith, "The question 'Is Confucianism a religion?' is one that the West has never been able to answer and China never able to ask."[2]

*Confucianism*, as an English word used to denote a particular religious tradition, owes an obvious debt to Western terminology and worldviews. This is evident in the writings of famed Scottish missionary and pioneering Sinologist James Legge (1815–97), whose influential definition of Confucianism identified it as "first of all the ancient religion of China, and then the views of the great philosopher himself . . . much as when we comprehend under Christianity the records and teachings of the Old Testament as well as those of the New."[3]

Legge's seminal use of the term suggests a single system of doctrines revealed by or identified with a divine or otherwise exemplary founder, much like *Marxism* or the now-antiquated *Mohammedanism*. It also explicitly links itself with a Christian hermeneutic that subsumes diverse traditions into one monolithic entity. The term *Confucianism* thus enshrines "Confucius" as the founder of a self-contained, uniform religion. But Kong Qiu 孔丘 (better known as Kongzi 孔子, Master Kong), the fifth century B.C.E. Chinese teacher whose later title *Kong Fuzi* 孔夫子 (Revered Master Kong) was Latinized as "Confucius" by sixteenth-century Jesuit missionaries to China, doubtless would have been surprised to learn that a set of traditions that began in China and then spread to Korea, Vietnam, and Japan was labeled "Confucianism" by these same foreign visitors.[4] Kongzi famously asserted that he simply transmitted the teachings of the sages of the past and did not create any sort of novel or personal teaching.[5] Moreover, he took great delight in learning about antiquity, by which he meant the history, customs, and literature of the Zhou 周 dynasty (twelfth through third centuries B.C.E.), which he assumed had preserved the best of the wisdom of earlier sages and kingdoms.[6] From his perspective—and there is no reason to doubt his sincerity—he believed that he was reviving the teachings of the Zhou dynasty founders to restore culture during the troubled times of the *Chunqiu* 春秋 (Spring and Autumn) period (722–481 B.C.E.). The most common term for someone like Master Kong was *Ru* 儒, a word that came to define a scholar or erudite expert in ritual. The *Ru* were the ritual masters and teachers of the courts of the various "warring states" that were, after the death of the master, to contend for the violent reunification of north China into a new imperial order. Moreover, historically there never has existed a single, uniform system of *Ru* doctrine and practice that might be called Confucianism; the third-century B.C.E. writer Han Fei 韓非 describes eight *Ru* factions (*rujia bapai* 儒家八派), and such internal diversity within Confucianism persists into the present day.[7] Thus, it might be said that Confucianism is not an authentic East Asian religious tradition because as a standardized revelation bequeathed by or associated with a divine or semi-divine founder, it is an alien construct imposed by Westerners.

Regardless of whether "Confucius" is the creature of Western Christian missionaries, a true equivalent to Chinese representations of their revered teacher, or somehow both, what about the understanding of "religion" embedded within and expressed by the *-ism*? The Chinese term *zongjiao* 宗教 (ancestral teachings), though formally cognate with the English term *religion* in contemporary usage, appears to have been developed as a way to distinguish among various Buddhist views by sixth-century C.E. Chinese monks, from whom the Japanese borrowed the term, eventually reintroducing it to China sometime in the late nineteenth century.[8] Prior to this, the term *jiao* 教 alone was used by Chinese and other East Asian literati in the sense of "teachings," as in the medieval Chinese phrase *sanjiao* 三教 (three teachings), a byword for Buddhism, Daoism, and Confucianism. It is unclear whether Buddhism and Daoism were regarded as religions by their adherents prior to Western commentators labeling them as such in the early modern era or even afterward. Indeed, this problem is hardly unique to the study of Confucianism or Chinese religions in general.[9] Whatever else *jiao* may have meant to premodern Chinese, it expressed a normative understanding of what Westerners call religion as eclectic, pluralistic, and syncretic—hardly the sort of canonical, sectarian orthodoxy usually denoted by the word *religion* in the West, to which the static copula "is" may be attached (e.g., "Confucianism is a religious tradition").[10] Indeed, from its inception amid the spiritual ferment of the late Zhou 周 era (fifth–third century B.C.E.) through the present day, Confucianism has never existed alone, but as *Lunyu* 4:25 says of those who possess *de* 德 (virtue), it "must have neighbors" (*bi you lin* 必有鄰).[11]

Historically, Confucianism has proven to be quite compatible both doctrinally and liturgically with its religious neighbors across East Asia—even, in present-day South Korea, for example, with Christianity[12]—and this might be interpreted as evidence that Confucianism has no religious content of its own, making it an ideal partner for or adjunct to any religious tradition.[13] Although Confucian discourse has entailed belief and practice related to the supernatural, such as *tian* 天 (Heaven), the very early notion of tian as a powerful theovolitional monotheistic force never became the sole or dominant Confucian interpretation of *tian*, which in any case fails to resemble the God of Moses, Jesus, or Mohammad. Thus, it might be argued that Confucianism is not an authentic East Asian religious tradition because there is no such thing: traditional East Asian cultures lack any such concept.

Finally, even if the conceptual and etymological problems related to the term *Confucianism* were disregarded, it still would be encumbered by what might be called ideological or institutional difficulties related to who uses the term and why. Like any other category, Confucianism is value-laden, but the values with which it is invested depend on who deploys it. Those who have described the tradition as "religious" include sociologist Max Weber (1864–1920) (who saw Confucianism as China's obstacle on the path to modernization), Chinese Marxists (who felt the same way), and so-called New Confucians (twentieth-century Chinese intellectuals, mostly from outside mainland China), who conversely advocate Confucianism as the foundation of cultural and economic success stories from Singapore to South Korea. Those who have rejected the categorization of Confucianism as "religious" include sixteenth-century Christian missionaries (who sought thereby to minimize conflicts between Chinese culture and Christian faith), twentieth-century Chinese communist bureaucrats (who did not wish to enfranchise Confucians politically, which official recognition of their tradition as a "religion" regulated by the government and represented at People's Political Consultative Congresses would have entailed), and many contemporary East Asians (for whom "religion" often connotes dogmatic narrow-mindedness, superstition, the West, and/or premodernity).[14] In other words, politics—in both loosely cultural and tightly institutional senses—has played a crucial role in the definition or nondefinition of Confucianism as a religious tradition. Thus, it might be claimed that Confucianism is not an authentic East Asian religious tradition because its classification (or lack thereof) has always been an epiphenomenon of larger political struggles within East Asia, chiefly vis-à-vis the West and modernity.

So there are many reasons for rejecting the union of the terms *Confucianism* and *religion*: Either Confucianism does not exist as an emic term or social reality, or it exists only as a political palimpsest on which other, more vivid discourses are inscribed. Why, then, do many (nearly all) Western scholars of religion—most of whom are neither missionaries, nor Marxist bureaucrats, nor Confucians, nor East Asians—continue to describe and teach Confucianism as an authentic East Asian religious tradition, worthy of inclusion in world religions surveys and other courses?[15]

Seeing Confucianism as a Religious Tradition

The persistent identification of Confucianism as a religious tradition cannot be traced to a consistent self-identification of East Asians as "Confucian." Hardly any contemporary East Asian would be comfortable uttering the Chinese (or equivalent) sentence *woshi yige rujiaotu* 我是一个儒教徒 (I am a follower of Confucianism), even though it differs by only two characters from very similar statements affirmed by many East Asians today: *woshi yige fojiaotu* 我是一个佛教徒 (I am a follower of Buddhism) and *woshi yige jidutu* 我是一个基督徒 (I am a follower of Christianity).[16] Outside of South Korea, Confucianism as a religious category plays virtually no formal role and is practically invisible to government data gatherers and scholarly investigators who ask questions such as, "What is your religion?"[17] If, however, a different question is posed—"To whom do you sacrifice?"—many East Asians will respond that they owe such sacrifice to their parents and ancestors, and will generally display a keen and comprehensive understanding of the duties of family ritual devotions. Of course, it is a completely different question as to whether they assiduously follow the formal family rituals as described by a Confucian authority such as Zhu Xi 朱熹 (1130–1200 C.E.). Most contemporary East Asians find the question about ritual practice intelligible and sensible (unlike the question about religious identity), even if they do not make an immediate connection between this distinctive Confucian dimension of religious practice and the complex forms of worship and clerical hierarchy found in Judaism, Christianity, or Islam. Sociologist C. K. Yang (1911–99) famously asserted that Chinese religion is marked by its diffuse character when compared to the highly organized structures of West Asian religious traditions.[18] In their level of religious participation, Chinese and other East Asian Confucians can be as scrupulous and pious as any Western Jew, Christian, or Muslim—or they can just as easily be backsliders.

Intellectual historian Qian Mu 錢穆 (1895–1990) put his finger on the issue of trying to see Confucianism as a religious tradition when he argued that

> Confucius was not a religious founder in China. What he had his faith and took delight in, as well as what he transmitted, was antiquity itself. His focus was on mankind, not on God, who is supernatural. Hence he never thought of himself as superior to the ancients. This is the spirit of Chinese learning and civilization. In fact, the position of Confucius in China surpasses that of Jesus in the West.[19]

Such a view of Confucianism recognizes within it a religious dimension, a faith stance, yet one that is distinctively different from the religious visions of the West Asian traditions. This stance entails an orientation of reverence for the cultural past. To be a Confucian is to look to this past for hope and other spiritual resources in shaping the cultural present and future. The work of Julia Ching, Rodney Taylor, Tu Wei-ming, and other modern scholars suggests that one should not simply label Confucianism a religion in the same sense in which one might call Christianity an organized "world religion."[20] Rather, one should recognize that the *Ru* path has profound religious dimensions as integral aspects of its historical, philosophical, cultural, and spiritual developments as major East Asian and world tradition. We take the word *religious* as descriptive of human attempts to develop a unified (though not necessarily uniform) set of beliefs, institutions, and practices in response to fundamental questions about the universe (cosmology), human beings (anthropology), and how to live (ethics). By this definition of *religious*, there clearly are elements of the Confucian Way (*dao* 道) that are religious in nature, even if not all aspects of the *Ru* path conform to standard (i.e., Western) definitions of religion. The most famous contemporary definition of the religious dimension of the Confucian project was penned by Tu Wei-ming as part of his commentary on the Confucian classic known as the *Zhongyong* 中庸 (Doctrine of the Mean):

> Being religious, in the Confucian perspective, informed by sacred texts such as the *Chung-yung* [*Zhongyong*], means being engaged in the process of learning to be fully human. We can define the Confucian way of being religious as ultimate self-transformation as a communal act and as a faithful dialogical response to the transcendent.[21]

We should note that other scholars will immediately contest this definition. For instance, many able scholars argue that Tu makes a fundamental category mistake when he writes about a Confucian sense of transcendence (see chapter 7). The more common note struck is that Confucianism is a path of immanent transcendence or transcendent immanence, depending on how one views divine–world relations.

Furthermore, given the adaptability of Confucianism and its coexistence with other traditions, what makes someone a Confucian rather than a Daoist or Buddhist who happens to practice family rituals (as most traditional East Asians do)? A Confucian is one who reveres and orders life around the collection of books known as the Confucian classics. This collection began with five major texts from the Han 漢 dynasty (202 B.C.E.–220 C.E.), but by the Song 宋 dynasty (960–1279 C.E.), it had been expanded to include thirteen early works that were considered the reliable records of the thoughts, history, poetry, divinations, words, rituals, and deeds of the early sage rulers of China. Does this mean that only an erudite scholar could become a true Confucian? In practice, it probably did mean that Confucians were scholars and that anyone recognized as a Confucian in East Asia would have to be literate; this has led most observers to see Confucianism as an elite tradition. Nonetheless, most Confucians would recognize even the uneducated if they cultivated their *xin* 心 (mind-hearts) to manifest in individual and social conduct the five cardinal virtues of *ren* 仁 (humanness), *yi* 義 (righteousness), *li* 禮 (ritual propriety), *zhi* 智 (wisdom), and *xin* 信 (faithfulness). Because Confucians believe that every person has this potential to become a worthy or even a sage, they hold that is possible for one to be endowed at birth with a refined moral sense such that, even without a formal education, one can manifest the humane heart and conduct of a true sage—and thus become truly Confucian. Moreover, until relatively recently in East Asian history, it was impossible for the illiterate to avoid the influence of Confucianism, especially in China, where Confucianism was the basis of official ideology from the second century B.C.E. to the early twentieth century C.E..

## Historicizing Confucianism as a Religious Tradition

The enduring argument about whether Confucianism is a religious tradition illustrates another important point about trying to teach about it as a religious path among other faith traditions. It is crucial to know something about the development of the history of Confucian thought and practice to decide whether Tu is right to include the notion of transcendence in his definition of the Confucian way of being religious. Hence we need an excursus into the intellectual-historical matrix of Confucian discourse to be able to think creatively about teaching the *Ru* path.

During Confucianism's process of expansion throughout East Asia, the tradition has undergone six paradigmatic historical transformations, which may be called periods or "epochs."[22]

1. The *classical period* (c. 500–221 B.C.E.) is when Kongzi and other famous warring states thinkers all lived.
2. The *early imperial period* (202 B.C.E.–200 C.E.) is when the classical texts attained their present form, the commentarial traditions arose, and Confucianism gained state support.
3. The *late antique period* (220–907) was characterized by the proliferation of Daoist movements, the introduction of Buddhism, and the waning of elite support for Confucianism.
4. The *renewal period* (960–1644) witnessed the renaissance of Confucianism (often called Neo-Confucianism), the reformulation of the Confucian canon, and the spread of the renewed tradition into Korea and Japan.
5. The *reactive period* (1644–1911) was distinguished by the refinement and rejection of much Neo-Confucian thought in China even as the tradition continued to grow in Korea and Japan.
6. The *postcolonial period* (1912–present) is shaped by the impact of Western powers, the disappearance of Confucianism's imperial sponsorship, and the reform movement known as New Confucianism.

This periodization challenges the hypothesis that the Confucian tradition was and is a perpetually rigid moral formalism of ritual and social domination—a perennial tradition without transformation or significant change over time and place. The first or classical period begins with Kongzi (551–479 B.C.E.), is reshaped by Mengzi 孟子 (Master Meng, often Latinized as Mencius) (372–289 B.C.E.), and is concluded by Xunzi 荀子 (310–220 B.C.E.) (see chapters 2, 5, and 8). In framing his vision of the dao, Kongzi relied on a number of early traditions, including historical documents, governmental decrees, poetry, and ritual texts that were later given the title "classics" (*jing* 經). The number of classics grew from the initial recognition of five to thirteen in their final canonization during the Song dynasty. Most of these texts were assumed to have been in existence prior to Kongzi's lifetime. Modern scholarly opinion views these texts in their present versions largely as products of the second or early imperial period, but Confucian tradition maintains that Kongzi was the first commentator and editor of the classics. Kongzi, Mengzi, and Xunzi are commemorated by Confucians as the foundational masters of their tradition, and in fact, their legacies provide the basic structure for Confucian thought throughout its long development in East Asia.

The second period, or transformation, began with the founding of the Han dynasty in 202 B.C.E. The second stage was marked by the formulation of a state-supported imperial Confucian ideology to replace the discredited legalism (*fajia* 法家) of the Qin 秦 dynasty (221–206 B.C.E.). This is also the grand era of commentary as the preferred technique for understanding the words and meanings of the sages (see chapter 2). In one form or another, the Han mixture of legalist realpolitik, Confucian ethics, and correlative cosmology dominated the Chinese political, social, and intellectual world right up to the end of the imperial state and the founding of the Chinese republic in 1911. However, many Confucians were extremely disconcerted about the inevitable misuse of Confucian symbols by state authority. Balancing this fear of serving an unworthy prince was the perennial Confucian desire to bring good government and social order to the world through governmental service. Three of the most representative of the Han Confucians were Dong Zhongshu 董仲舒 (c. 179–104 B.C.E.), Yang Xiong 揚雄 (53 B.C.E.–18 C.E.), and Xun Yue 荀悅 (148–209 C.E.). These men saw that governmental service must be tied closely to the state for it to be effective.

The late antique period begins with the fall of the Han dynasty in 220 and the commencement of the "period of disunity" (220–581) (see chapter 3). During this time, the rulers of a number of former Han territories fought for mastery of a reunified empire, sustaining centuries of disruptive conflict. The eclecticism and syncretism of the Han era continued as a form of Daoist speculation called *xuanxue* 玄學 (abstruse [or dark] learning, sometimes called Neo-Daoism) flourished and intellectuals such as the precocious Wang Bi 王弼 (226–249) mixed their Confucian reflections with Daoist cosmology and metaphysics. Even more momentous was the arrival of Buddhism in China. The

Chinese intellectual world was not the same after the introduction of the Buddha's teachings. Although Confucianism never lost its pride of place in the Chinese state or family, it is accurate to say that the most acute religious, artistic, and philosophical mind-hearts in China from the third to the tenth centuries devoted themselves to the appropriation and Chinese transformation of the Buddhist *dharma* (law or teaching). Great temples were created; the huge Buddhist *sangha* (monastic community) was formed; entirely new and elaborate schools of Buddhist thought such as Tiantai 天台, Huayan 華嚴, Pure Land 淨土, and Chan 禪 (better known by its Japanese moniker, Zen) were created and sustained. The rise and flourishing of this Chinese Buddhist world formed the backdrop for new epochs of transformation of the Confucian Way.

Toward the end of the Tang 唐 dynasty (618–907), a number of Confucian scholars saw their task as defending the Confucian Way against the challenge of Buddhism (see Chapter 6). The three most famous of these scholars were Han Yu 韓愈 (768–824), Li Ao 李翱 (772–841), and Liu Zongyuan 柳宗元 (733–819). Along with continuing the Han Confucian interest in government service, commentary, family ritual, and historical writing, these scholars framed the major lines of the Confucian response to the Buddhist philosophical and religious challenge with a renewed interest in cosmology, self-cultivation, and social ethics.

The fourth period of Confucianism's development is the renewal of Confucian thought (known in the West as the Neo-Confucianism) during the Northern and Southern Song Dynasties (960–1279) (see chapters 4 and 6). The Song scholars invented a new name for their teachings, calling it *daoxue* 道學 ("Learning of the Way"). The revival itself began in the Northern Song period (960–1127) and reached its conclusion with the synthesis of Zhu Xi (1130–1200). Regarding the scope and influence of his work, Zhu has been likened to St. Thomas Aquinas in the West, and there is little doubt that except for Kongzi, no one has been more important in defining the course of the Confucian tradition. Zhu Xi's form of Confucianism, which he based on the writings of the Northern Song masters Zhou Dunyi 周敦頤 (1017–1073), Shao Yong 邵雍 (1011–1077), Zhang Zai 張載 (1020–1077), and the brothers Cheng Hao 程顥 (1032–1085) and Cheng Yi 程頤 (1033–1107), was spread by his followers to Korea and Japan. This Neo-Confucianism actually replaced Buddhism as the principal form of elite Chinese thought from the Song to the modern period.

According to Confucian scholars, the reformers of the Song, Yuan 元 (1279–1368), and Ming 明 (1368–1644) Dynasties are second only to the classical Zhou founders in terms of their impact on Chinese culture. From the Confucian point of view, no higher praise can be given. If the classical Confucians—Kongzi, Mengzi, and Xunzi—defended the learning of the sages during the

Spring and Autumn and Warring States periods of the late Zhou dynasty, the Song, Yuan, and Ming Confucian masters did the same in countering the challenges of Daoism and Buddhism in their own age. Even though there were great changes and transformations of the Confucian Way after Zhu Xi, no one can deny the pivotal role he played in the renewal and definition of the tradition. Although others could contest Zhu's synthesis in the name of the tradition, no one could overlook his contribution to it.

Because the variety of Confucianism associated with Zhu Xi is the basis for much of Confucianism as a contemporary, living tradition today, it seems worthwhile to devote special attention to his vision of the Way. The diagram in figure I.1 visually outlines the interrelationships between human and cosmic forces and features as understood by Zhu.

Zhu achieved a critical philosophical insight when he was pondering the correct way to understand the relationship of *li* 理 and *qi* 氣 via meditating on Zhang Zai's statement, "The mind-heart unites [or unifies] nature and emotion [*xin tung xing qing* 心 統 性 情]." The proper unity of human nature or dispositions with the emotions leads, through the discipline of proper self-cultivation, to the desired goal of *cheng* 誠 as manifested in harmony (*he* 和) and centeredness (*zhong* 中) revealed through an exemplary moral life. Moving from this concrete human path of self-cultivation, Zhu argued that the Confucian path of self-cultivation illuminated the guiding principles of the primordial functioning of *Dao* 道 as a form of cosmic creativity. A person begins with the mind-heart and then discerns that the properly cultivated mind-heart is a principle of change (*yi* 易) that melds the Way with the emotion of spirit (*shen* 神). Even more abstractly, mind-heart becomes the supreme polarity 太極 that regulates principle 理 and vital force 氣. This can be thought of three expanding triangles moving from (1) the concrete mind-heart, (2) the process of change, (3) to the triad of the supreme polarity, principle, and vital force as the most abstract matrix that Zhu employed to explain his mature cosmology.

The most important challenge to Zhu Xi's summation of the Way came during the Ming dynasty in the form of Wang Yangming's 王阳明 (1472–1529) epic struggle to come to terms with Zhu Xi's rationalistic approach. Wang is remembered as the founder of the *xinxue* 心學 (School of Mind-Heart) in contradistinction to Zhu Xi's *lixue* 理學 (School of Principle). Not only was Wang a brilliant critic of Zhu's thought, he was also an outstanding general and civil servant, poet, and teacher. Wang held that *li* 理 (principle), the rationale of *Dao* in human nature, was in the mind-heart of the sincere student of the Confucian Way. He further taught a doctrine of the unity of thought and action based on this understanding of true principle being in the mind-heart.

## Zhu Xi's Schematic of Form, Dynamics, Unification, and Goal

*Li* 理 as principle, pattern, order
*Dao* 道 as the Way
*Xing* 性 as nature, dispositions, tendencies

*Qi* 氣 as vital force, matter-energy
*Shen* 神 as spirit, the function of feeling
*Qing* 情 as emotion, desire, passion

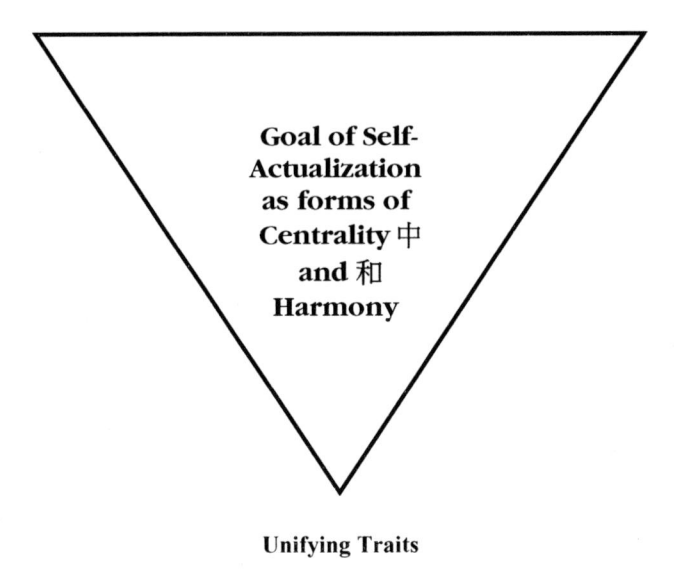

**Goal of Self-Actualization as forms of Centrality 中 and 和 Harmony**

**Unifying Traits**

*Xin* 心 as mind-heart unifying human *xing*/nature and *qing*/emotion
*Yi* 易 change/transformation as *xin*/mind-heart
*Taiji* 太極 as supreme ultimate/polarity
*cheng* 誠/self-actualization as *he* 和/harmony and *zhong* 中/centrality

The reactive period of Confucian learning is itself a response to and transformation of the Neo-Confucian achievement of the fourth period. The Qing 清 dynasty (1644–1911) movement known as *hanxue* 漢學 (School of Han [or sometimes Evidential] Learning) is unique in its concerns and self-conscious rejection of a great deal of Song-Ming scholarship. Its leaders were thinkers such as Wang Fuzhi 王夫之 (1619–1692), Huang Zongxi 黃宗羲 (1610–1695), and Dai Zhen 戴震 (1723–1777). By turns, these scholars castigated what they saw as the needlessly abstract thought of the Song and the equally debilitating subjectivism of Wang's thought in the late Ming as wrong turns for the Confucian Way. They believed that Confucianism must be of some concrete, practical use for the people. Hence, they often stressed strict, accurate, and what might be called empirical historical research. Likewise, they argued that much Song and Ming thought was infected with an unhealthy Buddhist and Daoist love of meditation without proper attention to what ought to be Confucian self-cultivation—namely, the practice of service to self and others in practical ways. Their empirical studies of the history of taxation and flood control were defended as being more in tune with the true nature of Confucian thought than Buddhist or Daoist sensibilities.

The postcolonial period of the Confucian Way is dramatically different from the first five periods. With the arrival of the expansive and aggressive Western powers, the Confucian tradition, like every other aspect of Chinese culture, was disrupted. This agitation continues today as Chinese intellectuals, along with their Korean, Japanese, and Vietnamese colleagues, struggle to come to grips with the interruption of the West and the modern question of globalization (see chapter 8 and 9). Although there is a historical analogy to the introduction of the Buddhist *dharma*, there are profound differences; for example, the Buddhists never arrived with such overwhelming military, political, and economic power. East Asian Confucian intellectuals have responded to this Western challenge by searching for a modern identity for the Confucian Way. This modern movement is called New Confucianism to distinguish it from the earlier Neo-Confucian synthesis. Contemporary Confucian scholar Tu Wei-ming has described the New Confucian movement as the "third wave" of the Confucian tradition. Tu uses the metaphor of a great ocean wave to express the movement of the tradition within the East Asian cultural world and into the broader world of the modern global city—an arena in which Confucianism is viewed and taught as (among other things) a distinctive religious tradition (albeit clearly not without controversy).

Teaching Confucianism as a Religious Tradition

One of the most interesting aspects of teaching about Confucianism in North America is that most students (unless they happen to be of East Asian descent) know little or nothing about it. Although this might seem like a drawback, in reality it is not. For instance, because learners know little about Confucianism, this means that they do not bring negative conditioning or prejudices that must be undone before the presentation of the tradition begins. (The one major exception, of course, is the general perception that Confucianism was a burden to East Asian women; of course, the same argument is used by many feminist scholars when discussing all world religions.) The perfect counterexample to this is the situation facing those who teach about Islam. Most people in the West think they know something about Islam; the sad fact is that most of what passes for commonly accepted knowledge about Islam is false or misleading. At least in the case of Confucianism, students often begin with a clean slate. Furthermore, most North Americans have a fascination with East

Asia that is fueled by increasing business and professional contacts with this politically, economically, and culturally resurgent region. In short, teaching about Confucianism (like teaching about Daoism and Buddhism) tends to begin with positive expectations all around.

Given that the history of Confucianism is so vast, even when presented in a schematic matrix such as the six epochs described, it is impossible to speak about teaching Confucianism as a whole. Any particular statement would demand so much clarification that the vagueness of the presentation would become all-encompassing in its vacuity. (Doubtless this is true with regard to teaching about any religious tradition.) Nonetheless, it is important to help learners see that Confucian texts and thinkers share a common sensibility that marks them as different from other Asian religious traditions. Although there is nothing like an enduring essence or timeless form to Confucian spirituality, there are such features as the veneration of a set of classical texts as normative for any Confucian and the arrangement of a set of concept clusters that arise from reflection on these classics.

Of course, undergraduate and even graduate courses devoted entirely to Confucianism are rare; for the most part, those who teach it do so within broader survey courses on Chinese religions, Asian religions, or world religions. There are several strategies available to the instructor who wishes to do justice to the Confucian tradition within the confines of a particular curriculum.

One way forward is to present Confucian thought through a particular case study. Many teachers, following the Confucian proclivity to honor the classical texts (and probably also responding to a Western bias toward canonical scripture as the optimal voice of a religious tradition), prefer to teach about the early masters such as Kongzi, Mengzi, and Xunzi. There is much to be said for this approach, especially if students are able to encounter these thinkers in their historical contexts—that is, as participants in a broad, vigorous, and varied conversation about how best to resolve the cultural crises of early China. In this volume, chapters 2, 5, and 8 offer three different yet complimentary strategies for teaching Confucianism through its earliest texts and traditions.

Although every Confucian has seen these early figures as foundational to the tradition, it is nonetheless vital to remember that it is some form of post-Song Confucianism that provides the cultural DNA for contemporary East Asians. For this reason, it is just as important to teach about the complex systems of the Neo-Confucians as it is to teach about the masters of the Zhou dynasty. Few teachers of Jewish, Christian, or Islamic traditions would fail to begin at the beginning, but when it comes to talking about contemporary religious theory and practice, they also would include attention to the state of contemporary religious institutions, thought, and practice. In all religious traditions, a great deal has happened since the Axial Age. For this reason, we suggest an alternative approach to the presentation of Confucianism that focuses on Zhu Xi, whose importance throughout East Asia is affirmed by his posthumous title, Zhuzi 朱子 (Master Zhu), for no higher compliment can be paid to a Confucian thinker than the honorary designation of *zi* 子 (master). In terms of modern life, the dominant form of Confucianism achieved its primary form in the Song dynasty and was received, modified, transformed, and sometimes even rejected in the later Yuan, Ming, and Qing Dynasties; moreover, this form of Confucianism became part of the vital intellectual life of Korea and Japan from the fourteenth century to the present. Finally, among the Song masters, Zhu Xi proved the paradigmatic architectonic vision of the Confucian Way. Therefore, at least one plausible way to teach Confucianism as a religious tradition is to guide students through the basic structure of Master Zhu's vision, which clearly has all the various dimensions of the Confucian religious path sheltered under the vast canopy of what Zhu called *daoxue*. Chapters 4 and 6 show how the life and work of Zhu Xi can help students understand and appreciate Confucianism as a religious tradition.

Finally, two of the most exciting venues in which Confucianism is taught today are in the Christian theological classroom and the Western philosophical seminar. Although there is resistance to the inclusion of Confucianism in both theological and philosophical curricula, increasingly globally minded instructors are turning to the tradition as a way of contextualizing, challenging, and comparing Western thought and practice. Chapter 7 as well as chapter 8 focus explicitly on issues arising from philosophical encounters with Confucianism, whereas chapter 9 discusses ways Confucianism can be incorporated into Christian theological education for the mutual benefit of both traditions and especially for the educational and spiritual welfare of Christian students preparing for service in the "Asian" twenty-first century.

NOTES

1. If one replaces "religious tradition" with "philosophy" in this sentence, similar problems arise. See Bryan W. Van Norden's letter to the editor published in *Proceedings and Addresses of the American Philosophical Association* 70, no. 2 (November 1996): 161–63 (available online at faculty.vassar.edu/brvannor/apaletter.html), as well as Ronnie Littlejohn, *Internet Encyclopedia of Philosophy* entry on "Comparative Philosophy" (www.iep.utm.edu/c/comparat.htm).

2. Wilfred Cantwell Smith, *The Meaning and End of Religion* (Minneapolis: Fortress Press, 1991), p. 69.

3. James Legge, *The Religions of China* (London: Hodder and Stoughton, 1880), p. 4.

4. See Lionel M. Jensen, *Manufacturing Confucianism: Chinese Traditions and Universal Civilization* (Durham, NC and London: Duke University Press, 1997), chap. 1.

5. See *Lunyu* 論語 (*Analects*), 7:1.

6. Ibid., 7:20.

7. Anne Cheng, "Rujia Bapai," in Xinzhong Yao, ed., *RoutledgeCurzon Encyclopedia of Confucianism* (London: RoutledgeCurzon, 2003), p. 2:511.

8. See Anthony C. Yu, *State and Religion in China* (Peru, Ill.: Open Court, 2004), chap. 2.

9. The classification of most non-Abrahamic traditions as "religions" usually is problematic. The problem is dealt with in general terms by Tomoko Masuzawa in *The Invention of World Religions, Or, How European Universalism Was Preserved in the Language of Pluralism* (Chicago: University of Chicago Press, 2005); for specific cases, see Jonathan A. Silk, "The Victorian Creation of Buddhism," *Journal of Indian Philosophy* 22, no. 2 (June 1994): 171–96; David N. Lorenzen, "Who Invented Hinduism?" *Comparative Studies in Society and History* 41 (1999): 630–59; and N. J. Girardot, "'Finding the Way': James Legge and the Victorian Invention of Taoism," *Religion* 29, no. 2 (1999): 107–21.

10. On religious pluralism and syncretism as normative in traditional Chinese culture, see Judith A. Berling, *The Syncretic Religion of Lin Chao-en* (New York: Columbia University Press, 1980), chap. 2 and passim.

11. See Randall Collins, *The Sociology of Philosophies: A Global Theory of Intellectual Change* (Cambridge, Mass.: Harvard University Press, 1998), for an account of the development of global philosophy in this era.

12. See James H. Grayson, *Korea: A Religious History* (Oxford: Oxford University Press, 1989), chap. 12.

13. Tim H. Barrett argues that Confucianism's "flexibility with regard to religion . . . does not reduce [it] to a system of ethics, but actually builds in a measure of strength and adaptability within shifting religious environments." See Barrett, "Confucianism and Religion," in *RoutledgeCurzon Encyclopedia of Confucianism*, p. 1:140.

14. For a useful overview and analysis of contemporary attitudes toward Confucianism as a religious tradition in mainland China, see Anna Xiao Dong Sun, "The Fate of Confucianism as a Religion in Socialist China: Controversies and Paradoxes," in Fenggang Yang and Joseph B. Tamney, eds., *State, Market, and Religions in Chinese Societies* (Leiden: Brill, 2005), pp. 229–53.

15. An unscientific survey of best-selling books on world religions advertised on Amazon.com reveals that *all* include Confucianism in their catalog of such traditions. Philip Novak, *The World's Wisdom: Sacred Texts of the World's Religions* (San Francisco: HarperSan Francisco, 1995)—ranked number 3,513 among Amazon.com's overall book sales as of January 18, 2007—confidently asserts, "We can promptly shelve the old debate about whether the Confucian social ethic amounts to a religion. . . . No student of our planetary religious heritage . . . can afford to ignore Confucius" (p. 111).

16. See Sun, "The Fate of Confucianism," p. 236.

17. Sun cites a 1995 government survey in South Korea in which 0.5 percent of South Koreans identified themselves religiously as Confucians (ibid., p. 246).

18. See C. K. Yang, *Religion in Chinese Society: A Study of Contemporary Social Functions of Religion and Some of their Historical Factors* (Berkeley and Los Angeles: University of California Press, 1967), p. 20.

19. Cited in Wing-tsit Chan, ed., *Chu Hsi and Neo-Confucianism* (Honolulu: University of Hawaii Press, 1986), p. 40.

20. See Julia Ching, *The Religious Thought of Chu Hsi* (Oxford and New York: Oxford University Press, 2000); Rodney L. Taylor, *The Religious Dimensions of Confucianism* (Albany: State University of New York Press, 1990); and Tu Wei-ming, *Centrality and Commonality: An Essay on Confucian Religiousness* (Albany: State University of New York Press, 1989).

21. Tu, *Centrality and Commonality*, p. 94.

22. The "epochal" periodization of Confucianism's history owes much to Tu Wei-ming's account in "Confucianism," in Arvind Sharma, ed., *Our Religions* (New York: HarperCollins, 1993), pp. 141–60. This account is not without its critics; for one critical view, see chapter 7.

RECOMMENDED RESOURCES

Over the past forty or so years, there has been a vast and growing body of literature on all aspects of the Confucian tradition in East Asia, including a burgeoning Internet presence for Confucian studies. What is listed herein is a small but representative sample of the kind of materials a teacher can use in presenting basic information to undergraduate and graduate students.

## Basic Introductions and Reference Works

Berling, Judith A. "Confucianism." *Focus on Asian Studies* 2, no. 1 (Fall 1982): 5–7. Also available online at www2.kenyon.edu/Depts/Religion/Fac/Adler/Reln270/Berling-Confucianism.htm.

Berthrong, John H., and Evelyn Nagai Berthrong. *Confucianism: A Short Introduction*. Oxford: Oneworld, 2000.

Cua, Antonio S., ed. *Encyclopedia of Chinese Philosophy*. New York and London: Routledge, 2003.

Ebrey, Patricia Buckley, ed. *A Visual Sourcebook of Chinese Civilization*. University of Washington. Online document available at /depts.washington.edu/chinaciv.

Eno, Robert. *Glossary of Chinese Philosophical Terms*. Indiana University at Bloomington. Online document available at www.indiana.edu/~p374/gloss.html.

Ivanhoe, Philip J. *Ethics in the Confucian Tradition*, 2nd ed. Indianapolis: Hackett, 2002.

Taylor, Rodney L. *The Religious Dimensions of Confucianism*. Albany: State University of New York Press, 1990.

Tu, Weiming, and Mary Evelyn Tucker, eds. *Confucian Spirituality*, 2 vols. New York: Crossroad Publishing, 2003–2004.

Yao, Xinzhong. *An Introduction to Confucianism*. Cambridge: Cambridge University Press, 2000.
———, ed. *RoutledgeCurzon Encyclopedia of Confucianism*, 2 vols. London and New York: RoutledgeCurzon, 2003.
Zhang, Dainian. *Key Concepts in Chinese Philosophy*, trans. and ed. Edmund Ryden. New Haven, Conn.: Yale University Press, 2002.

## Thematic Studies: Ecology, Gender, Human Rights

de Bary, W. Theodore. "Neo-Confucianism and Human Rights." In Leroy S. Rouner, ed., *Human Rights and the World's Religions*. Notre Dame, Ind.: University of Notre Dame Press, 1988, pp. 183–98.
He, Xiang, and James Miller. "Confucian Spirituality in an Ecological Age." In James Miller, ed., *Chinese Religions in Contemporary Societies*. Santa Barbara, Calif.: ABC-CLIO, 2006, pp. 281–300.
Kang, Hildi. "The Legacy Lingers On: Korean Confucianism and the Erosion of Women's Rights." Institute of East Asian Studies, University of California at Berkeley. Available online at ieas.berkeley.edu/cks/k12/kang1_paper.pdf.
Kennedy, Thomas L., trans. *Confucian Feminist: Memoirs of Zeng Baosun (1893–1978)*. Philadelphia: American Philosophical Society, 2002.
Ko, Dorothy. *Teachers of the Inner Chambers: Women and Culture in Seventeenth-Century China*. Stanford, Calif.: Stanford University Press, 1994.
Ko, Dorothy, Jayhun Kim Haboush, and Joan R. Piggott, eds. *Women and Confucian Cultures in Premodern China, Korea, and Japan*. Berkeley: University of California Press, 2003.
Mann, Susan, and Yu-Yin Cheng, eds. *Under Confucian Eyes: Writings on Gender in Chinese History*. Berkeley: University of California Press, 2001.
Rosemont, Henry Jr. "Why Take Rights Seriously? A Confucian Critique." In Leroy S. Rouner, ed., *Human Rights and the World's Religions*. Notre Dame, Ind.: University of Notre Dame Press, 1988, pp. 167–82.
Tucker, Mary Evelyn, and John H. Berthrong, eds. *Confucianism and Ecology: The Interrelation of Heaven, Earth, and Humans*. Cambridge, Mass.: Harvard University Press/Harvard University Center for the Study of World Religions, 1998.

## Primary Sources in Translation

Chan, Wing-tsit, ed. *A Source Book in Chinese Philosophy*. Princeton, N.J.: Princeton University Press, 1963.
———, trans. *Instructions for Practical Living and Other Neo-Confucian Writings by Wang Yang-ming*. New York: Columbia University Press, 1963.
Chen, Chun. *Neo-Confucian Terms Explained: The Pei-hsi tzu-i by Ch'en Ch'un (1159–1223)*. Trans. and ed. Wing-tsit Chan. New York: Columbia University Press, 1986.
*Chinese Literature in Translation*. East Asia Center, University of Virginia. Available online at faculty.virginia.edu/cll/chinese_literature.

Chu Hsi [Zhu Xi] and Lü Tsu-ch'ien. *Reflections on Things at Hand: The Neo-Confucian Anthology.* Trans. Wing-tsit Chan. New York: Columbia University Press, 1967.

Chu Hsi [Zhu Xi]. *Chu Hsi's Family Rituals: A Twelfth-Century Chinese Manual for the Performance of Cappings, Weddings, Funerals, and Ancestral Rites.* Trans. and ed. Patricia Buckley Ebrey. Princeton, N.J.: Princeton University Press, 1991.

———. *Introduction to the Study of the Classic of Changes (I-hsüeh ch'i-ming).* Trans. Joseph Adler. New York: Global Scholarly Publications, 2002.

Csikszentmihalyi, Mark, trans. and ed. *Readings in Han Chinese Thought.* Indianapolis: Hackett, 2006.

de Bary, William Theodore, Irene Bloom, and Richard Lufrano, eds. *Sources of Chinese Tradition,* 2nd ed., 2 vols. New York: Columbia University Press, 1999–2000.

de Bary, William Theodore, Donald Keene, George Tanabe, and Paul Varley, eds. *Sources of Japanese Tradition,* 2nd ed., 2 vols. New York: Columbia University Press, 2001.

Gardner, Daniel K., trans. *Learning to Be a Sage: Selections from the Conversations of Master Chu, Arranged Topically.* Berkeley: University of California Press, 1990.

Gihwa. *Exposition of the Correct (Hyeonjeong non).* Trans. Charles Muller. Toyo Gakuen University. Available online at www.acmuller.net/jeong-gihwa/index.html.

Ivanhoe, Philip J., and Bryan W. Van Norden, eds. *Readings in Classical Chinese Philosophy,* 2nd ed. Indianapolis: Hackett, 2003.

Jeong, Dojeon. *Array of Critiques against Buddhism (Bulssi japbyeon).* Trans. Charles Muller. Toyo Gakuen University. Available online at www.acmuller.net/jeong-gihwa/index.html.

Knoblock, John, trans. *Xunzi: A Translation and Study of the Complete Works,* 3 vols. Stanford, Calif.: Stanford University Press, 1988–1994.

Lau, D. C., trans. *Mencius.* New York: Penguin Books, 1970.

Lee, Peter H., ed. *Sourcebook of Korean Tradition,* 2 vols. New York: Columbia University Press, 1997–2000.

Makra, Mary Lelia, trans. *The Hsiao Ching.* New York: St. John's University Press, 1961.

Muller, Charles, trans. *The Analects of Confucius.* Toyo Gakuen University. Available online at www.hm.tyg.jp/~acmuller/contao/analects.html.

———, trans. *The Great Learning.* Toyo Gakuen University. Available online at www.hm.tyg.jp/~acmuller/contao/greatlearning.htm.

———, trans. *The Doctrine of the Mean.* Toyo Gakuen University. Available online at www.hm.tyg.jp/~acmuller/contao/docofmean.htm

———, trans. *Mencius (Selections).* Toyo Gakuen University. Available online at www.hm.tyg.jp/~acmuller/contao/mencius.html.

Slingerland, Edward, trans. *Analects with Selections from Traditional Commentaries.* Indianapolis: Hackett, 2003.

Sure, Heng, trans. "The Twenty-four Paragons of Filial Respect: Their Stories & Verses In Praise." Available online at www2.kenyon.edu/Depts/Religion/Fac/Adler/Reln270/24-filial2.htm.

## Classical Confucianism

Chan, Alan K. L., ed. *Mencius: Contexts and Interpretations.* Honolulu: University of Hawaii Press, 2002.

Ch'en, Ch'i-yün. "Confucian, Legalist, and Taoist Thought in Later Han." In Denis C. Twitchett and Michael Loewe, eds., *The Cambridge History of China, Vol. 1: The Ch'in and Han Empires, 221 BC–AD 220.* Cambridge: Cambridge University Press, 1986, pp. 766–807.

Colvin, Andrew. "Yang Xiong." *Internet Encyclopedia of Philosophy.* Available online at www.iep.utm.edu/y/yangxion.htm.

Elstein, David. "Xunzi." *Internet Encyclopedia of Philosophy.* Available online at www.iep.utm.edu/x/xunzi.htm.

Fingarette, Herbert. *Confucius—The Secular as Sacred.* New York: Harper Torchbooks, 1972.

Graham, A. C. *Disputers of the Tao: Philosophical Argument in Ancient China.* La Salle, Ill.: Open Court, 1989.

Kline, T. C., and Philip J. Ivanhoe, eds. *Virtue, Nature, and Moral Agency in the Xunzi.* Indianapolis: Hackett, 2000.

Knapp, Keith N. *Selfless Offspring: Filial Children and Social Order in Medieval China.* Honolulu: University of Hawai'i Press, 2005.

Kramers, Robert P. "The Development of the Confucian Schools." In Denis C. Twitchett and Michael Loewe, eds., *The Cambridge History of China, Vol. 1: The Ch'in and Han Empires, 221 BC–AD 220.* Cambridge: Cambridge University Press, 1986, pp. 747–65.

Lee, Janghee. *Xunzi and Early Chinese Naturalism.* Albany: State University of New York Press, 2005.

Machle, Edward J. *Nature and Heaven in the Xunzi.* Albany: State University of New York Press, 1993.

Nivison, David S. "The Classical Philosophical Writings." In Michael Loewe and Edward L. Shaughnessy, eds., *The Cambridge History of Ancient China: From the Origins of Civilization to 221 B.C.* Cambridge: Cambridge University Press, 1999, pp. 745–99.

Richey, Jeffrey L. "Confucius." *Internet Encyclopedia of Philosophy.* Available online at www.iep.utm.edu/c/confuciu.htm.

———. "Mencius." *Internet Encyclopedia of Philosophy.* Available online at www.iep.utm.edu/m/mencius.htm.

Schwartz, Benjamin. *The World of Thought in Ancient China.* Cambridge, Mass.: Belknap Press of Harvard University, 1985.

Shun, Kwong-loi. "Mencius." *Stanford Encyclopedia of Philosophy.* Available online at plato.stanford.edu/entries/mencius.

Tu, Weiming. *Centrality and Commonality: An Essay on Confucian Religiousness.* Albany: State University of New York Press, 1989.

Van Norden, Bryan W., ed. *Confucius and the Analects: New Essays.* Oxford: Oxford University Press, 2002.

Wilson, Thomas A., ed. *On Sacred Grounds: Culture, Society, Politics, and the Formation of the Cult of Confucius.* Cambridge, Mass.: Harvard University Asia Center, 2002.

Wong, David. "Confucius." *Stanford Encyclopedia of Philosophy.* Available online at plato.stanford.edu/entries/confucius.

*Neo-Confucianism*

Abe, Yoshio. "Development of Neo-Confucianism in Japan, Korea, and China." *Acta Asiatica* 19 (1970): 16–39.

Bellah, Robert. *Tokugawa Religion: The Cultural Roots of Modern Japan.* New York: Free Press, 1985.

Berthrong, John H. "Neo-Confucianism." *Internet Encyclopedia of Philosophy.* Available online at www.iep.utm.edu/n/neo-conf.htm.

Bol, Peter K. *"This Culture of Ours": Intellectual Transition in T'ang and Sung China.* Stanford, Calif.: Stanford University Press, 1992.

Chan, Wing-tsit, ed. *Chu Hsi and Neo-Confucianism.* Honolulu: University of Hawaii Press, 1986.

Chen, Victor W. "The Korean Neo-Confucianism." *Asian Culture Quarterly* 18, no. 2 (Summer 1990): 75–77.

Ching, Julia. *The Religious Thought of Chu Hsi.* Oxford: Oxford University Press, 2000.

———, ed. *To Acquire Wisdom: The Way of Wang Yang-ming.* New York: Columbia University Press, 1976.

Chung, Edward Y. J. *The Korean Neo-Confucianism of Yi T'oegye and Yi Yulgok.* Albany: State University of New York Press, 1995.

DeBary, William Theodore and JaHyun Kim Haboush, eds. *The Rise of Neo-Confucianism in Korea.* New York: Columbia University Press, 1985.

Elstein, David. "Zhang Zai." *Internet Encyclopedia of Philosophy.* Available online at www.iep.utm.edu/z/zhangzai.htm.

Hooker, Richard. "Japanese Neo-Confucianism." Washington State University. Available online at www.wsu.edu/~dee/TOKJAPAN/NEO.HTM.

Kassel, Marleen. *Tokugawa Confucian Education: The Kangien Academy of Hirose Tanso (1782–1856).* Albany: State University of New York Press, 1996.

Kim, Youngmin. "Wang Yangming." *Internet Encyclopedia of Philosophy.* Available online at www.iep.utm.edu/w/wangyang.htm.

Nosco, Peter, ed. *Confucianism and Tokugawa Culture.* Honolulu: University of Hawai'i Press, 1997.

Palais, James B. *Confucian Statecraft and Korean Institutions: Yu Hyŏngwŏn and the late Chosŏn Dynasty.* Seattle: University of Washington Press, 1996.

Peterson, Willard. "Confucian Learning in Late Ming Thought." In Denis C. Twitchett and Frederick W. Mote, eds., *The Cambridge History of China, Vol. 8: The Ming Dynasty, 1368–1644, Part Two.* Cambridge: Cambridge University Press, 1998, pp. 708–88.

Ro, Young-chan. *The Korean Neo-Confucianism of Yi Yulgok*. Albany: State University of New York Press, 1989.
Sawada, Janine Anderson. *Confucian Values and Popular Zen: Sekimon Shingaku in Eighteenth Century Japan*. Honolulu: University of Hawai'i Press, 1993.
Selover, Thomas W. *Hsieh Liang-tso and the Analects of Confucius: Humane Learning as a Religious Quest*. Oxford: Oxford University Press, 2005.
Setton, Mark. *Chong Yagyong: Korea's Challenge to Orthodox Neo-Confucianism*. Albany: State University of New York Press, 1997.
Standaert, Nicholas. *Yang Tingyun: Confucian and Christian in Late Ming China: His Life and Thought*. Leiden and New York: Brill, 1988.
Thompson, Kirill O. "Zhu Xi." *Internet Encyclopedia of Philosophy*. Available online at www.iep.utm.edu/z/zhu-xi.htm.
Tiwald, Justin. "Dai Zhen." *Internet Encyclopedia of Philosophy*. Available online at www.iep.utm.edu/d/dai-zhen.htm.
Tran My-Van. *A Vietnamese Scholar in Anguish: Nguyen Khuyen and the Decline of Confucian Tradition, 1884–1909*. Singapore: Dept. of History, National University of Singapore, 1992.
Tucker, Mary Evelyn. *Moral and Spiritual Cultivation in Japanese Neo-Confucianism: The Life and Thought of Kaibara Ekken (1639–1714)*. Albany: State University of New York Press, 1989.
Wilson, Thomas A. *Images of the Temple of Culture*. Hamilton College. Available online at academics.hamilton.edu/asian_studies/home/TemplCultno.html.
Yun, Sa-soon. *Critical Issues in Neo-Confucian Thought: The Philosophy of Yi T'oegye*. Honolulu: University of Hawai'i Press, 1991.

## Contemporary Confucianism

Bell, Daniel A., and Hahm Chaibong, eds. *Confucianism for the Modern World*. Cambridge: Cambridge University Press, 2003.
Bresciani, Umberto. *Reinventing Confucianism: The New Confucian Movement*. Taipei, Taiwan: Taipei Ricci Institute for Chinese Studies, 2001.
Cheng, Chung-ying, and Nicholas Bunnin, eds. *Contemporary Chinese Philosophy*. Oxford: Blackwell, 2002.
Chung, Chai-shik. "Confucianism: Tradition and Transformation in Korea." *Transactions of the Korea Branch of the Royal Asiatic Society* 63 (1988): 37–56.
Elman, Benjamin A., John B. Duncan, and Herman Ooms, eds. *Rethinking Confucianism: Past and Present in China, Japan, Korea, and Vietnam*. Los Angeles: Asia Institute, University of California, Los Angeles, 2002.
Jiang, Joseph P. L., ed. *Confucianism and Modernization: A Symposium*. Taipei: Freedom Council, 1987.
Keum, Jang-tae. "The Confucian Religion Movement in the Modern History of Korean Confucianism." *Korea Journal* 29, no. 5 (May 1989): 4–12.
Koh, Byong-ik. "Confucianism in Asia's Modern Transformation." *Korea Journal* 32, no. 4 (Winter 1992): 46–64.

Levenson, Joseph R. *Confucian China and Its Modern Fate: A Trilogy.* Berkeley: University of California Press, 1968.

Liu, Shu-hsien. *Essentials of Contemporary Neo-Confucian Philosophy.* Westport, Conn.: Praeger, 2003.

Makeham, John, ed. *New Confucianism: A Critical Examination.* New York: Palgrave Macmillan, 2003.

Neville, Robert C. *Boston Confucianism: Portable Tradition in the Late-Modern World.* Albany: State University of New York Press, 2000.

Palmer, Spencer J. *Confucian Rituals in Korea.* Berkeley, Calif.: Asian Humanities Press, 1984.

Reid, T. R. *Confucius Lives Next Door: What Living in the East Teaches Us about Living in the West.* New York: Random House, 1999.

Rozman, Gilbert, ed. *The East Asian Region: Confucian Heritage and Its Modern Adaptation.* Princeton, N.J.: Princeton University Press, 1991.

Seith, Andrew. "Ancestors and Ideologues: Confucianism and Communism in Korea." *Asian Studies Review* 7, no. 2 (November 1983): 87–93.

Setton, Mark. "Is There a Post-Neo-Confucianism? Jeong Yagyong, Ito Jinsai, and the Unraveling of *li-qi* Metaphysics." *Sungkyun Journal of East Asian Studies* 2, no. 2 (August 2002): 156–71.

Sun, Anna Xiao Dong. "The Fate of Confucianism as a Religion in Socialist China: Controversies and Paradoxes." In Fenggang Yang and Joseph B. Tamney, eds., *State, Market, and Religions in Chinese Societies.* Leiden: Brill, 2005, pp. 229–53.

Tu, Wei-ming. *Humanity and Self-Cultivation: Essays in Confucian Thought.* Berkeley, Calif.: Asian Humanities Press, 1979.

Tu, Wei-ming, Milan Hejtmanek, and Alan Wachman, eds. *The Confucian World Observed: A Contemporary Discussion of Confucian Humanism in East Asia.* Honolulu: University of Hawai'i Press, 1992.

Yao, Souchou. *Confucian Capitalism: Discourse, Practice and the Myth of Chinese Enterprise.* New York: RoutledgeCurzon, 2002.

Zhang, Wei-bin. *Confucianism and Modernization: Industrialization and Democratization of the Confucian Regions.* New York: St. Martin's, 1999.

PART I

# Teaching Confucianism in Practice

# The Social and Religious Context of Early Confucian Practice

*Mark Csikszentmihalyi*

Whether it is the most suitable text with which to approach either the historical Confucius or the religious tradition of Confucianism, there is no escaping the fact that the introduction most students today are likely to receive to both topics is the *Analects* (*Lunyu* 論語). That text, composed using short texts and brief snippets of conversation dating from the centuries following the death of Confucius in the fifth century B.C.E., was most likely edited in the second and first centuries B.C.E. Because the *Analects* purports to record the actual words of the master, an analogy to other religions may well imply to first-time readers that this single text not only may but *should* be sufficient to understand the basic principles of Confucianism.[1] After all, in some circles, questioning the authority of a scriptural passage is tantamount to calling into question its sacred status.

Even a cursory reading of the *Analects* suggests that Confucius used a different standard with his disciples, because he often taught his students to turn to more ancient traditions and texts he transmitted to them. The *Analects* alone does not spell out the ritual background of Confucius's ethical teachings. Although a student might know about the role of ancestor worship in early China, and the importance of music and the *Classic of Odes* to the earliest Confucians, the nature of the connection between these practices and the ethical teachings is not one that the *Analects* explores in a rigorous way. The aim of this chapter is to contextualize the *Analects* by providing a brief overview of what early texts—both those that have been continuously passed down over generations and those that have been recently excavated from tombs—tell us about the ritual, literary, and self-cultivation curriculum of the community of Confucius and his disciples. Each section begins with a translation of a text from the early tradition that grew up around Confucius. These quotations are then read against the *Analects* and serve to elucidate some of the central social and religious claims of the text.

Ritual Training

> 孔子曰 君子之道譬猶防與 夫禮之塞亂之所從生也 猶防之塞 水之所從來也 故以舊防為無用而壞之者 必有水敗 以舊禮為無所用而去之者 必有亂患 故昏姻之禮廢 則夫婦之道苦 而淫辟之罪多矣 鄉飲酒之禮廢 則長幼之序失 而爭鬥之獄繁矣 聘射之禮廢 則諸侯之行惡 而盈溢之敗起矣 喪祭之禮廢 則臣子之恩薄 而倍死忘生之禮眾矣
> (Confucius said: "I might compare the Way of the Gentleman to an embankment dam. When ritual is blocked, chaos comes about in the same way that when [the regulated flow of water through] an embankment dam is blocked, a flood comes about. So if you think an old embankment dam is useless and destroy it, that will certainly result in flooding and loss, just as if you think the old rites are obsolete and get rid of them, that will certainly result in chaos and disaster."
>
> That is why if the rite of marriage is abandoned, then the Way of husband and wife will be bitter, and many people will be guilty of illicit relations. If the rite of serving wine in the village is abandoned, then the hierarchy of elder and junior will be lost, and conflict and fighting will proliferate. If the rite of diplomatic gifts and ceremonies are abandoned, then the actions of the feudal lords will become evil, and they will start to take part in improperly lavish displays. If the rites of funeral and ancestral sacrifice are abandoned, then the kindness of subjects will wear thin and rituals that multiply death and destroy life will predominate.)[2]

Reading chapter 10 of the *Analects* provides a quick introduction to the different kinds of ritual practice in which Confucius and his disciples routinely participated. It illustrates the breadth of the community's involvement in ritual, encompassing concerns that stretch from etiquette to performance of purification rites and sacrifice. The former may be seen in the expectation of seeing a guest out and remaining outside until one could report that 賓不顧

矣, "the guest has stopped looking back" (*Analects* 10.3).[3] The latter is evident in passages like: 齊必變食 居必遷坐, "During ritual purification he changes his regular diet, and when at home, he did not sleep in his usual place" (10.7) and 祭於公 . . . 出三日 不食之矣, "After assisting at a public sacrifice . . . [Confucius] did not eat the sacrificial offerings after it had been out for three days" (10.9). Clearly, Confucius was concerned with establishing a standard of correct ritual performance.

On the most literal level, these passages indicate that the ancient practice of ancestral sacrifice was still an important part of the ritual environment Confucius was trying to preserve. Ancestral sacrifice was a means of demonstrating reverence for the ancestors and also a way of asking for their assistance. The relationship between the living and the ancestral world was predicated on the assumption of reciprocity. The descendants lay out a sacrifice to make sure their ancestors are satisfied. The ancestors, though predisposed to taking care of the living members of the clan, expect their descendants to enter into purification and reverently make sacrifices.

The purification rites that Confucius carried out were preparation for sacrificing to his ancestors. A ritual text that probably dates to the Han Dynasty explains that the ten-day rite of "retreat and abstinence" (*zhaijie* 齋戒) is further divided into two parts. The first seven days of abstinence from music, wine, meat, fish, sex, participation in marriage or funeral rites, and other forms of social interaction are the "dispersing" (*sanzhai* 散齋) and take place outside the retreat. The last three days are the "arriving" (*zhizhai* 致齋) and take place in the retreat itself, involving what one source calls "communicating with the spirit intelligences" (*jiao yu shenming* 交於神明), the postmortem continuations of the ancestors. Although the question of whether Confucius believed in the continued existence of the ancestors is one that cannot be answered, there is no doubt that he expected his followers to continue practicing ancestral sacrifices in the ritually correct way.[4]

To assume Confucius was intent only on preserving these rites would be to ignore the many diverse rationales for ritual performance included in works like the *Analects*. His early followers promoted a variety of theories about the benefits of ritual practice that go far beyond explicit rationales such as the propitiation of ancestral spirits. In particular, the same word that means *rite* is used to express the proper disposition to ritual, the attitude of "ritual propriety" that becomes a central part of Confucian ethics. In the *Analects*, many discussions of ritual assume the importance of correctly observing the rite, but they go further and emphasize the importance of the psychological state of the practitioner. In *Analects* 3.26, Confucius raises the possibility of performing ritual "without reverence" (*wujing* 無敬), a possibility he condemns. In the context of the rites just described, ritual propriety may be seen as the secularization of the reverence involved in the ritual process, a generalization that adapts it to situations wherein the ancestors are not directly involved, even though they might be watching.

By isolating the psychological state of the performer from the explicit ends of the rites, the early followers of Confucius were able to graft their normative ethical program onto the ritual practices they had inherited. Although there are numerous explanations of the effect of ritual performance by writers like Xunzi 荀子 (early third century B.C.E.) and Jia Yi 賈誼 (early second century B.C.E.), one of the central metaphors in discussions of this topic centers on the rites' ability to form a boundary that restricts or suppresses socially detrimental reactions and feelings.

In some early discussions of ritual, a particular metaphor is used to describe the psychological effect of ritual practice. The Chinese term *fang* 防 (dyke or dam) is used in the passage from the Han Dynasty *Elder Dai's Record of Ritual* that begins this section. Confucius likens the rites to an old earthen dyke or dam that was set up by previous generations to regulate the flow of water and protect against flooding. It might be tempting to conclude such barriers are "obsolete and get rid of them," but that would certainly result in disaster and chaos. The passage goes on to explain how society would also drown in chaos if socially destructive desires for sex, power, and violence were no longer held in check by ritual. The same metaphor occurs in the "Fangji" 坊記 (literally, Record of the Dykes) chapter of the *Records of Ritual* (*Liji* 禮記), when the rites are described as an embankment dam for the people. Ritual distinctions in dress preserve the hierarchy between noble and common, just as ritual positions at court teach the people the importance of yielding.[5] This second passage places a higher value on social harmony and argues that the genius of the rites is their preservation of useful inequalities in society. What both uses of the metaphor illustrate is the prevalence of the theory that participation in the rites prevents a person from acting in ways that lead to conflict and pain.

Understanding the relationship between rites and ritual propriety is crucial to appreciating the way that the message of Confucius grew out of the social norms of his time. The famous twentieth-century scholar Hu Shi 胡適 (1891–1962) wrote that this progressive transformation of ritual had three stages. The first stage was the rite as religious ceremony. The second stage occurred once the rules of the ceremony had become acknowledged as customary across the society. The third stage was when these rules became aligned with moral principles and thus became subject to adaptation and modification.[6] A contemporary student, perhaps one approaching the Chinese tradition for the first time, may never have considered the possibility that ritual might have a potentially positive social aspect. Yet for Confucius, ritual propriety was neither a willingness to submit to a set of symbolic conventions nor simply a matter of giving up personal autonomy. Rather, he held that by restricting appetites and desires, the rites allowed their practitioners cognitive space to reflect, and so allowed them the freedom to cultivate personal moral virtues.

Hu's account of how Confucius adapted ancient rites of purification and sacrifice into a nuanced and dynamic ethical system is only one way of relating his practice of the rites to his theory of the role of ritual practice in ethics. Today, scholars disagree about whether the *Analects* admits of genuine flexibility in the rites, that is, whether that text shows evidence of the third of Hu Shi's three stages. Whether or not Hu's explanation is adequate or its notion of progressive stages reasonable, it draws attention to the important way in which Confucius's ethical system is rooted in the ritual system he taught and practiced.

## Mastery of the *Classic of Odes*

關關雎鳩　在河之洲
窈窕淑女　君子好逑
參差荇菜　左右流之
窈窕淑女　寤寐求之
求之不得　寤寐思服
悠哉悠哉　輾轉反側
參差荇菜　左右采之
窈窕淑女　琴瑟友之
參差荇菜　左右芼之
窈窕淑女　鍾鼓樂之

("Guan, guan!" cry the ospreys on the river's sandbar.
An elegant and kindhearted woman—a good match for a gentleman.
The duckweed grows unevenly, she selects it from the left and right.
An elegant and kindhearted woman—dreaming in bed, seeking her out.
Seeking but not getting her—dreaming in bed, thinking of her.
Interminable, interminable, is the tossing and turning.
The duckweed grows unevenly, she gathers it to the left and right.
An elegant and kindhearted woman—play the lute, befriending her.
The duckweed grows unevenly, she picks it to the left and right.
An elegant and kindhearted woman—play the drums, giving her joy.) ("'Guan!' cry the ospreys," from the *Classic of Odes*)

子曰 關雎 樂而不淫 哀而不傷
(The Master said:
"[The song] 'Guan! cry the ospreys,' is joyous but not depraved, grieving but not to the point of injury.") (*Analects* 3.20)
以琴瑟之悅擬好色之願
以鍾鼓之樂[擬婚姻之]好
反納於禮不亦能改乎
(The "pleasure of the lute," describes the urge of sexual attraction, and the "joy of the drums" describes the attraction [of being married]. By channeling them back into the rites couldn't one change them?) (The excavated text known as "Confucius discusses the *Odes*" [Kongzi shilun 孔子詩論], dating to c. 300 B.C.E.)[7]

Within the disciple community that formed around Confucius, a knowledge of the *Classic of Odes* (*Shijing* 詩經) was a cardinal goal of education. These 305 songs, derived from a variety of traditional sources, provided, in Michael Nylan's words, "not just a storehouse of memorable phrases to play with and master, but a host of antique moral exemplars and an avenue to appropriate pleasures."[8] Although the *Odes* are often understood as poetry, early descriptions indicate that they were to be memorized and chanted. As such, they were at the core of the literacy that Confucius tried to impart and formed a background to the ethical lessons he taught to his students.

What may be unclear to the modern reader is how this devotion to a fixed repertoire of lyrics is connected with the religious dimension of early Confucianism. Part of the connection likely has to do with the way the form of the song lends itself to certain tasks better than historical prose or pedagogical dialogues. In the recorded conversations of Confucius, the *Classic of Odes* did function to evoke images and narratives, drawing connections in a way that a modernist like Ezra Pound found to be essentially poetic in nature. Confucius, Pound wrote, "collected *The Odes* to keep his followers from abstract discussions. That is, *The Odes* give particular instances. They do not lead to exaggerations of dogma."[9] This reading is consistent with Pound's emphasis on the importance of poetic imagery, but it is incomplete because it assumes an aesthetic that historical sources indicate was not shared by the early Confucians. Although the imagery of the *Classic of Odes* allowed those who memorized it to exploit its metaphorical vocabulary, it would be a mistake to think that Confucius insisted on productive ambiguities and avoiding dogmatic applications of the songs.

The early use of the *Classic of Odes* involved both a type of poetic abstraction and knowledge of a "correct" interpretation. This is clear from a dialogue between Confucius and his disciple Zixia 子夏 in *Analects* 3.8. When Zixia asks him about a passage from the song "Bamboo pole" (*Zhugan* 竹竿) that contrasts dark and light features of a beautiful face, the first response Confucius makes draws attention to an abstract feature of the image. He summarizes the poem by telling Zixia 繪事後素, "the matter of painting comes after the plain foundation." Then, Zixia asks Confucius about a particular application of this abstract reading: 禮後乎 (Is it the rites that come after?) His instructor answers affirmatively: 起予者商也 始可與言詩已矣 (You are the one who inspires me! Now, I may begin to discuss the *Odes* with you.) The song in question is not to be interpreted on the most literal level as a poem of longing, but neither are its images to be read without reference to its ritual and ethical connotations. Zixia's method is an example of a reading that is neither simply literal nor strictly abstract but is based on the use of metaphors to inspire a more profound understanding of the other elements of the religious program of Confucius.

This method of reading is even more clearly illustrated in a recently discovered set of short texts dedicated to interpretation of the *Classic of Odes* that found their way into a tomb at the beginning of the third century B.C.E. One of these texts treats seven *Classic of Odes* songs by critically explaining their utility using the vocabulary of the disciple community's program. The quotations at the beginning of this section include the very first work in the *Classic of Odes*, called "' *Guan!*' cry the ospreys" (*Guanju* 關雎), as well as what is said about it in both the *Analects* and the recently discovered tomb text. A close look at this song and the way that it was read by the early Confucians reveals a complex theory of interpretation that integrated the *Classic of Odes* into a theory of ritual and ethical cultivation.

The song "'*Guan!*' cry the ospreys," alternates between two registers. The first might be described as naturalistic, including the image of ospreys and a woman gathering duckweed by the Yellow River. Because this was traditionally a woman's task, these images might be read as metonymic for the woman, who then becomes the object of longing in the rest of the poem. The second register is more psychologistic, recording the longing of a man for the woman. It is not a stretch to read this poem as being about unrequited romantic and sexual longing, although traditionally it has been read as King Wen of the Zhou's appreciation of the virtues of his wife Taisi 太姒. Neither of these readings would cause Confucius to exclaim, "Now, I may begin to discuss the *Odes* with someone!" That is because neither reading integrates the poem into the ritually based system of ethical self-cultivation that Confucius promoted.

Rather, the earliest extant interpretation of the song "'*Guan!*' cry the ospreys," is explicitly about sublimating sexual desire and acting with ritual propriety. In "Confucius discusses the *Odes*," the lutes and drums of the poem are read as descriptions of sexual desire that may be "changed" or "reformed" (*gai* 改).[10] The transformation of desires through ritual practice is not unlike the ritual transformation described in the first section, and it allows the disciple to move closer toward the goal of responding not according to desires but according to ritual propriety, one of the virtues at the core of the self-cultivation program.

The palette provided by the 305 songs in the *Classic of Odes* gave the disciples a set of classical illustrations of transformations and attitudes that were part of their ritual program of self-cultivation. Though the songs provided useful descriptions, they were not explicit as normative instructions to individual disciples found in the *Analects*. For this reason, their role for the earliest Confucians was not unlike that of the hexagrams of the *Classic of Changes* (*Yijing* 易經) for divination. Each song was a resource that might be applied to a particular case or problem. In *Analects* 3.8, Zixia not only understood one of the songs but further understood the proper case to which to apply it.

## Self-Cultivation Practice and the Mind

不遠不敬不敬不嚴. 不嚴不尊不尊不恭 不恭無禮
(If one is not (suitably) distant, then one will not be reverent. If one is not reverent, then one will not be in awe. If one is not in awe, then one will not be respectful. If one is not respectful, then one will not be humble. If one is not humble, then one will be without ritual propriety.) (The *Five Kinds of Action* [Wuxing 五行], excavated at Guodian, copied at the end of the fourth century B.C.E.)

不遠不敬 遠心也者 禮氣也.
("If one is not (suitably) distant, then one will not be reverent." A distant mind is (due to) the *qi* of ritual propriety.) (The commentary on the *Five Kinds of Action* unearthed at Mawangdui, copied in the second century B.C.E.)[11]

In the early twenty-first century, readers tend to identify the ideals of the early community that developed around Confucius as primarily ethical. As a result, the *Analects* and related texts are often mined for information about the ethical program for attaining the ideal of the gentleman, or *junzi* 君子. The preceding sections have already shown how ritual practice and the use of the

*Classic of Odes* in the community were closely connected to this ideal, but the specific way these practices facilitated the gentleman's development of the virtues remains to be described. This is, perhaps, the area in which the *Analects* provides the least guidance. Indeed, the absence of a detailed account of the original state of the virtues and the best means of their development occasioned a celebrated theoretical schism between Mengzi 孟子 (fourth century B.C.E.) and Xunzi on the quality of human's innate nature.[12] There is no question that teaching the cultivation of these virtues was a primary concern of Confucius as portrayed in the *Analects*, but he engages in almost no theoretical discussion of the nature of emotional, intellectual, or psychological changes corresponding to this development.

The *Analects* only uses the word *mind* (*xin* 心), a term that means both the organ of the heart and the seat of intelligence, six times. Although later Confucian texts use it with much greater frequency, clearly changes in the mind are required for the process of self-cultivation to succeed. One of these six instances is Confucius's description of the disciple Yan Hui's devotion to benevolence in *Analects* 6.7: 其心三月不違仁 其餘則日月至焉而已矣 (In his mind he will not oppose benevolence for months at a time, while the others can only get there for a day or so.) What accounts for Yan Hui's powers of moral concentration? And the other disciples' lack thereof?

The *Analects* does not spell out Yan Hui's secret, but we do know that he was "fond of learning" (*hao xue* 好學, 6.3). If we recall the cardinal aspects of the curriculum of the disciple community, the content of this learning incorporated both ritual practice and chanting the *Classic of Odes*. From the foregoing analysis, we may conclude that these two activities aided Yan Hui's capacity for engaging in the cultivation of virtue, because the *Classic of Odes* taught him to sublimate his desires into ritually proper action, and ritual performance served as a barrier to selfish or immoral actions. These practices gave him the cognitive space in which he could develop the virtues, but how did he actually develop the moral concentration for which he was known?

Here, a metaphor more familiar to students of East Asian medical traditions provides one account of how Yan Hui developed his virtue. The metaphor of *qi* 氣, variously translated as pneuma, energy, or even psycho-physical stuff, is similar to the European concept of the bodily humor in that it is a quasi-material substance whose accretion in the body causes feelings, behaviors, health, and disease. In traditional Chinese medicine, the balance of different kinds of *qi* is a key to health, but the term can also stand in for "life force" in that its absence or stilling can signify death. This metaphor has the advantage of having been used in several of the earliest extant Confucian texts to describe the development of the virtues. Beginning with the recently excavated *Five Kinds of Action*, these texts support the idea that the virtues are gradually constructed through practice that enhances their material dimension. That text explains the development of ritual propriety as beginning from an attitude of "distance" (*yuan* 遠), an attitude that Confucius elsewhere uses to describe the attitude to the spirits.[13] In a six-stage process, the initial feeling during ritual performance is developed into a full-fledged disposition to ritual propriety via the intermediary feelings of reverence, awe, respect, and humility. A separate commentary to the text, also excavated in the past few decades and dating to the second century B.C.E. at the latest, describes how the initial stage of distance is a result of the *qi* of ritual propriety. In other words, a small amount of this kind of *qi* leads to the ability to sacrifice to one's ancestors with a suitably distant attitude. Participating in such practice, in turn, further enhances that kind of *qi*. When enough is accrued, one is able to act out of ritual propriety, presumably for months at a time.

The commentary to the *Five Kinds of Action* makes the tie between ritual performance and the accretion of the *qi* of virtue even more explicit. In a discussion of how the attitude of distance becomes that of reverence, the first steps along the path to developing the virtue of ritual propriety, the commentary observes: 左麾而右飯之 未得敬[心者也] (There has never yet been a person who, directing with the left hand and eating with the right hand, was able to attain a reverent [mind]).[14] The almost humorous picture of a person directing the sacrificial rite with one hand while holding food in the other illustrates how proper practice both is a result of a certain degree of propriety and is needed to reach the next level of the progression to full propriety. Although this model for the development of the virtues is not necessarily the one that Confucius had in the back of his mind, it is one example of how some early writers imagined the practices we have already examined, culminating in the development of virtue.

This metaphor of *qi* is an important aspect of the justification of Confucius's ethics. Numerous passages in the *Analects* appear traditionalist or even reactionary with respect to the precedent of the Zhou, but this account of the way ritual benefits society stresses the intermediary transformation of the individual. Though we saw how the *Records of Ritual* justified the ritual order in terms of the social goods that particular rites ensured, that is not the entire picture, according to the *Analects* and the writers of the *Five Kinds of Action*, who sought to explain the mental dimension of the *Analects*' self-cultivation picture. Ritual functions to restrict desires, but it also builds virtue in the individual practitioner and in doing so creates an ethical actor in the society.

## Conclusion

I have reexamined three topics in the *Analects* in light of other early texts to better understand and contextualize their practical dimension for the early disciple community. Taking the example of the disciple Yan Hui, is it possible to rearrange these observations so as to imagine his daily practice?

After completing the purification rites of fasting and abstinence, Yan Hui emerges from the retreat, having communicated with the spirits of the ancestors. Throughout the process he has tried to maintain the proper attitude of distance and reverence. Yan Hui remembers how the ritual codes warned him against abandoning the ritual because of the way that ritual offerings model the kindness necessary for other spheres of society to function. He begins to direct the newer members of the disciple community in laying out the sacrifice to the ancestors. Yan Hui is intent on rechanneling his deepest desires into ritual practice, using the model of the gentleman in "*'Guan!'* cry the ospreys." He, too, is trying to reform his desires by adhering to ritual. Confucius observes the ritual performance and voices his approval. It strikes him that Yan Hui never stops to eat while directing the sacrifice, proving his disciple's powers of concentration and attesting to Yan Hui's growing accumulation of ritual propriety.

This reconstruction only begins to locate the *Analects* within the ritual and cultural universe in which it was written. This context is not inseparable from the ethical system of the text, and indeed there is little question that the *Analects* would lose its appeal to most readers today should ancestral sacrifice and memorization of 300 songs be considered a prerequisite for its contemporary application. At the same time, to understand the text's appeals to the transformative power of ritual and its reliance on the canon of the *Classic of Odes*, a modern reader might do well to turn to other early works and the newest archeological material. By doing so, it is possible to better understand the practical curriculum of the early community that formed around Confucius, and thus better understand their discussions as they have come down to us today.

NOTES

The author acknowledges the helpful comments of Guo Jue on an earlier draft of this chapter.

1. The use of the term *Confucianism* creates problems in that it implies a single tradition that grew out of the teachings of a single founder. On both the strengths and shortcomings of this model, and what it owes to the sociologist Max Weber, see Mark Csikszentmihalyi, "Confucius," in David Noel Freedman and Michael J. McClymond,

eds., *The Rivers of Paradise: Moses, Buddha, Confucius, Jesus, and Mohammad as Religious Founders* (Grand Rapids: Eerdmans, 2001), pp. 233–308.

2. Chapter 46 of the *Elder Dai's Record of Ritual* (*DaDai Liji* 大戴禮記). In the "Licha" 禮察 chapter, see Wang Pinzhen 王聘珍, *DaDai Liji jiegu* 大戴禮記解詁 (Beijing: Zhonghua shuju, 1985), p. 21.

3. See D. C. Lau, trans., *Confucius: The Analects* (London: Harmondsworth, 1979), pp. 101–105. Here, the actions of Confucius are in the context of his service as an usher (bin 擯).

4. The "Suburban sacrifice of Cattle" (Jiao te sheng 郊特牲) in Sun Xidan 孫希旦 (1736–1784), *Liji jijie* 禮記集解 (Beijing: Zhonghua, 1989), pp. 670–723. This was translated by James Legge in *Li Ki*, 2 vols. (New York: University Books, 1967), pp. 1:416–48.

5. See *Liji jijie* 50.1283 and Legge, p. 2:285.

6. *Zhongguo zhexue shi dagang* 中國哲學史大綱 (Shijiazhuang: Hebei jiaoyu, 2001), p. 105.

7. This bamboo slip text was acquired by the Shanghai Museum in 1994, and my transcription is based on Huang Huaixin's 黃懷信 study, *Shanghai bowuguan cang Zhan'guo Chu zhushu Shilun jieyi* 上海博物館藏戰國楚竹書詩論解義 (Beijing: Shehui kexue wenxian, 2004), p. 19. This is the earliest extant edition of the songs that are quoted in the text, and so the use of *yue* 悅 instead of *you* 友 suggests that the original song might have read "play the lute, giving her pleasure," instead of "befriending her."

8. *The Five "Confucian" Classics* (New Haven, Conn.: Yale University Press, 2001), p. 104.

9. *Confucius: The Unwobbling Pivot, The Great Digest, The Analects* (New York: New Directions, 1951), p. 191.

10. Here, I follow Huang's reading of *gai* instead of the more common reading of *fei* 妃 (spouse) because although *fei* may be more consistent with the traditional reading of the poem, *gai* is more consistent with the context in "Confucius discusses the *Odes*."

11. See Mark Csikszentmihalyi, *Material Virtue: Ethics and the Body in Early China* (Leiden: Brill, 2004) for translations of both texts. Specifically, these translations may be found on pp. 294–95 and 329–30.

12. For an overview of these early Confucian writers, see Philip J. Ivanhoe, *Confucian Moral Self Cultivation* (Indianapolis: Hackett, 2000). An excellent survey of the reading of Confucian ethics in a comparative context as an ethics of virtue may be found in Bryan van Norden, "What Should Western Philosophy Learn from Chinese Philosophy?" in Philip J. Ivanhoe, ed., *Chinese Language, Thought and Culture: Nivison and His Critics* (LaSalle: Open Court, 1996), pp. 224–49.

13. *Analects* 6.22. For this reading, see *Material Virtue*, p. 295.

14. *Material Virtue*, p. 331. The same text also explains how "Guanju" is to be read as a process of extrapolating desire for sex into an understanding of ritual. See *Material Virtue*, pp. 366–67, and Jeffrey K. Riegel, "Eros, Introversion, and the Beginnings of *Shijing* Commentary," *Harvard Journal of Asiatic Studies* 57 (1997): 143–77.

# Learning Confucianism through Filial Sons, Loyal Retainers, and Chaste Wives

*Keith N. Knapp*

In the postmodern world, heroes do not exist. Popular and scholarly historiography are both devoted to proving that larger-than-life great men, such as John F. Kennedy, Franklin Delano Roosevelt, and Martin Luther King Jr., had aspects of their lives that were as sordid as that of any person on the street. Telltale biographies level the great so that they appear no better than the ordinary person. No doubt the fervent egalitarianism that industrialism has produced is responsible for this trend. Our history now focuses on impersonal social and economic trends that are greater than any individual. Despite living in an era in which individualism is king, we rivet our historical attention on patterns, institutions, and ideas that formed individuals, rather than individuals themselves. This certainly was not the case, though, in the premodern world. In preindustrial societies, history was the stuff of remarkable people who shaped events, instead of being shaped by them. History books related the lives of that society's most significant people; their paramount aim was to provide readers with exemplars after whom they could model their lives. History was human; thus, it could best be summed up in the lives of the finest people.

The postmodern negation of heroes has given us a sharper view of the complexity of reality, but it has also made history less human and interesting. In the same manner, it has made religious traditions, such as Confucianism, less inspiring as well. To many of our students, Confucianism appears stodgy, unappealing, and detached from real life. This happens because we only introduce students to the theoretical works of the tradition, such as the *Analects, Mencius,* and the *Xunzi,* disclosing our proclivity for ideas rather than individuals. These texts reveal the richness and complexity of the Confucian message —they are truly the heart of the tradition. Nevertheless, even though they are far from impenetrable, these works are by no means a breeze to read. This was true even in the Chinese past. The *Analects,* the simplest of the three, was often used as a classical primer in premodern China and could still only be approached after one gained a basic mastery of characters through word books. In other words, even the easiest of these books could only be read by people who had some basic training.

The vast majority of Chinese became acquainted with Confucianism not through these philosophical texts but through stories of notable men and women whose actions embodied the Confucian teachings. These figures were usually noted for their filiality and loyalty (in the case of men) or chastity (in the case of women). Very much like Christian saints, their lives were dramatic, often punctuated by miracles, and they sometimes were the recipients of cult admiration. Moreover, because images of their exploits often adorned the walls of public buildings and shrines, even the unlettered could readily identify these tales. For most Chinese, these filial heroes, loyal retainers, and chaste heroines were the human face of Confucianism, perhaps even more so than Confucius or his beloved disciple Yan Hui. Hence, the most ubiquitous book in late imperial China was not the *Analects* or *Mencius,* but the *Twenty-Four Filial Exemplars.*

Due to the immense popularity and social reach of these tales, this chapter's primary contention is that in addition to the philosophical texts, instructors should expose students to a healthy dose of Confucian exemplar stories and images. The reasons for doing so are many. First, because their purpose was to make Confucian ideas readily understandable, they not only explain the tradition's values in a clear and straightforward manner, they also reveal to us how later Confucians interpreted *Ru* (Confucian, or more precisely, scholars of the Kingly Way) teachings and the way they transmitted them to others.[1] Second, because these stories and images were accessible to a much wider audience than were the philosophical texts, they offer students a sense of how the vast majority of people understood and perceived Confucianism. Third, illustrations of the tales give undergraduates a chance to see how Confucian ideas were visually constructed and furnish them with vivid images of Confucianism in action. Fourth, because the stories are narratives, they are fascinating and fun to read in themselves, they will certainly pique nearly any student's interest and enliven a discussion of Confucianism. Finally, by showing supernatural agents rewarding virtuous actions, they also reveal a sense of the religious overtones of popular Confucianism. Before discussing the benefits of using this material in the classroom, I first narrate the nature and importance of these materials to premodern Chinese.

## The Nature and Place of Confucian Exemplars in Chinese Society

The central *Ru* values of *ren* (compassion), *li* (propriety), *xiao* (filial piety), and *yi* (righteousness) are of such complexity and profundity that they are hard to translate, let alone explain. Moreover, their realization comes about through the practice of complicated and elaborate ceremonies that are exhaustively described in Confucian ritual codes. For laypersons, whether they are early Chinese or modern North Americans, it is difficult to obtain a good understanding of these concepts, much less believe that anyone could perform all of the attendant rites. Due to the intricacy of the messages, ever since *Ru* began to propagate the views of their school in the Warring States period, the masters sought to clarify the teachings by putting forth examples of individuals whose behavior captured both the spirit and the letter of their doctrines and rituals. The first exemplars were Confucius's disciples, such as Yan Hui, Zengzi, Min Ziqian, Zixia, and Ziyou. As time went on, proponents of Confucianism proselytized its doctrines further afield. To facilitate their new audiences' comprehension of Confucian doctrine, more exemplars were created, many of whom were contemporary in time with their audiences.

On Confucianism becoming the Han dynasty's guiding philosophy (c. 138 B.C.E.), the government itself took a hand in publicizing the lives of people that embodied these teachings. It did so through the creation of special chapters in the standard dynastic histories that were dedicated to the lives of Confucian heroes. As a result, the imperial era witnessed the creation of large numbers of Confucian paragons, especially in the form of filial sons, loyal retainers, and chaste women. Privately compiled works that carried the titles of *Accounts of Filial Offspring* (*Xiaozi zhuan*), *Accounts of Exemplary Women* (*Lienü zhuan*), *Accounts of Loyal Retainers* (*Zhongchen zhuan*), and the *Twenty-Four Filial Exemplars* (*Ershisi xiao*) also propagated tales of these exemplars. These texts were so important for learning Confucianism that they were seen as indispensable supplements to philosophical teachings. For instance, the only reading material that Southern Qi (479–502 C.E.) princes were allowed to read were the *Five Classics* and the *Accounts of Filial Offspring*.[2] This fact illustrates not only the stories' orthodoxy but also that contemporaries viewed them as complementary to the *Ru* classics.

42   TEACHING CONFUCIANISM IN PRACTICE

The importance of exemplars as educational matter is most visibly evident in the popularity of the primer *Inquiries of the Ignorant* (*Meng Qiu*), which circulated widely from the eighth through thirteenth centuries. This text consists of 298 rhymed couplets that mention the names and allude to the stories of paired exemplars. For example, "Kuang Heng bore a hole in the wall; Sun Jing shut his door" (*Kuang Heng zao bi; Sun Jing bi hu*). Students memorized these two four-character couplets, and their teacher narrated the tale associated with each man. Kuang was so poor that he could not afford candles. So to study at night, he bore a hole in his neighbor's wall to borrow some of his candlelight. Sun Jing was so devoted to his studies that he always stayed in his room. To prevent drowsiness, he would tie a noose around his neck and attach the other end to a ceilingbeam.[3] Needlessly to say, both anecdotes drive home the point that students should be extremely diligent in their studies. By memorizing this primer, students not only learned about noteworthy historical figures but also imbibed each story's moral lesson.

The usefulness of this type of instructional tool was not lost on later generations. The *Mengqiu* had many spin-offs, such as *Inquiries of the Ignorant into the Seventeen Histories* (eleventh century), *Inquiries of the Ignorant into [the history of] the Two Han Dynasties*, and *Inquiries of the Ignorant of Names and Things* (thirteenth century). These texts had a wide following in late imperial times.[4] The importance of using exemplars to teach was such that, in his primer, *Elementary Learning* (*Xiaoxue*), the great synthesizer of Neo-Confucianism Zhu Xi (1130–1200) felt it necessary to dedicate an entire chapter to anecdotes of people who embodied the principles expounded on in earlier chapters.[5] Inspired by the significance that Chinese have traditionally placed on exemplars, North American historians have even written introductory surveys of Chinese history that consist entirely of biographies of China's most noteworthy individuals.[6] Because premodern Chinese placed so much emphasis on exemplars and found them to be such a useful teaching tool, it only makes sense that we should, too.

Tales to Teach

So which tales should we teach our students? To give them a sense of what anecdotes Chinese found truly inspiring, we should furnish those stories that were most reproduced in both text and images. Students will then be able to see the narratives that people knew best and found most compelling. An excellent place to start is with the *Twenty-Four Filial Exemplars*. Works with this name first appeared in the late ninth century and became widespread after

## FILIAL SONS, LOYAL RETAINERS, AND CHASTE WIVES    43

1000. Western observers from the early 1900s note that if a family only possessed one book, it would be the *Twenty-Four Filial Exemplars*. This is also a good text to use for class because it is short and several Web sites contain downloadable translations of it.[7] Have your students read the text before class and simply ask about their reactions to the stories. A vigorous discussion of how weird and outlandish these tales are will surely ensue. You can use the students' negative reactions to delineate modern assumptions of what the parent-child relationship should be like and how we define rationality. You can dig deeper by asking your students the following questions: Why have Chinese found these stories to be so poignant that before 1949 every Chinese child was taught them? How did these tales shape expectations about children's behavior? Keeping the ages of the narratives' protagonists in mind, were these anecdotes just for children? Having students formulate answers to these questions will hopefully transport them from their modern assumptions to premodern Chinese suppositions.

I find it particularly helpful to focus on the stories that modern students find the hardest to fathom. For instance, nothing could be more shocking to modern sensibilities than the story of Guo Ju, who wants to bury his infant son alive to ensure that his aged mother has enough to eat. When he is in the process of digging the hole, he finds a pot of gold that Heaven has caused to be there as a reward for his filial intentions. As a child, Lu Xun (1881–1936), China's greatest modern writer, found this tale to be especially frightening. Here he conveys the dismay he felt on first reading it:

> At first I broke into a real cold sweat for that child, not breathing freely again until the crock of gold had been dug up. But by then not only did I no longer aspire to be a filial son myself, I dreaded the thought of my father acting as one. At that time our family fortunes were declining, I often heard my parents worrying as to where our next meal was to come from, and my grandmother was old. Suppose my father followed Guo Ju's example, wasn't I the obvious person to be buried? If things worked out exactly as before and he too dug up a crock of gold, naturally that would be happiness great as Heaven; but small as I was at the time I seem to have grasped that, in this world, such a coincidence couldn't be counted on.[8]

Nevertheless, for premodern Chinese, this was one of the most poignant and frequently illustrated filial tales. Hence, one should push his or her students to think about why Chinese found this tale to be so compelling. Why would Guo Ju sacrifice a child who has his whole life ahead of him for an elderly woman whose life is near its end? While discussing the answer, the instructor should point out that Guo's actions did not signal that he was bereft of feelings for his son; on the contrary, precisely because people then and now dote on young children, this made his sacrifice even greater. Note, too, the role of Guo's wife. Guo tells her that to save his mother, they must bury their son. Instead of trying to protect her son, who in the future will provide her with status and subsistence, she obediently follows her husband's command and agrees that the child must die. What could be more emblematic of filial piety than a couple who sacrifices their future happiness to requite past kindness? Finally, if you want to give students a sense of how the *Twenty-Four Filial Exemplars* version of this text has been modified for a popular audience, you can have them compare this version of the Guo Ju story to an earlier version.[9]

Another figure who will surely look strange to our students is Old Master Lai (Lao Laizi). At the age of seventy, he was afraid that his ninety-year-old parents might be feeling old, so he often dressed up in multicolored children's robes and played with toys in front of them. Sometimes he would carry water and intentionally slip. He would then cry like a baby, which sent his parents into peals of laughter. He did these things so that his parents would forget about their age. Even as a child, Lu Xun found this tale to be completely absurd because he could not countenance an adult behaving in such a ridiculous manner.[10] In contrast, most Chinese since the first century C.E. have found this tale to be immensely meaningful and moving. It is especially important to have students look at how premodern artists depicted this narrative. Without exception, in all the premodern representations I have seen, Lao Laizi is depicted as either a child or a young man.[11] Ask your students why artists chose to portray him that way, especially since from his name and the written text of the story, most people probably knew he was an old man. I think the answer is that the artists were trying to suggest that in loving his parents so much, Old Master Lai had retained the heart of a child. It is important to point out, too, that the artists might have been suggesting that filial sons and daughters should forever serve as ageless children on their parents' behalf.[12]

As for loyal retainers, there are many dramatic examples from which to choose. Due to its unparalleled fame, one of the best choices has to be that of Jing Ke, the would-be assassin of Qin Shihuang, the First Emperor of the Qin dynasty (221–207 B.C.E.). In this tale, Prince Dan of the state of Yan in the northeast was insulted by the First Emperor and feared that he would soon conquer the state of Yan. He thereupon lavished attention and honors on Jing Ke, a knight-errant, in hopes that he would undertake a suicide mission to assassinate the First Emperor. During an audience with the First Emperor, Jing had the opportunity to stab the emperor, but he hesitated so he could extract a promise from him to stop the Qin's wars of conquest. The emperor broke away from his grasp, but he was too scared to order anyone to his rescue. Jing Ke chased him around a pillar, but he was stunned by a blow from the court doctor's medicine bag. The emperor finally unsheathed his sword and wounded Jing's leg. Before the others could finish him off, Jing threw his dagger at the emperor, which missed and struck a bronze pillar. Images of this story usually show a fleeing emperor, an exasperated Jing, and a dagger stuck into a pillar.[13]

This tale is so famous that at least two recent blockbuster Chinese films (both available with English subtitles) have been devoted to it: Zhang Yimou's *Ying Xiong* (*Hero*; 2002) and Chen Kaige's *Jing Ke Ci Qin Wang* (*The Emperor and the Assassin*; 1999). One of the earliest and best-known versions of this story is found in Sima Qian's (145–86? B.C.E.) monumental *Records of the Grand Historian* (*Shiji*). Translations of this tale are readily available in a number of sources.[14] I suggest, then, that instructors have students read Sima Qian's version of it and ask students to watch one of the two recent films on their own time. Then put the following questions to them. According to the earliest version, why is Jing Ke willing to give up his life on Prince Dan's behalf? Does he die based on a feeling of loyalty toward his adopted state of Yan? Why would Confucians, who generally viewed knights-errant as unlawful ruffians, view Jing Ke positively? How have modern films changed the story? What type of loyalty does Jing Ke express in contemporary movies? How have Chinese definitions of virtue changed from the first century B.C.E. to the present? Endeavoring to answer these questions not only allows students to gain an understanding of Confucian loyalty but also gives them a sense of how Chinese values have changed due to the influence of nationalism.

Now that you have some understanding of what sort of behavior Confucians expected of men, what do you think was expected of women? A well-known text that provides many biographies of Confucian female role models is Liu Xiang's (77–6 B.C.E.) *Accounts of Exemplary Women* (*Lienü zhuan*). Anne Behnke Kinney is working on a new translation of this text, which will be available online. Her Web site already has a wealth of information on this text.[15] Until that translation is finished, one can still consult Albert Richard O'Hara's full translation.[16] Because the biographies of the *Accounts of Exemplary Women* are longer than those in the *Twenty-Four Filial Exemplars* and are not yet fully available electronically, having students read a couple of the narratives from this work should be sufficient to stimulate discussion of Confucian notions of female behavior.

The best-known and most widely available tale of a virtuous woman is that of Mencius's mother (Mengmu).[17] Mencius (c. 372–289 B.C.E.), of course, was the second greatest Confucian philosopher. Several anecdotes set forth his mother's virtuous motherhood. When Mencius was just a child, his family lived next to a graveyard. As a result, Mencius pretended to construct graves and perform funerals. Not being pleased with this behavior, his mother then moved the family to a new residence near a market. Soon Mencius was pretending to sell goods and haggle over prices. This displeased his mother as well, so she again moved the family; this time to the vicinity of a school. Soon Mencius was pretending to offer sacrifices and bow to everyone in a respectful manner. She knew she had found the right environment for him. Once when he showed apathy toward his learning, his mother took a knife and cut apart the cloth she was weaving. When a startled Mencius asked her why, she replied, "In what way does what you are doing differ from spinning thread and weaving in order to provide food? A woman who neglects the work that provides food is like a man who falls short in cultivating his virtue. If he does not become a thief, then he will become a servant."[18] Clearly, Mencius's mother is a worthy model because she made her son's moral upbringing the center of her attention and efforts. Her every moment and place was an opportunity for teaching her son how to act correctly. She also shows us that for any self-respecting man the only acceptable profession was that of scholar. Because her account has a number of other anecdotes as well, it is truly rich teaching material. Nevertheless, for at least the first thousand years after it was propagated in the *Accounts of Exemplary Women*, it was rarely depicted pictorially.

For me, the most evocative stories concern chaste wives; unfortunately, because modern analysts do not think these stories put women in a complimentary light, they tend to omit them from anthologies of Chinese historical writings.[19] Once it is revealed that Confucians thought women should never remarry and applauded those who either mutilated or killed themselves to prevent that from happening, Confucianism loses much of its charm for modern audiences. Ignoring these narratives is a shame because premodern Chinese held them in high esteem, which is manifest in that they were frequently the exemplary tales of women that were illustrated. Consequently, I do not think students can truly understand Confucian attitudes toward women until they are exposed to these stories. Moreover, because Confucians believed that the husband-wife relationship was parallel to that between a lord and his retainer—to the point where some analysts believe that the *Accounts of Exemplary Women* was largely written to teach men about loyalty[20]—to sidestep these tales is tragic.

One of the best-known early tales of the chastity that Confucians hoped widows would maintain is that of a woman who was given the title *Gaoxing* (Exalted Conduct). When her husband died early, she refused to remarry. Due to her extraordinary beauty and flawless conduct, the noblemen of her state vied with each other for her hand in marriage. She refused each one. When the king sent an envoy with betrothal gifts, she decided the only way for her to maintain her virtue was to make herself unattractive. She used a knife to cut off her nose.[21] Indicative of this tale's popularity is the fact that this was one of exemplary women tales that was most often depicted on objects.[22] Discussion of this tale will quickly dispel any notion that Confucianism is easily reconcilable with feminism. It thereby forces students to see that Confucians viewed women quite differently than modern Westerners do.

Confucians even hoped that women with unworthy husbands would maintain the same high standard of conduct. After being married for only five days, Qiu Huzi left home to take up office in a faraway place. After five years, he returned. As he neared home, he spied a beautiful woman picking mulberry leaves. He propositioned her to lie down with him; when she refused, he offered her money to do so. She would have nothing to do with him. When he arrived home, he discovered that the woman he had propositioned was his own wife. Scandalized by his licentious behavior, his wife castigated him. However, since a woman should never remarry, divorce was out of the question. Rather than remain the wife of such a contemptible husband, she drowned herself in a river.[23] Concerning this narrative, the first question we can ask is why the author felt compelled to have such a virtuous woman commit suicide. Was not her avoidance of temptation enough? Why were women expected to have such a high standard of behavior? To what extent did women actually behave in this manner? Discussing these questions allows students to avoid looking at Confucianism solely through the rosy but distorted lenses of contemporary Confucian apologists. At the same time, answering the last question will make students appreciate that there was always a wide gap between Confucian ideals and social practice.

An excellent resource that combines both images and stories of exemplary women is a late sixth-century scroll titled "Admonitions of the Instructress to the Court Ladies," which is attributed to Gu Kaizhi (c. 344–406). This scroll contains images that depict four stories of outstanding women and six groups of illustrated precepts that indicate how women should behave. Shane McCausland's *First Masterpiece of Chinese Painting: The Admonitions Scroll* handsomely reproduces those images and conveniently translates and interprets their accompanying text.[24] Three out of the four stories of outstanding women illustrated in the scroll are taken from Liu Xiang's *Accounts of Exemplary Women*; moreover, those three tales are all from the "Accounts of the Sagacious and Wise" chapter.

## Advantages of Teaching with Exemplars

One of the frustrations of teaching Confucianism is the vagueness of some of its key concepts. Anyone who has used the *Analects* to talk about ren (humaneness) will know what I mean. Even Confucius seems to have a hard time putting its meaning in words. The exemplar tales, in contrast, provide explicit models of how one should embody Confucian values. Unlike the philosophical texts, the biographies of exemplars leave little room for interpretation. Consequently, the stories present Confucian ideas in a concrete manner that is easily understandable, which is precisely why they were so popular. Moreover, because the paragons express Confucian ideals through their discrete behavior, others can do the same by imitating their actions. In other words, the exemplars make Confucian ideas more accessible and simplify them to the point that others can undertake them. Hence, in premodern China, if one asked how one should live, rather than list Confucian do's and don'ts, most Chinese would have said that one should model his or her life after so-and-so.

Another important aspect of these tales is that they were written long after the Confucian philosophical texts. Hence, they provide us with not only a simplified version of these teachings but also a later understanding of them. Moreover, they tell us what parts of the tradition later people valued and did not value. One very striking thing is that the values that the historical biographies champion are neither *ren* (humaneness) nor *li* (ritual propriety); instead they champion *xiao* (filiality), *zhong* (loyalty), *yi* (righteousness), and *zhen* (chastity). Although the philosophical texts also affirm these values, in them these virtues are merely secondary. For instance, the philosophical texts rarely mention the value of *zhen* and never connect it with women. In these texts, it means "steadfast" more than it does "chaste." One should note that the values touted by the historical biographies were precisely those that most benefited the state and social relations, rather than self-cultivation. Consequently, looking at the accounts of exemplars immediately reveals that there was a deep chasm between what the classical philosophers advocated and what their later adherents found attractive within the tradition. No doubt, changing historical conditions account for these differences. To make students aware of the historical development of the tradition, one can ask them what some of those changed historical circumstances might have been.

The exemplar accounts are especially valuable because they provide students with a different kind of Confucianism—one that was aimed at a much less elevated audience than those of the philosophical texts. Because the tales simplify Confucian messages and are brief, self-contained narrative units in themselves, they were easily transmitted orally in both elite circles and in the village square. Furthermore, many of the tales were illustrated, meaning that the unlettered could readily know them. That images of these stories appeared on everyday goods, such as mirrors, baskets, and screens, and the walls of government offices, schools, and funerary shrines ensured that they had a large and diverse audience. The inscriptions within the cartouches that accompany many of these images merely identify the name of the story's protagonist. Obviously, the artisans expected that the images' audience already knew the plots of the tales. Hence, by reading these accounts and looking at the images, students are exposed to Confucianism as it was understood by most people.

Our students are visually oriented, so they should find the images quite attractive. One of the few places where one can find images of filial sons, loyal retainers, and virtuous women together in one place is the appendix of Wu Hung's *Wu Liang Shrine*. Unfortunately, there is no English Web site that contains the illustrations of *the Twenty-Four Filial Exemplars* text. One Chinese site, however, contains modern depictions of all twenty-four filial exemplars.[25] As for images of exemplary women, the University of Virginia's E-text Initiative contains an illustrated Ming copy of the *Accounts of Exemplary Women (Lienü zhuan)*.[26] These images of the exemplar tales serve as snapshots of ideology that will undoubtedly stamp vivid images of Confucianism on your students' minds.

One last important aspect of the exemplar stories is that they also shed light on the religiosity of popular Confucianism. In many ways these tales are reminiscent of the hagiographies of Christian saints. Like hagiographies, they are meant to commemorate the life of a great individual, and in so doing, they are meant to inspire others to imitate that outstanding life. Like the saintly heroes of the hagiographies, Confucian exemplars practiced a form of asceticism in which they denied themselves ordinary pleasures, daily necessities, and in some cases even their lives, all to benefit others. As a result, people sometimes established shrines to give them cult and honor their deeds. The divine world sometimes confirmed the sanctity of their lives by favoring them with miracles. We have already seen how Heaven rewarded Guo Ju for his murderous yet filial intentions.

What precise form did this religiosity take? The exemplar tales exhibit what I have called elsewhere "correlative Confucianism," which is based on the principles of *Tianren ganying* (Heaven and People mutually respond to each other) and *Tianren heyi* (Heaven and People become one).[27] What this means is that the writers of these stories believed that people live in a moral universe, in which a morally good Heaven and Earth produce all things in the world. Because people have the essence of Heaven and Earth within them,

50 TEACHING CONFUCIANISM IN PRACTICE

each person has the potential to be heavenly—that is, to do good. Based on the principle that things of the same kind affect each other, when people perform an especially good or sincere act, they realize their heavenly nature, thereby causing Heaven to respond with an auspicious sign or reward. Hence, when Guo Ju was about to bury his son, his act of pure devotion moved or caused Heaven to react by making a pot full of gold appear. On a simpler level, many of the stories make it apparent that heavenly deities closely observe our behavior and reward and punish us for our especially good or bad deeds. For example, when Xiang Sheng was away from home, his wife treated his blind mother badly by feasting on the tastiest morsels while giving her mother-in-law the less choice pieces. When her mother-in-law reprimanded her for this, Xiang Sheng's wife mixed pig excrement with the food she served her. When Heaven saw this unfilial behavior, it struck her dead with a bolt of lightning. On her back were written the following words: "Xiang Sheng's wife committed [one of] the Five Deviances, hence Heaven has struck her dead with a lightning bolt."[28] Here, Heaven's role as a conscious agent who intervenes in this world is readily apparent. Note that the text stresses that Heaven took notice of her actions. That the wife's death is not a coincidence is made obvious by the fact that Heaven has made known its will by inscribing its punishment on her back. For the authors and audiences of these narratives, good deeds were not only a method of self-cultivation, but they were also a means by which to gain the favor of the celestial deities that keep close watch on our actions.

In short, just as one cannot talk about medieval European religion without mentioning the cult of the saints, one cannot talk about premodern Chinese religion without mentioning the veneration of ethical paragons. The religiosity that the Confucian exemplar tales convey is that of a spirit world that deeply cares about human moral behavior and sanctions adherence to *Ru* values with supernatural rewards; at the same time, it reviles those who transgress Confucian norms and punishes them with thunderbolts and bad fortune.

Conclusion

The purpose of this chapter was to provide instructors with a means of introducing an alternate and more popular view of Confucianism. While teaching the philosophical texts is essential to conveying the tradition's main tenets, one should also expose students to documents that indicate how most people understood those ideas. For this purpose, nothing is better than the exemplar stories, which were widely known and transmitted throughout Chinese society. Having students read these tales will benefit them in many ways. First, it will indicate that for most Chinese, *Ru* values were not just abstract intellectual notions but forms of concrete behavior that should be embodied by its practitioners. Second, it will give them a better sense of how the Confucian tradition changed over time. Whereas the early philosophers were most interested in virtues that ultimately benefited the self, such as ren and li, the virtues that later Confucian adherents promoted were those that benefited the state or the family, such as *zhong*, *xiao*, and *zhen*. Third, the tales reveal a popular form of Confucian religiosity that emphasized a caring Heaven that zealously observed people's moral behavior. Fourth, because the narratives are interesting to read and surprising, they should enliven any discussion of Confucianism. That many were illustrated also provides students with the ability to examine how Confucians presented their ideas through images. Fifth, because the tales (through their images) were accessible to the unlettered, these tools of propaganda furnish us with a sense of how the great majority of premodern Chinese understood and viewed the Confucian tradition. Hence, even though these narratives are short and simple, for the student of Confucianism, they pack quite a punch.

NOTES

1. For a short discussion of what the word *Ru* means, see Keith Knapp, "New Approaches to Teaching Early Confucianism," *Teaching Theology and Religion* 2, no. 1 (1999): 45–46.

2. See Li Yanshou, *Nan shi*, ed. Zhonghua shuju (Taipei: Dingwen shuju, 1980), p. 43.1088.

3. Li Han and Hsü Tzu-Kuang, *Meng Ch'iu: Famous Episodes from Chinese History and Legend*, trans. Burton Watson (Tokyo: Kodansha, 1979), p. 23.

4. Regarding these texts and their popularity, see Thomas H. C. Lee, *Education in Traditional China* (Leiden: Brill, 2000), pp. 447–55, and Limin Bai, *Shaping the Ideal Child: Children and Their Primers in Late Imperial China* (Hong Kong: Chinese University Press, 2005), pp. 29–32.

5. See M. Theresa Kelleher, "Back to Basics: Chu Hsi's *Elementary Learning* (*Hsiao-hsüeh*)," in William Theodore de Bary and John W. Chaffee, eds., *Neo-Confucian Education: The Formative Stage.* (Berkeley: University of California Press, 1989), pp. 234–37.

6. See John E. Wills, *Mountain of Fame: Portraits in Chinese History* (Princeton, N.J.: Princeton University Press, 1994), and Kenneth J. Hammond, ed., *The Human Tradition in Premodern China* (Wilmington, Del.: SR Books, 2002).

7. The following Web sites have full translations of the *Twenty-Four Filial Exemplars*: www.ruf.rice.edu/~asia/24ParagonsFilialPiety.html, www2.kenyon.edu/Depts/Religion/Fac/Adler/Reln270/24-filial2.htm, and weber.ucsd.edu/~dkjordan/scriptorium/xiao/xiaointro.html.

8. Lu Xun, "The Picture-book of the Twenty-four Acts of Filial Piety," in *Dawn Blossoms Plucked at Dawn*, trans. Gladys and Hsien-yi Yang (Peking: Foreign Languages Press, 1976), pp. 34–35.

9. See Keith Knapp, "Early-Medieval Stories of Filial Piety," in Victor H. Mair, Nancy S. Steinhardt, and Paul R. Goldin, eds., the *Hawai'i Reader in Traditional Chinese Culture* (Honolulu: University of Hawai'i Press, 2005), p. 280.

10. Lu, "The Picture-book," pp. 31–33.

11. See Wu Hung, *The Wu Liang Shrine: The Ideology of Early Chinese Pictorial Art* (Stanford, Calif.: Stanford University Press, 1989), pp. 280–82; Keith N. Knapp, *Selfless Offspring: Filial Children and Social Order in Medieval China* (Honolulu: University of Hawai'i Press, 2005), p. 150.

12. On this point, see Wu Hung, "Private Love and Public Duty: Images of Children in Early Chinese Art," in Anne Behnke Kinney, ed., *Chinese Views of Childhood* (Honolulu: University of Hawai'i Press, 1995), pp. 99–101. This article also has a good discussion of illustrations of exemplary women.

13. Wu, *The Wu Liang Shrine*, p. 316.

14. See Burton Watson, trans., *Records of the Historian: Chapters from the SHIH CHI of Ssu-ma Ch'ien* (New York: Columbia University Press, 1969), pp. 55–67, and his *Records of the Grand Historian: Qin Dynasty* (New York: Columbia University Press, 1993), pp. 167–78; Sima Qian, *The Grand Scribe's Records: Volume VII The Memoirs of Pre-Han China*, ed. William H. Nienhauser Jr. (Bloomington: Indiana University Press, 1994), pp. 325–33. For a more fantastic version of this story, see "Prince Tan of Yen," in Wolfgang Bauer and Herbert Franke, eds., *The Golden Casket* (New York: Harcourt, Brace and World, 1964), pp. 30–41.

15. The URL of her Web site is jefferson.village.virginia.edu/xwomen.

16. See his *The Position of Women in Early China: According to the Lieh Nü Chuan "Biographies of Eminent Chinese Women* (reprint, Westport, Conn.: Hyperion Press, 1981).

17. Besides being translated by Albert O'Hara, it has also been rendered into English by Pauline C. Lee in Robin Wang, ed., *Images of Women in Chinese Thought and Culture: Writings from the Pre-Qin Period through the Song Dynasty* (Indianapolis: Hackett, 2003), pp. 149–55, and by Nancy Gibbs in Patricia Buckley Ebrey, *Chinese Civilization: A Sourcebook* (New York: Free Press, 1981), pp. 72–74.

18. Wang, *Images of Women*, p. 151.

19. For example, in Wang, *Images of Women*, Pauline C. Lee has only translated the tale of Mencius's mother and two tales from the chapter on those who are good at argument. In other words, the only texts translated are those that show women who are esteemed because of their intellect.

20. Catherine Gipoulon, "L'Image de l'épouse dans le *Lienü zhuan*," in Jacques Gernet, Marc Kalinowski, and Jean-Pierre Diény, eds., *En Suivant la Voie Royale* (Paris: École Française d'Extrême-Orient, 1997), pp. 109–11.

21. O'Hara, *The Position of Women in Early China*, pp. 122–24.

22. Wu, *The Wu Liang Shrine*, pp. 253–54 and 258.

23. O'Hara, *The Position of Women in Early China*, pp. 141–43. For the depiction of this story at Wu, *The Wu Liang Shrine*, pp. 254–56 and 259.

24. See his *First Masterpiece of Chinese Painting: The Admonitions Scroll* (New York: George Braziller, 2003), pp. 32–81.
25. See news.xinhuanet.com/health/2005-03/08/content_2666176.htm.
26. See etext.lib.virginia.edu/etcbin/chinesebin/lienu.
27. See Knapp, *Selfless Offspring*, chap. 4.
28. Wang Chongmin, *Dunhuang bianwen* (reprint, 2 vols.; Taipei: Shijie shuju, 1980), p. 2:909.

BIBLIOGRAPHY

Bai Limin. *Shaping the Ideal Child: Children and Their Primers in Late Imperial China.* Hong Kong: Chinese University Press, 2005.
Bauer, Wolfgang, and Herbert Franke, eds. *The Golden Casket.* New York: Harcourt, Brace and World, 1964.
Ebrey, Patricia Buckley, ed. *Chinese Civilization: A Sourcebook.* New York: Free Press, 1981.
Gipoulon, Catherine. "L'Image de l'épouse dans le *Lienü zhuan.*" In Jacques Gernet, Marc Kalinowski, and Jean-Pierre Diény, eds., *En Suivant la Voie Royale.* Paris: École Française d'Extrême-Orient, 1997, pp. 97–111.
Hammond, Kenneth J., ed. *The Human Tradition in Premodern China.* Wilmington, Del.: SR Books, 2002.
Kelleher, M. Theresa. "Back to Basics: Chu Hsi's *Elementary Learning (Hsiao-hsüeh).*" In William Theodore de Bary and John W. Chaffee, eds., *Neo-Confucian Education: The Formative Stage.* Berkeley: University of California Press, 1989, pp. 219–51.
Knapp, Keith N. "New Approaches to Teaching Early Confucianism." *Teaching Theology and Religion* 2, no. 1 (1999): 45–54.
———. "Early-Medieval Stories of Filial Piety." In Victor H. Mair, Nancy S. Steinhardt and Paul R. Goldin, eds., *Hawai'i Reader in Traditional Chinese Culture.* Honolulu: University of Hawai'i Press, 2005, pp. 278–81.
———. *Selfless Offspring: Filial Children and Social Order in Medieval China.* Honolulu: University of Hawai'i Press, 2005.
Lee, Thomas H. C. *Education in Traditional China.* Leiden: Brill, 2000.
Li Han and Hsü Tzu-Kuang. *Meng Ch'iu: Famous Episodes from Chinese History and Legend,* trans. Burton Watson. Tokyo: Kodansha, 1979.
Li Yanshou. *Nan shi* (History of the Southern Dynasties). Reprint; Taipei: Dingwen shuju, 1980.
Lu Xun. "The Picture-book of the Twenty-four Acts of Filial Piety." In *Dawn Blossoms Plucked at Dawn,* trans. Gladys and Hsien-yi Yang. Peking: Foreign Languages Press, 1976, pp. 26–35.
McCausland, Shane. *First Masterpiece of Chinese Painting: The Admonitions Scroll.* New York: George Braziller, 2003.
O'Hara, Albert Richard. *The Position of Women in Early China: According to the Lieh Nü Chuan "Biographies of Eminent Chinese Women.* Reprint; Westport, Conn.: Hyperion Press, 1981.

Sima Qian. *The Grand Scribe's Records: Volume VII, The Memoirs of Pre-Han China*, ed. William H. Nienhauser Jr. Bloomington: Indiana University Press, 1994.

Wang Chongmin. *Dunhuang bianwen* (Dunhuang's Transformation Texts). Reprint, 2 vols.; Taipei: Shijie shuju, 1980.

Wang, Robin R., ed. *Images of Women in Chinese Thought and Culture: Writings from the Pre-Qin Period through the Song Dynasty.* Indianapolis: Hackett, 2003.

Watson, Burton, trans. *Records of the Historian: Chapters from the SHIH CHI of Ssu-ma Ch'ien.* New York: Columbia University Press, 1969.

———. *Records of the Grand Historian: Qin Dynasty.* New York: Columbia University Press, 1993.

Wills, John E. *Mountain of Fame: Portraits in Chinese History.* Princeton, N.J.: Princeton University Press, 1994.

Wu Hung. *The Wu Liang Shrine: The Ideology of Early Chinese Pictorial Art.* Stanford, Calif.: Stanford University Press, 1989.

———. "Private Love and Public Duty: Images of Children in Early Chinese Art." In Anne Behnke Kinney, ed., *Chinese Views of Childhood.* Honolulu: University of Hawai'i Press, 1995, pp. 79–110.

# Divination and Sacrifice in Song Neo-Confucianism

*Joseph A. Adler*

Confucianism is assumed by most students and by many teachers to be fundamentally a socioethical tradition in which ritual (*li*) is primarily a method and legitimation of social control. The theme of moral self-cultivation, especially in the Neo-Confucian movement, is likewise often regarded as something akin to contemporary humanistic psychology or "self-help" regimens. Thus neither ritual nor self-cultivation is commonly understood to be essentially religious. Yet as we shall see in this chapter, Confucian ritual included two particular forms, divination and sacrifice, which are clearly religious in character and are systematically related to the Confucian theory and practice of self-cultivation.

Divination (the formal questioning of ancestors or gods and the reception and interpretation of their responses) and sacrifice (offerings of various sorts to spiritual beings) are rituals that have become highly marginal in Judeo-Christian culture. Students may be familiar with tarot, Ouija boards, and perhaps even the *Yijing*, but they do not encounter anything of the sort in their own religious communities. Sacrifice, once central to the Jewish (or ancient Israelite) tradition, disappeared with the destruction of the Second Temple in 70 C.E. and was consciously replaced by the study of Torah and living according to its commandments (the Word of God). Although these two rituals are clearly religious because they generally involve divinities, their deeper significance may elude students without some guidance.

In China, divination and sacrifice as a ritual dyad constitute the earliest known form of Chinese religion (that of the rulers of the Shang dynasty at least as early as the fourteenth century B.C.E.) and have continued throughout Chinese history to the present day as central features of popular religious life. They can be considered a model of the fundamental Chinese way of orienting the human world to the sacred: a kind of ritual *axis mundi* rooting our world in something that transcends it, thereby making it meaningful. This chapter explores the continuity of the Confucian tradition with this central core of Chinese religiosity and suggests ways by which its forms and meanings can be conveyed in the classroom.

The major forms of sacrifice and divination practiced by Confucians for over two thousand years have been offerings to ancestors and sages and divination using the *Yijing* (Scripture of Change). Both forms of ritual will be discussed here, but the focus will be on *Yijing* divination practiced by the Neo-Confucians of the Song dynasty (960–1279 C.E.), and in particular on Zhu Xi (1130–1200), who was the first to fully integrate the theory and practice of divination into the Confucian religious process of transformation into a sage. Zhu Xi's version of the Confucian tradition, which came to be called *Daoxue*, the Learning of the Way, exerted tremendous influence on all levels of Chinese society into the twentieth century. Zhu Xi understood *Yijing* divination to be a ritual aid to the cultivation of "spiritual clarity" (*shen-ming*), or the capacity of the human mind/heart to penetrate to the ultimate source of moral creativity underlying the phenomenal world. This is one aspect of the religious character of Confucianism, which can easily be missed by observers taking a narrowly defined perspective of the tradition, a perspective based largely on a limited number of texts and a bias for a model of religion derived from Western prototypes.

Before turning to the Song dynasty, let us briefly consider the roles of sacrifice and divination in the aristocracy of the Shang dynasty (fourteenth to eleventh centuries B.C.E.) and in the popular religion of the present day.[1] The religion of the Shang royal court centered on the relationship of the king with his departed ancestors, who served a higher being called Di (Lord) or Shangdi (High Lord, or Lord Above). There were also various nature deities representing heavenly bodies, mountains, rivers, and so on, who likewise served under Di. The ancestors had power over the king and his family in such matters as childbirth and illness, and they could intercede on behalf of the king with Di, who had broader powers over weather and the success of crops, hunting, and warfare. The king had a two-way channel of communication with Di and his ancestors: Through sacrifice he could influence them to use their powers for the welfare of his family and the state, and through divination he could determine which ancestors should be given offerings, whether they received them with good favor, whether certain courses of action were advisable, and so forth.

Sacrificial offerings usually consisted of wine or food items placed in beautifully cast bronze vessels. Sacrifices were made to the Shang royal ancestors according to a strict ritual calendar, much like the feast days of Roman Catholic saints, although they could also be made at any time for specific reasons. For example, if the king fell ill, it would be determined through divination which ancestor was the cause and what kind of sacrifice would assuage him or her. The ancestors were ranked hierarchically by generation, sex, and nearness to the main descent line, and they were given offerings appropriate to their rank. All the ritual details were strictly prescribed, and what made the sacrifice efficacious, besides the appropriateness of the sacrifice (as in the case of illness, when it was necessary to determine which ancestor was causing it) was the correctness of the ritual's performance.

Shang divination took the form of pyromancy (fire divination) using two kinds of bones: the broad scapulae (shoulder blades) of cattle and the plastrons (ventral bones) of tortoises, about one foot in length. The bone would be prepared by gouging out two parallel columns of small hollows. The divination itself involved a specialist posing a question in the form of two alternative statements, such as "The princess's childbirth will be auspicious" (i.e., it will produce a son) and "The princess's childbirth will not be auspicious." After each statement or "charge" was uttered, a red-hot stick or poker was inserted into one of the gouges, producing a sideways T-shaped crack on the reverse side of the bone. This might be repeated five or ten times. Using criteria that have not been identified with certainty by scholars, the crack-making was interpreted as either positive or negative. When the process was completed, the date, the names of the diviner and the king, and the question were inscribed on the bone, sometimes followed by the king's interpretation and the outcome of the event.

These oracle bones—the earliest Chinese written documents—were first excavated and identified beginning in 1928 at the site of the last Shang capital, the city of Yin (near present-day Anyang in Henan Province). From them scholars have extracted most of what we know about the culture of Bronze Age China. The other major form of written inscriptions from this period were inscriptions on some of the bronze ritual vessels that held the sacrificial offerings. These or similar specially cast vessels were sometimes given as gifts to commemorate military victories or to mark such special occasions as marriages. This practice continued for roughly a thousand years after the end of the Shang period.[2]

The picture that emerges of this earliest known form of Chinese religion is one that is highly ritualistic, bureaucratic, and family-centered. Sacrifice and divination constituted the central linkage between the heavenly and earthly realms, and the king was the pivotal figure ensuring their harmonious coexistence. Through sacrifice he acknowledged the higher status of the ancestors and gods and provided for their needs; through divination he received confirmation that their needs were being met and that they were willing to act in favor of the king, his family, and the state he represented. The ultimate goal was to ensure the harmony and welfare of the heavenly, earthly, and social realms.[3]

One of the more remarkable aspects of the history of Chinese religions is the extent to which these general themes and specific forms of religious practice (sacrifice and divination) are still clearly evident in contemporary Chinese society. Today sacrifice is practiced in homes and in temples. Most Chinese families have an altar table or shelf in the home, holding ancestral plaques on which are written the names and dates of the ancestors (in most cases no more than two or three generations back) alongside images of gods, Buddhas, and/or bodhisattvas. Offerings may be made either daily, weekly, every fifteen days (according to an ancient agricultural calendar), on holidays, or on anniversaries of the ancestor's death. Offerings always include incense—the smoke rising heavenward symbolizes a burnt offering and carries the wishes of the subject to the gods and ancestors—and some kind of food item such as fresh fruit or, for ancestors only, cooked rice. In Taiwan today and in mainland China before the communist crackdown on religion, some extended families have or had family or lineage temples (*jia miao*), whose altars hold plaques going back to their earliest known ancestor. Since the 1990s, lineage temples have begun to reappear in mainland China.[4]

Offerings to ghosts (the dangerous yet pitiable spirits who lack descendants to worship them as ancestors) in many Chinese communities are made every fifteen days by householders and businesses, always outside the home or business. (Ghosts, like the beggars with whom they are often compared, are never invited inside the home.) Offerings to gods in temples are made by ordinary people and, less frequently, by priests in more elaborate rituals. The ornate altars in Chinese temples always have incense and food offerings on them, put there by temple attendants and visiting worshippers. The larger temples have offering tables in their courtyards on which visitors place all sorts of packaged and fresh food items for the gods enshrined in the temple. In Confucian temples, which are typically found only in larger cities and in towns where descendants of Confucius live (the largest being the Confucian family complex in Qufu, Shandong Province, Confucius's birthplace), the atmosphere is more restrained and the visitors much fewer, but the same kinds of offerings are made both to Confucius himself and to the officially designated sages, worthies, and erudites of the past (i.e., Confucian scholars in descending ranks). On Confucius's birthday, conventionally observed as September 28, there is an annual grand sacrifice to him in Confucian temples in the People's Republic of China, Taiwan, and other Chinese communities. This hugely elaborate ceremony, conducted at dawn, includes ritual musicians, dancers, and priests, and is attended by local government officials and perhaps a few hundred "ordinary" people.[5]

Oracle bone divination became obsolete during the Western Zhou dynasty (1045–771 B.C.E.) that followed the Shang, but divination in other forms took its place. The earliest of these new forms was the use of the *Zhou Yi* (Changes of Zhou), today more commonly called the *Yijing*. This divination manual (the original *Zhou Yi*) and the early commentaries that were eventually incorporated into the text as appendices (called the "Ten Wings") is still used,[6] primarily by intellectuals but also by less highly educated people who might pay a diviner operating a stall or a small storefront, offering several forms of divination, to cast a hexagram and interpret it for them. Other forms of divination are more common today, especially the use of "moon-blocks" (*bei*) and "divination slips" (*qian*) by worshippers in Chinese temples. More elaborate forms of divination, requiring the hiring of specialists, include shamanistic spirit-mediums (*tongji*) and palanquin or chair divination (*jiaozi*).[7] But the Song dynasty Confucian scholars to be discussed regarded the *Yi* (as it was usually referred to) as the most suitable form of divination for the educated elite.

Although today's Chinese communities are of course worlds apart from the warlike aristocracy of Bronze Age China, in certain respects what we would call their religious goals are quite similar: healthy families with strong connections to their ancestors, prosperous communities that maintain good relations with the powers of nature and their deities, and a secure state whose government takes the welfare of its people as its first and highest duty. Harmony within society, with the natural world, and with the various types of spiritual beings still pretty much defines the ideal Chinese state of things.

Although there are elements of this worldview that clearly qualify as "religious" by Western standards—for example, the worship of spiritual beings—there are also aspects that, from a Western perspective, appear at first to be irreducibly secular, such as social harmony and good government. It is these elements that are most closely related to Confucianism. But it is crucially important to recognize that understanding "the secular as sacred" (as Herbert Fingarette put it three decades ago)[8] is precisely the key to grasping the meaning of Confucian religiosity.

## Confucian Ritual in the Song

### Sacrifice

The forms of ritual that most concerned Confucian scholars throughout the history of imperial China were those practiced within the family, all of which revolved around ancestor worship. Indeed, communication and participation with ancestors has been one of the characteristic features of Chinese culture as a whole for millennia. As Patricia Ebrey has put it, "The mutual dependence of the living and the dead, of ancestors and their descendants, had been a central feature of Chinese culture from ancient times," and "the links of the living and the dead needed to be renewed on a fixed schedule through offerings and sacrifices to ancestors."[9]

Family rituals included the capping and pinning of young adult males and females, respectively; marriage; funerals; and a wide variety of rituals that we can collectively call ancestor worship. Capping and pinning were varieties of late puberty rituals, transformations into adulthood, described in such classical texts as the *Yili* (Etiquette and Ritual) and *Liji* (Record of Ritual), as well as in later ritual texts up through the Song dynasty. Capping/pinning and marriage were commonly understood not only as rites of passage, effecting and marking the major transitions between life stages, but also as rituals that ultimately served the purpose of continuing the family line. Likewise, funeral rituals, including a series of sacrifices extending over a twenty-five-month mourning period, were understood as the transformation of the deceased into an ancestor. When this process was completed and the ancestor was installed in the family shrine, ancestor worship involved—at least according to the prescriptive or normative texts—daily activities such as a respectful looking in, occasional reports to the ancestor about important family events, regular offerings of food and wine, and more elaborate sacrificial rituals on specified dates.[10]

Interest in family rituals reached a peak during the Confucian revival of the Song, a movement that gave rise to what today is commonly referred to as Neo-Confucianism. After the fall of the Han dynasty in 220 C.E.—a dynasty that had adopted Confucianism as its official ideology—Buddhism (recently arrived from India) and Daoism attracted the most creative Chinese intellectuals. Part of the impetus of the Neo-Confucian revival was the view held by many Song intellectuals that China's infatuation with Buddhism and Daoism had contributed to the political weakness of the Song state in relation to its neighboring nomadic peoples to the north. One of these, the Jurchen, did in fact conquer the northern half of Song China in 1127.[11] So the Neo-Confucian revivalists felt that by rejecting the "foreign" religion of Buddhism, by restoring the family descent line as the core of Chinese society, and by returning to what they believed were the original sources of Chinese culture—the wisdom of the ancient sages preserved in the Confucian scriptures (or "classics")—the Song state could recover the glory and success of the early Zhou and Han periods.

One of the strongest proponents of this view was Zhu Xi, who was born three years after the Northern Song fell to the Jurchen and the capital was relocated to the south. He and other like-minded Confucians regarded Buddhism as a threat to China's social fabric because of what they claimed was its disrespect for the family. Because Buddhism encouraged a monastic vocation—which to Confucian eyes appeared to go against the very grain of the Chinese social order, which was based on the family—Buddhism was seen as a serious threat to the social cohesion and strength of Chinese society and hence to the very survival of Chinese culture. This and the more obvious threat of invasion constitute a good part of the sociopolitical background of Zhu Xi's efforts to synthesize the teachings of the Confucian tradition, from the earliest mythic sages right up to his immediate predecessors in the Northern Song period.

Perhaps the most broadly influential book among the many written by Zhu Xi was his *Family Rituals* (*Jia li*). The book quickly became authoritative after his death and was republished in various editions many times during the ensuing Yuan, Ming, and Qing Dynasties. It was part of Zhu Xi's effort to strengthen the moral fiber of Chinese society by standardizing the major social rites of passage according to his reconstruction of the orthodox Confucian forms and principles. His lifelong mission was to construct a comprehensive system of education and personal moral cultivation—beginning in the family—by which individuals could approach as closely as possible the ultimate Confucian goal of sagehood. The larger sociopolitical goals depended, for him, on a class of educated elite comprised of such individuals, who would strengthen and transform Chinese society through the force of their "moral power" or virtue (*de*).[12] One became a Confucian sage, according to this system, by transforming one's imperfect psychophysical nature into a condition of "spiritual clarity" (*shen-ming*), which would allow one's inherent "Heaven-endowed" moral nature to fully express itself. This was an extremely difficult process, in Zhu Xi's view, and required all the help one could muster. As we shall see, *Yijing* divination was a powerful tool that he believed could be employed to this end.

In addition to sacrificial offerings to ancestors within the family, Song Confucians also made offerings, accompanied by praise and prayer, to earlier

Confucian sages. These were conducted in official Confucian temples; in smaller temples and shrines to some of the prominent sages of the past, such as Mencius (Mengzi, who lived in the fourth century B.C.E.) and Zhou Dunyi (1017–1073); and in Confucian academies. Education was expanding greatly in the Song, in part because of the decreasing cost of printing books;[13] the central government was establishing schools in every county, and many individual Confucian scholars (including Zhu Xi) built and ran their own private academies. In these academies prayers and offerings to the sages of the past were daily practices.[14]

*Divination*

Just as in the Shang period, Song communication or participation with spiritual beings through sacrificial offerings was complemented by various methods of divination, including divining blocks, geomancy, and the hexagrams of the *Yijing*. All are still practiced today. Divining blocks, or moon-blocks, are crescent-shaped painted wooden blocks, about three or four inches long, flat on one side and convex on the other. The subject drops a pair of blocks onto the floor, and the answer to the question is determined by whether they come to rest on the flat side or the convex side: one of each is a positive response; both on the same side is negative. This is the simplest and most common form of divination and can easily be demonstrated in class if a pair of moon-blocks is available.[15] Geomancy, or *feng-shui*, is a complex art, practiced by specialists and used to determine auspicious locations for houses, temples, tombs, and businesses. It is based on the theory that *qi*, the psychophysical stuff of which all things are composed, flows through the Earth according to certain natural laws and influences the success of human life (and death).

Song Confucian attitudes toward these popular forms of divination were mixed, although generally positive. Divination blocks were commonly used for questions such as selecting the proper day for a ritual. Some of the more conservative Confucians, such as Sima Guang (1019–1086) and Cheng Yi (1033–1107), were opposed to geomancy in general (although Zhu Xi was not) and opposed to the use of divination blocks in certain circumstances;[16] when important moral principles were involved, they felt that the *Yijing* should be used instead. In general the *Yijing* was considered the most powerful and nuanced oracle, the one most appropriate for the educated elite.[17]

The *Yijing* was part of the earliest Confucian textual canon, commonly known as the Five Classics (*Wu jing*), more accurately translated as the Five Scriptures. The others are the *Shujing* (Scripture of Documents), *Shijing* (Scripture of Odes), *Chunqiu* (Spring and Autumn Annals), and the *Li* (Ritual, actually comprising three different ritual texts: *Liji* or Record of Ritual, *Zhouli* or Rituals of Zhou, and *Yili* or Etiquette and Ritual). Although the versions of these texts that we have today are only partially the same as those that existed in Confucius's time, texts corresponding to them were apparently taught by Confucius. In the second century B.C.E., when King Wu of the Han dynasty made Confucianism the official ideology of his government, he established an academy for the training of government officials in those texts, and bureaus of government were established for each one. Other scriptures were later added to the original five, eventually (by the Song dynasty) resulting in a Confucian canon of Thirteen Scriptures, although the original five had the greatest prestige and until the Song were considered to be the core of Confucian education.

However, a shift took place during the Song, largely as a result of the Confucian curriculum systematized by Zhu Xi. In this new curriculum, the core was no longer the Five Classics but the Four Books (*Sishu*). These were the *Daxue* (Great Learning), *Zhongyong* (Centrality and Commonality), *Lunyu* (Analects of Confucius), and *Mengzi* (Book of Mencius).[18] Zhu Xi considered the Four Books to be more important than the Five Scriptures because they focused more on the issues in moral psychology and moral cosmology that he considered most crucial in the achievement of sagehood. So he published the Four Books in a single volume with his commentaries and made them the core of the advanced Confucian curriculum.[19]

But the statement that the Four Books replaced the Five Scriptures in importance should be qualified, because one of the Five Scriptures actually became *more* important in Song and later Confucianism than it had been before. That was the *Yijing*. Two of the five masters of Northern Song—a group of eleventh-century scholars who initiated the intellectual movement that Zhu Xi later promoted and synthesized into a coherent system—focused much of their scholarly attention on and gained much of their inspiration from the *Yijing*.[20] These two were Shao Yong (1011–1077) and the aforementioned Zhou Dunyi. Both were particularly interested in a tradition of diagrammatic explication of the *Yi* that had begun in Daoist religious circles. In particular, Zhou Dunyi's "Explanation of the Diagram of the Supreme Polarity" (*Taijitu shuo*), an originally Daoist diagram based on the *Yi*, became—through the efforts of Zhu Xi—the fundamental text in Neo-Confucian moral cosmology.[21]

The *Yijing* is a multilayered text. The original core is a series of sixty-four diagrams, called *gua* or hexagrams, each composed of six lines, either solid or broken. The solid lines represent *yang*, the principle of light, Heaven, activity, and so on; the broken lines represent *yin*, the principle of darkness or shadow, Earth, stillness, and so forth. Each hexagram has a name and is thought to represent an archetype of a social or natural situation in which the questioner can be involved. The hexagrams may or may not have evolved from three-line diagrams (also called *gua*, but commonly translated as "trigrams"), which in any case are treated as meaningful units within the hexagrams. The eight trigrams all have symbolic meanings and names based on their configurations of *yin* and *yang*, as do the sixty-four hexagrams.[22] The *gua* are said to have been conceived by the mythic culture-hero Fuxi (traditionally dated to the twenty-ninth century B.C.E.), who abstracted them from the patterns he observed in the natural world. He is also credited with the divination system by which the dried stalks of the milfoil (or yarrow) plant (*Achillea millefolium*) are manipulated and counted off to derive a number that determines each of the six lines of a hexagram.[23]

The next layer of the *Yijing* is composed of the short, oracular texts given with each hexagram. For example, hexagram 24 (*Fu*, "Return") and its text are as follows.

> Return. Success.
> Going out and coming in without distress.
> Friends come without blame.
> The Way reverts and returns.
> On the seventh day comes the return.
> It is beneficial wherever one goes.[24]

These texts are traditionally said to have been composed by the first king of the Zhou dynasty, King Wen, while he was imprisoned by the corrupt last king of the Shang dynasty in the eleventh century B.C.E. King Wen's son, King Wu, later conquered the Shang, and King Wu's brother, the duke of Zhou, continued his father's work on the *Yi* by composing further explanatory texts for each line of each hexagram. The texts attributed to King Wen and the duke of Zhou constitute the second and third layers of the *Yijing*.

The final layer is the appendices, or Ten Wings, which are attributed to Confucius but were more likely written long after his death. They vary greatly in style and content.[25] Philosophically, the most important part of the *Yijing* for the Song Neo-Confucians was the longest of the appendices, the *Xici* or Appended Remarks—also called the *Dazhuan* or Great Treatise—and certain closely related parts of a shorter appendix, the *Shuo-gua* (Explaining the Trigrams). The *Xici*, dating probably from the third century B.C.E., is basically a collection of reflections, from a Confucian perspective, on the theory of *yin-yang* change that underlies the *Yi*.[26] Some of the concepts it covers that were incorporated into the Neo-Confucian synthesis during the Song are *dao* (Way), *qi* (psychophysical stuff), *Taiji* (Supreme Polarity), *yin-yang* (dark-light), *shen* (spirit), the sage (*shengren*), change (*yi*), alternation (*bian*), transformation (*hua*), mind (*xin*), activity and stillness (*dong-jing*) (of things and the mind), and of course divination using the dried stalks of the milfoil plant (*shi*). All of these terms figured into Zhu Xi's theory of moral self-cultivation.[27]

During the Zhou dynasty, of course, the *Yi* had been used primarily for divination—not as the wisdom book that it eventually became after the addition of the Ten Wings. The *Zuozhuan* (Mr. Zuo's Commentary), one of the first major commentaries on the *Spring and Autumn Annals*, contains numerous instances of rulers and other aristocrats practicing divination to help decide important personal and political issues.[28] Zhu Xi clearly regarded these as normative, because his collaborator on one of his two books on the *Yi* refers to many of them, with Zhu's implicit agreement.[29]

Zhu Xi saw in the *Yijing* trigrams/hexagrams a formal representation of the fundamental ordering principle (*li*), which has two dimensions: natural principle (*tian-li*) and moral principle (*dao-li*). Because of the extreme difficulty, in Zhu Xi's view, of clarifying one's psychophysical nature (*qizhi zhi xing*) enough to enable one to fully apprehend moral principle and put it into practice, he believed that ordinary humans needed to investigate things, patterns, and principles in the natural world. Because it is often easier to understand natural principle than moral principle, one can first study the natural patterns and then extend them, or infer from them, the moral connotations. But ultimately the natural and moral patterns are consistent or continuous; they imply each other. This view—that moral value is inherent, at least incipiently, in the natural world—is one of the bedrock claims of Confucianism, going back to the pre-Confucian theory of the "mandate of Heaven" (*tianming*).

Fuxi had first intuited the linkage between natural principle and moral principle, and this was the first representation of the Confucian Way (*dao*). He had represented that linkage in the form of the hexagrams, which were intended to function as a divination method for those who came later. This would enable ordinary people—people without his level of spiritual clarity—to learn to detect the most subtle patterns of change, or "incipiences" (*ji*) in the natural and social worlds. By learning to detect those changes and respond (*ying*) to them in morally appropriate ways, ordinary people could become more spiritual (*shen*), authentically (*cheng*) human and therefore sage-like. Thus Zhu titled his own commentary *The Original Meaning of the Zhouyi* (*Zhouyi benyi*), intending it to provide access for ordinary people to the "mind of the sage" (Fuxi).[30] In Zhu Xi's terminology, the sage's "human mind" (*renxin*) perfectly reflects the "moral mind" (*daoxin*), which in most people is obscured by selfish desires and other consequences of our physical nature.

Fuxi was also important to Zhu Xi because one of the myths recounting his creation of the *Yi* was a paradigm of one of the central methods in Zhu's system of self-cultivation, the "investigation of things" (*ge wu*):

> In ancient times, when Baoxi [= Fuxi] ruled the world, he looked up and contemplated the images in heaven; he looked down and contemplated the patterns on earth. He contemplated the markings of the birds and beasts and their adaptations to the various regions. From near at hand he abstracted images from his own body; from afar he abstracted from things. In this way he first created the Eight Trigrams, to spread the power of [his] spiritual clarity and to classify the dispositions of the myriad things.[31]

The purpose of this kind of objective examination of the natural world, or investigation of things, for Zhu Xi was to fully understand the principles (*li*) of things, including the principle of one's own mind, which is the principle of being human—the principle of human nature (*xing*).[32] Of this Mencius had said: "To fully develop one's mind is to know one's nature. To know one's nature is to know Heaven. Preserving one's mind and nourishing one's nature is how one serves Heaven" (7A.1).

Thus to cultivate and perfect one's innate moral nature, in the Mencian tradition of Confucianism, is clearly a religious matter. It is a way of relating oneself (or more precisely, realizing or actualizing one's inherent relation) to the unconditioned absolute, Heaven (*tian*). Moreover, this is more than *self*-realization; it is to realize the moral potential of the cosmos. Only humans have this capacity and therefore this moral responsibility. As the *Zhongyong* (Centrality and Commonality) puts it:

> Only that one in the world who is most perfectly authentic [*cheng*] is able to give full development to his nature. Being able to give full development to his nature, he is able to give full development to the nature of other human beings and, being able to give full development to the nature of other human beings he is able to give full development to the natures of other living things. Being able to give full development to the natures of other living things, he can assist in the transforming and nourishing powers of Heaven and Earth; being able to assist in the transforming and nourishing powers of Heaven and Earth, he can form a triad with Heaven and Earth.[33]

Human beings are therefore "co-creators" of the cosmos.

But how does divination figure into all this? First, it is important to realize that because of the scriptural prestige and authority of the *Yijing*, which at its core is a divination manual, *Yijing* divination had always been accepted and practiced by Confucians. Although some Confucians disdained certain popular religious practices, such as the reliance on spirit mediums for divination, the unquestioned authority of the *Yijing*—and especially the tradition that Confucius himself had written the Ten Wings[34]—outweighed any "rationalistic" doubts they might have had about this form of divination. For Zhu Xi, another compelling point was the story of the creation of the *Yi* by Fuxi, who was also credited with the invention of implements for hunting and fishing, animal sacrifice, and the institution of marriage. Such mythic culture-heroes were regarded as historical characters and the inventors, so to speak, of Chinese culture.[35] So Fuxi's creation of the hexagrams and divination method of the *Yi* placed that text and that particular method of divination at the very beginning of the history of Chinese culture. This, too, added to its prestige and authority.

More important for Zhu Xi, though, was his theory that *Yijing* divination could be used as a powerful aid in the process of self-cultivation. This was an original discovery by Zhu Xi, and one that he took quite seriously. Yet many later scholars, both in China and the West in modern times, have misunderstood his position on this point. To this day one still hears or reads statements to the effect that "Zhu Xi considered the *Yijing* to be *only* a divination manual"—that is, that he did *not* regard it as a significant component of the all-important process of self-cultivation. This view is actually an unexamined and uncritical assumption based on Zhu's often-repeated dictum, "The *Yi* was originally created for divination." But further examination reveals that Zhu meant that the *Yi* was originally created (by Fuxi) for divination; that this is how it should be used; and that because the *Yi* had been taken seriously by not only Fuxi but also by King Wen, the duke of Zhou, and Confucius, it must be part of the Confucian *dao*. For Zhu Xi, this meant that it was part of the process of self-cultivation aimed at the ultimate goal of becoming a sage.[36]

To make the *Yi* more accessible and useful as a manual of divination, Zhu wrote a book titled *An Introduction to the Study of the Yi* (*Yixue qimeng*), which provides detailed instructions on the *Yi*'s method of divination, as well as extensive commentary on the symbolic and numerological meanings of the lines, trigrams, hexagrams, and various diagrams associated with the *Yi*.[37] In the opening lines of his preface, referring to the story of Fuxi's creation of the *Yi*, he says:

> The Sage [Fuxi] contemplated the images [in Heaven and Earth] in
> order to draw the *gua*, and cast the yarrow stalks in order to determine
> the lines. This enables all people of later ages throughout the world to

68  TEACHING CONFUCIANISM IN PRACTICE

decide uncertainty and doubt, to settle indecision, and to be undeluded about following the auguries "auspicious," "inauspicious," "repentance" and "regret."[38] This achievement can be called glorious.[39]

Here he is announcing the basic themes of his interpretive approach to the *Yi*: the focus on Fuxi's original intention in creating it, the original form it took (i.e., the lines and *gua*), and its intended use by later people in using divination (when necessary) to guide their moral behavior.[40]

In his commentary, the *Zhouyi benyi*, Zhu took pains to interpret the text according to Fuxi's original intention in creating it—a hermeneutical approach not taken by other Neo-Confucians. As a result, his commentary focuses more closely than Cheng Yi's (for example) on the *yin-yang* meanings and relationships of the lines—that is, the original layer of meaning intended by Fuxi, and on the implications for the diviner. Both the original meaning (the literal denotation of the text, referring to the structural features, numerological characteristics, and symbolic associations of the hexagram and its component lines and trigrams) and the original intention (divination) are emphasized in the *Zhouyi benyi*. We can see this in Zhu's commentary to hexagram 14, *Dayou* (Great Possession). The hexagram text for this is simply "Great possession; primal success." Zhu comments:

Great possession is possession in great measure. Li [the upper trigram] comes to rest over Qian [the lower], fire over heaven. All is illuminated. The 6 in the fifth place [the broken line in the fifth position from the bottom] is a *yin* line abiding in respect. It attains the central position [in the upper trigram], while the five *yang* lines respond to it. Thus it is a great possession. Qian is strong and Li is bright. Abiding in respect and responding to heaven is a Way of success. If the diviner has these virtues, then there will be great goodness and success.[41]

In his two books on the *Yi*, the *Introduction to the Study of the Yi* and the *Original Meaning of the Zhouyi*, we see Zhu Xi's theory of the *Yi* in practice, but the theory itself is mainly to be found in his extensive recorded conversations and his numerous short essays.[42] Indeed, the *Yi* was one of the major topics of conversation between Zhu and his students, judging from the fact that roughly 11 percent of the *Zhuzi yulei* (Master Zhu's Classified Conversations) is devoted to it. In addition to the basic interpretive principles already discussed, there are several key terms at the heart of Zhu's understanding of *Yijing* divination and sagehood: responsiveness (*ying*), incipience (*ji*), and spirit (*shen*).

## Sagehood and Divination

What are the characteristics of Confucian sagehood? The term *shengren* (sage) was used by Confucius in a more limited and exalted sense than what Zhu Xi meant by it. For Confucius, the sages were primarily the mythical sage-kings of high antiquity (especially Yao, Shun, and Yu), although he may have also included the glorious founders of the Zhou dynasty (King Wen, King Wu, and the duke of Zhou). Although he regarded them all as historical figures, they were essentially semi-divine beings whose excellence was far beyond what ordinary humans could hope to achieve. The goal of human life for Confucius was to achieve humanity (*ren*), the cardinal virtue, which he dared not claim to have achieved himself but which everyone should strive for—not sagehood, an impractical goal.[43] That distinction between the humane person and the sage disappeared with Mencius, who said that any person theoretically could be a Yao or a Shun—by which he meant a humane person who transforms (*hua*) those around him, thereby transforming society itself. Mencius's rival, Xunzi, also said anyone could theoretically be a sage, even though he disputed Mencius's contention that human nature is inherently good.

The Neo-Confucians continued Mencius's usage; for them, the ultimate goal of human life was to become a sage. But the vocabulary they used to describe sagehood shifted from the terminology used by Confucius and Mencius. One of the more significant terms that entered the lexicon in this respect was *response* (*ying*). This term, particularly in the dyad "stimulus and response" (*gan-ying*), had become prominent much earlier in the Huang-Lao text *Huainanzi* (second century B.C.E.). There, the Daoist sage-ruler, or "True Man" (*zhenren*), "holds fast to the Responses of the Natural (*ziran zhi ying*)."[44] He therefore "is like a mirror, neither sending [things] away nor welcoming [things], responding (*ying*) but not storing."[45] This implies an "affinitive correspondence" between the sage and the natural world based on their common constitutive ground of *qi*.[46] Zhou Dunyi, in his *Tongshu* (Comprehensive Writing), defines the Confucian sage in the following way:

> That which is "silent and inactive"[47] is authentic (*cheng*). That which is "penetrating when stimulated"[48] is spiritual (*shen*). That which is active but not yet formed, between existence and not existence, is incipient (*ji*).

Authenticity is essential, and therefore clear. Spirit is responsive (*ying*), and therefore mysterious. Incipience is subtle, and therefore obscure. One who is authentic, spiritual, and incipient is called a sage.[49]

In his commentary on *Mencius* 7A.1 (already quoted), Zhu Xi says: "Mind is man's spiritual clarity (*shen-ming*). It is that by which one embodies the various principles and responds to the myriad phenomena."[50] And in his "Treatise on the Examination of the Mind" Zhu says: "The learning of the sages is to base one's mind on fully investigating principle, and to accord with principle by responding to things."[51]

So the sage, according to the Daoxue school of Confucianism, is a person whose mind is sensitive enough to be able to respond spontaneously and appropriately to even the most subtle, incipient (*ji*) changes in the human and natural environment. The response is appropriate to the situation, or morally correct, because the sage's inherent nature (*xing*) is part of the universal natural/moral order (*li*)—as is the inherent nature of every human being. But only the sage has clarified or purified his physical nature (*qizhi zhi xing*) to the point where it no longer clouds or interferes with his essential moral nature. That clarity (*ming*) renders the sage "spiritual" (*shen*) so that his responses sometimes seem superhuman, like those of gods and spirits. But in fact the sage is nothing more than fully human, which is why Zhou Dunyi says, "Sagehood is nothing more than being authentic (*cheng*)."[52]

In Zhu Xi's reading, authenticity means "actualized principle (*li*)."[53] That is, the sage's thought and behavior fully manifests his moral nature or the natural/moral order.[54] That order or principle is one of transformation and creativity. It is seen in the natural world as "birth and growth" (*sheng-sheng*),[55] and in the sage as his ability to transform (*hua*) others by the force (or virtue, *de*) of his moral example, that is,, to create a humane society.

How then is *Yijing* divination relevant to the process of becoming a sage? How exactly does the *Yijing* work (according to the Neo-Confucians)?

We might begin with the name itself. From earliest times the text was known as the *Zhou Yi*, or Changes of Zhou.[56] The changes indicated by the title are of three types.[57] The primary one, at least in Song usage, occurs in the process of constructing a hexagram and interpreting the oracle. The method of counting off the yarrow stalks, which is only sketchily given in the *Xici* but was reconstructed by Zhu Xi in the *Yixue qimeng*, involves four steps to derive each line of a hexagram. Each of these steps is called a change. The *Xici* says, "Therefore four operations completes a change (*yi*); eighteen changes (*bian*) completes a hexagram."[58] Second, when a single line transforms into its opposite (*yin*-broken to *yang*-solid or vice versa), or a hexagram changes into any other (depending on which of its lines are changing lines), that is also called a change (usually *bian*). Finally, change (usually *yi*) refers to the cosmic processes of change and transformation, as in "the Way of Change" (*yi dao*),[59] or one of the most significant lines in the text for the Daoxue synthesis, "In Change there is the Supreme Polarity" (*Yi you taiji*)—that is, the *yin-yang* principle.[60]

Clearly, the concepts of change (*bian* or *yi*) and transformation (*hua* or *bianhua*) are central to the *Yijing*. As an oracle, the *Yi* is regarded in a sense as an instrument for the detection of patterns of change, and those patterns are understood to be based ultimately on the simplest such pattern: *yin-yang* alternation or transformation. Of course, real-life situations are likely to be highly complex iterations or combinations of this fundamental ordering principle. The process of casting a hexagram enables the diviner—through the "spiritual" power of the milfoil stalks[61]—to detect patterns of change that might otherwise be too subtle or complex to perceive. By detecting them and applying the wisdom of the sages who created the *Yi* to interpret the pattern and directionality of change at the given moment, the diviner can better adapt his or her behavior to the dynamic exigencies of the situation. Action that is consistent with the changing flow of events is more likely to succeed because it becomes part of the normative pattern that constitutes the *dao* in Chinese religious cosmology. For Confucians, this *dao* is inherently moral.

So *Yijing* divination, as Neo-Confucians understood it, is only indirectly or secondarily concerned with fortune-telling. It is really more about apprehending the *present*, or the direction and character of the present flow of events, and choosing one's course of action to fit into and make use of the energy of that flow in the most appropriate (moral) manner. When a hexagram is derived through the manipulation of the yarrow stalks, it is conceived as an image (*xiang*) or reading of that current, dynamic situation. Depending on the numbers yielded by the complex process of manipulation and counting off, each line will be designated as one of four types: changing *yang*, unchanging *yang*, changing *yin*, or unchanging *yin*.[62] After reading and interpreting the hexagram text and the line texts for any changing lines, one then changes those lines into their opposite, yielding a second hexagram. (If no lines are changing, the situation is deemed to be relatively static, and no second hexagram is derived.) The second hexagram indicates the *potential* future state—provided that one's interpretation of the first hexagram was correct and one's subsequent behavior is appropriate to that situation. In other words, the second represents not necessarily the future, but rather the point toward which the present situation is tending.[63]

The basic connection between the functionality of the *Yi* and Confucian self-cultivation is expressed in the following passage from the *Xici* and Zhu Xi's comment on it.

> The virtue of the milfoil is round and spiritual; the virtue of the hexagrams is square and wise; the meanings of the six lines change in order to inform. With these the sage purifies his mind and retires into secrecy. He suffers good fortune and misfortune in common with the people. Being spiritual, he knows the future. Being wise, he stores up the past. Who is comparable to this? [It was] the ancients, with broad intelligence and astute wisdom; those who were spiritually martial and yet non-violent.[64]

Zhu Xi comments:

> "Round and spiritual" means the unboundedness of transformation. "Square and wise" means that things have definite principles.... The Sage concretely embodies the virtues of the three [milfoil, hexagrams, and lines], without the slightest worldly tie. When there is nothing happening, then his mind is silent, and no one can see it. When there is something happening, then the operation of his spiritual understanding responds when stimulated. This means he knows what is auspicious and what is inauspicious without divination. "Spiritually martial and yet non-violent" means he apprehends principle without recourse to things.[65]

Here Zhu Xi points out that this refers to the fully realized sage, not to the ordinary person. According to him, the sage in fact does not need to resort to divination. The sage himself, by virtue of his spirituality, can spontaneously respond to the incipient signs of good fortune and misfortune or the subtle tendencies of events, and thus can know their direction of change. This understanding is nonempirical in that it does not depend on prior exposure to things. He has the ability to transcend the usual limitations of cause and effect, for example, "To hurry without haste, to arrive without going" (A.10.6) and to know the future. This is one of his "god-like" characteristics.

The spirituality, or "spiritual clarity" (*shen ming*), of both the *Yi* and the sage is precisely their capacity to detect those otherwise undetectable subtle changes. According to the *Xici*, "To know incipience (*ji*) is spirituality" (B.5.11). The Confucian sage, who symbolizes the potential perfection of human nature, is attuned to the flow of change in the natural and social environment and responds spontaneously, directly, and appropriately, with no need for intervening calculation or cogitation.[66] For ordinary people, on the other hand, moral decisions usually require careful thought. When they have reached the limits of their current capacity to know the Way, the use of the *Yijing*, which embodies both the spiritual efficacy of the mechanism itself and the wisdom of the sages who devised it and contributed to the text, becomes appropriate.

## Confucianism as a Religious Tradition

The question of the "religious" character of the Confucian tradition has been debated at least since the Chinese rites controversy of the early eighteenth century, when the Vatican struggled with the question of whether Chinese Christian converts should be allowed to continue their practice of ancestor worship. In the nineteenth century, British missionary translator James Legge considered Confucius as something of a rational skeptic in regard to what Legge deemed to be religious belief, although he did perceive the original texts of the tradition—what he called the Five Classics—as sacred scriptures pointing back to an originally monotheistic faith. Since the late twentieth century, when the academic field of religious studies came of age in Western academia, scholars of religion have spilled much ink proposing definitions of *religion* that attempted to go beyond Western biases, and some of them have been broad enough to include Confucianism within their bounds. Yet scholars in other fields, as well as some Asian scholars unfamiliar with these fairly recent developments, have continued to insist that Confucianism is not a religion.

Part of the problem is with the reifying or essentializing presuppositions of the very question, "Is Confucianism *a religion*?" For that reason, recent scholarship has tended to shift away from the usage of "a religion" to the less essentialistic term "religious tradition."[67] It is indeed more fruitful to ask whether the Confucian tradition has any religious dimensions, and if so what they might be, than to ask whether it is or is not a religion. Still, this approach begs the question of what makes a particular aspect of the tradition religious, so it still relies on some kind of definition. I have elsewhere suggested that Frederick Streng's definition, "a means of ultimate transformation," can provide a useful basis for a definition of religion that includes Confucianism.[68] I would like to take another approach here and discuss the issue in terms of what may be a simpler criterion: a linkage to "something beyond," to something transcendent.[69]

Confucianism is a humanistic tradition. This means that the focus of interest and the fundamental reference point is the human being. Human beings are both individual and social creatures, and their sociality is experienced and expressed in families and in communities. On the individual level (1),

Confucianism is concerned with self-cultivation, with the ultimate aim of achieving sagehood. In the terminology of the Great Learning (*Daxue*), this involves extending one's knowledge, making one's intentions sincere, and "rectifying the mind"—that is, sorting out one's good desires and intentions from the bad and nourishing the former while eliminating the latter. On the level of the family (2), the focus is on cultivating and practicing love and respect with family members and ancestors—the latter involving the various forms of ancestor worship already discussed. On the community level (3), the focus is on building a humane society with behavior that is humane (*ren*), appropriate (*yi*), and ritually proper (*li*); working for the greater good in government, if possible, and practicing "reverence to ghosts and gods" (*jing gui shen*).[70]

On each of the three levels here outlined—self, family, and society—there is a corresponding "transcendent" focus: (1) sages, (2) ancestors, and (3) ghosts and gods. On the family and community levels, the Confucian emphasis on kinship and social relations includes maintaining good relationships with all three types of spiritual beings (gods, ghosts, and ancestors). Ancestors are still part of the family: They are kept informed of important family business, they symbolically join the living family at meals, and they are paid respects at regular intervals. Ghosts must be pacified with occasional offerings of spirit money or food, both out of pity for their homelessness and to keep them from harming the living. Gods must be respected and worshipped—as long as they fulfill their complementary obligations of protecting the community and helping it prosper. If they fail to do so, as Mencius says and common practice has always acknowledged, other gods can take their place.[71]

On the individual level, it is clear that sagehood (*sheng*) is a religious goal.[72] The word *sheng* itself has clear religious connotations. For example, as mentioned before, it is part of the Chinese name for the Judeo-Christian Bible (*sheng jing*, or Holy Scriptures), and the same word translated in a Confucian context as sage (*shengren*) is used as the Chinese translation of *saint*. And as I have shown, in the dominant school of Neo-Confucian thought, synthesized from earlier sources by Zhu Xi, the sage is a spiritual or god-like being, with "powers and abilities far beyond those of mortal men." But he is not a Superman—he is Everyman, because what he has perfected is the moral nature inherent in every human being.

This may be considered one of the central paradoxes of Confucian thought. It brings us back again to Fingarette's phrase, "the secular as sacred." The human nature that is common to us all and makes us what we are is also what makes us more than we are. The capacity for transcendence—becoming a sage—is immanent. All three of the secular foci of Confucian thought and practice—the individual, the family, and the community—are our links to a transcendent, unconditioned reality called Heaven (*tian*).

Heaven symbolizes the creative power that constitutes all that exists. As Cheng Yi put it, "The mind of Heaven and Earth is to produce things."[73] That creative power is manifested in human beings, and only in human beings, as "moral power" or "virtue" (*de*), the power to create ourselves as fully human (i.e., humane) beings, to create a humane society, and to bring to fruition the moral potential that is inherent in the cosmos. Although we need external help in this endeavor, that help comes from the human community, not from a god. The closest Confucian equivalent of Christian grace is the nurturance we receive from family members, friends, and teachers, all of whom transmit to us (through the cultural tradition, *wen*) the learning of the sages, who were people fundamentally just like us.[74]

The Neo-Confucian understanding of the *Yijing* developed by Zhu Xi gives ordinary human beings access to the very origin of that cultural tradition: Fuxi's creation of the *Yi*. The "mind of the sage," which is equivalent to the "moral mind" (*daoxin*) that is inherent in all humans but needs to be actualized or expressed through self-cultivation, is symbolized by Fuxi's mind as he surveyed the natural order, intuited or abstracted from it the moral order, and compassionately created a device by which ordinary humans could learn to recognize and internalize that same natural/moral order or principle (*li*). By learning to understand incipient change and how best to respond to it, according to Zhu Xi, one can move closer to the goal—perhaps an unreachable goal, but a goal nonetheless—of manifesting that creative principle in one's own action, as a sage.

Zhu Xi is typically regarded as one of the arch-"rationalists" of the Confucian tradition. The particular school of Confucian thought that he championed (referred to as the Cheng-Zhu school) is often called *lixue*, or "school of principle/reason," in contradistinction to *xinxue*, or "school of mind" represented by Lu Jiuyuan and Wang Yangming. This terminology is misleading for two reasons: First, the mind/heart is just as central in Zhu's Confucian synthesis as it is in the Lu-Wang school; second, it suggests a parallel with Western rationalism that brings with it the mistaken assumption that it is not fundamentally religious. But as we have seen, divination and sacrifice were systematically involved in Zhu Xi's system, and that system itself was fundamentally religious in its aim of becoming a sage. This, then, is part of the challenge of conveying the religious meaning of a tradition that does not easily fit within the more familiar Western model of what constitutes a religion.

## NOTES

1. Because of the limitations of the historical record, all we know of Shang religion is that of the royal family and court. It should not be assumed that common people at that time had the same beliefs or practices. The phrase "popular religion" (or "folk religion") refers to the religious practices of families and local communities independent of or only marginally connected with religious institutions such as Daoist priesthoods or Buddhist monastic establishments. See Joseph A. Adler, *Chinese Religious Traditions* (Upper Saddle River, N.J.: Prentice Hall, 2002).

2. Major art museums may have some of these bronzes on display; if a field trip is feasible, students can view and discuss them, and their inscriptions if translations are available, in their presence. Pictures, of course, are also readily available. An excellent source for rubbings and explanations of oracle bones is David N. Keightley, *Sources of Shang History: The Oracle-bone Inscriptions of Bronze Age China* (Berkeley: University of California Press, 1978). The preamble of this book (pp. 1–2) is Keightley's imaginative reconstruction of the scene of a divination session involving King Wuding of the Shang, based on an actual oracle bone inscription. This is short enough to read aloud in class. Color pictures of oracle bones can also be found on the Web. The major museum collections of oracle bones are in the National Palace Museum in Taipei and a number of museums in mainland China.

3. See Keightley, *Sources of Shang History*, and his *The Ancestral Landscape: Time, Space, and Community in Late Shang China, ca. 1200–1045 B.C.* (Berkeley: University of California Institute of East Asian Studies, 2000).

4. For the special case of the reconstruction of a Kong family temple by descendants of Confucius (Kongzi) in Gansu Province, see Jun Jing, *The Temple of Memories: History, Power, and Morality in a Chinese Village* (Stanford: Stanford University Press, 1996). More recent ethnographies focusing on popular religion include Thomas David Dubois, *The Sacred Village: Social Change and Religious Life in Rural North China* (Honolulu: University of Hawai'i Press, 2005) and Adam Yuet Chau, *Miraculous Response: Doing Popular Religion in Contemporary China* (Stanford, Calif.: Stanford University Press, 2006). A short scene of ancestor worship (albeit somewhat lighthearted) in a northern Chinese village in the 1980s can been seen in the film by Carma Hinton, *To Taste a Hundred Herbs: Gods, Ancestors, and Medicine in a Chinese Village* (Long Bow Group, 1986).

5. For an excellent multidimensional study of Confucian rituals, see Thomas Wilson, ed., *On Sacred Grounds: Culture, Society, Politics, and the Formation of the Cult of Confucius* (Cambridge, Mass.: Harvard University Asia Center, 2002). Pictures and films of the scenes described are not widely available, but if some can be found (e.g., on the Web), their showing in class can be accompanied by burning incense to convey something of the sensory experience of Chinese temples. Authentic Chinese incense can often be found in the United States in Chinese food markets.

6. Although this distinction is not used universally, one can say that the *Yijing* comprises the *Zhouyi* plus the Ten Wings. The Ten Wings date from the late Warring States and early Han periods (perhaps fourth to second century B.C.E.).

7. See Adler, *Chinese Religious Traditions*, pp. 11–12, 118–19, and David K. Jordan,

*Gods, Ghosts, and Ancestors: Folk Religion in a Taiwanese Village* (Berkeley: University of California Press, 1972), chap. 4; also available online at anthro.ucsd.edu/ ~dkjordan/scriptorium/gga/ggacover.html. A scene of an elaborate divination ritual in Taiwan, employing a red-hat Daoist priest, a spirit medium, and a divination chair can be seen in the film *A Question of Balance*, part of the 1970s BBC series *The Long Search*, which has been reissued on DVD (New York: Ambrose Video, 2001).

8. See Herbert Fingarette, *Confucius: The Secular as Sacred* (San Francisco: Harper and Row, 1972).

9. Patricia Buckley Ebrey, *Chu Hsi's Family Rituals: A Twelfth-Century Chinese Manual for the Performance of Cappings, Weddings, Funerals, and Ancestral Rites* (Princeton, N.J.: Princeton University Press, 1991), pp. xv, xiv.

10. See Ebrey, *Chu Hsi's Family Rituals*. This was the most influential ritual text of the last 800 years. Although it was widely circulated and regarded as the standard to strive for, it is important to bear in mind that it was a normative (not a descriptive) text. Actual practices varied considerably from family to family and rarely (if ever) followed Zhu Xi's recommendations in every detail. For ancestor worship in particular, see chaps. 1 and 5, and pp. xx–xxv.

11. The Jurchen were the ancestors of the Manchus, who conquered and ruled all of China from 1644 to 1911. After the calamity of the loss of northern China during the Song, the imperial capital was "temporarily" moved from Kaifeng in north-central China to Hangzhou on the southeast coast. Hence the period from 960 to 1127 is called the Northern Song, and 1127–1279 is the Southern Song. In 1234 the Jurchen were conquered by the Mongols, who proceeded in 1279 to conquer all the rest of China, which they ruled until 1368 under their Yuan dynasty.

12. Patricia Ebrey has suggested that part of the motivation behind the growing interest in family rituals during the Song was to legitimate the social status of those educated elite who did not have official positions in government—a group that increased in numbers extensively during this period. See Patricia Buckley Ebrey, *Confucianism and Family Rituals in Imperial China: A Social History of Writing about Rites* (Princeton, N.J.: Princeton University Press, 1991), p. 47.

13. Movable type printing was invented by the Chinese during the eleventh century, although because of the character-based writing system, carved woodblock printing remained the preferred method until modern times. Paper had been invented by the Chinese in the first century C.E.—long before its first use in Europe.

14. For more on shrines to past sages and worthies, see Ellen Neskar, "Shrines to Local Former Worthies," in Donald S. Lopez Jr., ed., *Religions of China in Practice* (Princeton, N.J.: Princeton University Press, 1996), pp. 293–305. For the religious aspects of Neo-Confucian academies, see Linda Walton, "Southern Sung Academies as Sacred Places," in Patricia Buckley Ebrey and Peter N. Gregory, eds., *Religion and Society in T'ang and Sung China* (Honolulu: University of Hawai'i Press, 1993). For education during the Song, see William Theodore deBary and John W. Chafee, eds., *Neo-Confucian Education: The Formative Stage* (Berkeley: University of California Press, 1989); Linda Walton, *Academies and Society in Southern Sung China* (Honolulu: University of Hawai'i Press, 1999); and Thomas H. C. Lee, *Education in Traditional China: A History* (Leiden: Brill, 2000).

15. They can be purchased at some of the shops surrounding major temples in Taiwan.

16. Patricia Ebrey, "Sung Neo-Confucian Views on Geomancy," in Irene Bloom and Joshua A. Fogel, eds., *Meeting of Minds: Intellectual and Religious Interaction in East Asian Traditions of Thought* (New York: Columbia University Press, 1997), pp. 75–107.

17. Sima Guang wrote a book on family ritual, called the *Shu yi* (Writing and Etiquette), which Zhu Xi relied on extensively for his *Family Rituals*. Cheng Yi, on whom Zhu Xi relied most heavily overall, discussed family rituals extensively but did not write a book on them. See Ebrey, *Chu Hsi's Family Rituals*, pp. xix–xx, 37n, 140n, 155n.

18. The Four Books were actually all contained in the Thirteen Classics: The *Daxue* and *Zhongyong* were two chapters in the *Liji* (Record of Ritual); the *Analects*, the collection of Confucius's sayings compiled by his disciples and followers after his death, had been added during the Latter Han dynasty; and the *Mencius* became a *jing* in the Song (the last to be added to the list).

19. See Daniel K. Gardner, "Principle and Pedagogy: Chu Hsi and the Four Books," *Harvard Journal of Asiatic Studies* 44, no. 1 (1984): 57–81.

20. The five masters were Shao Yong (1011–1077), Zhou Dunyi (1017–1073), Zhang Zai (1020–1077), and Cheng Hao (1032–1085) and his brother Cheng Yi (1033–1107). Sometimes a sixth is added, Sima Guang (1019–1086). They constituted the first generation of what later became known as the Cheng-Zhu school, which, through the prodigious scholarship, tireless efforts, and sometimes bitter political infighting of Zhu Xi in the twelfth century, became the dominant school of Confucian thought to the present day. See Hoyt Cleveland Tillman, *Confucian Discourse and Chu Hsi's Ascendancy* (Honolulu: University of Hawai'i Press, 1992).

21. See Joseph Adler, "Zhou Dunyi: The Metaphysics and Practice of Sagehood," in William Theodore de Bary and Irene Bloom, eds., *Sources of Chinese Tradition*, 2nd ed., (New York: Columbia University Press, 1999), pp. 1:669–78.

22. The Eight Trigrams (*Bagua*) are:

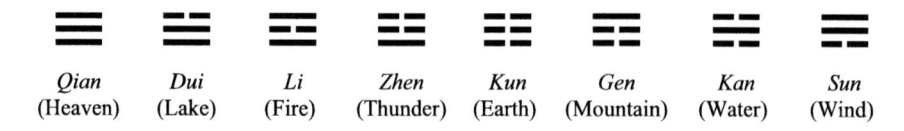

| Qian | Dui | Li | Zhen | Kun | Gen | Kan | Sun |
|---|---|---|---|---|---|---|---|
| (Heaven) | (Lake) | (Fire) | (Thunder) | (Earth) | (Mountain) | (Water) | (Wind) |

The sixty-four hexagrams can be derived by combining the trigrams in all possible pairs.

23. For a clear summary of this method, as systematized by Zhu Xi, see Richard Wilhelm and Cary F. Baynes, trans., *The I Ching, or Book of Changes*, 3rd ed. (Princeton, N.J.: Princeton University Press, 1967), pp. 721–23. For Zhu Xi's text, see Chu Hsi (Zhu Xi), *Introduction to the Study of the Classic of Change* (*I-hsüeh ch'i-meng*), trans. Joseph A. Adler (Provo, Utah: Global Scholarly Publications, 2002), chap. 3.

24. My translation, in Kidder Smith Jr., Peter K. Bol, Joseph A. Adler, and Don J. Wyatt, *Sung Dynasty Uses of the I Ching* (Princeton, N.J.: Princeton University Press, 1990), p. 251.

25. For brief descriptions. see Smith, Bol, Adler, and Wyatt, *Sung Dynasty Uses of the I Ching*, pp. 14–21.

26. See Gerald Swanson, "The Concept of Change in the *Great Treatise*," in Henry Rosemont Jr., *Explorations in Early Chinese Cosmology* (Chico: Scholars Press, 1984); and Willard Peterson, "Making Connections: 'Commentary on the Attached Verbalizations' of the *Book of Change*," *Harvard Journal of Asiatic Studies* 42 (1982): 67–116.

27. See Joseph A. Adler, "Varieties of Spiritual Experience: *Shen* in Neo-Confucian Discourse," in Tu Wei-ming and Mary Evelyn Tucker, eds., *Confucian Spirituality* (New York: Crossroad, 2005), pp. 2:120–48.

28. See Kidder Smith Jr., "*Zhouyi* Interpretation from Accounts in the *Zuozhuan*," *Harvard Journal of Asiatic Studies* 49, no. 2 (December 1989): 421–63.

29. Chu Hsi, *Introduction to the Study of the Classic of Change*, chap. 4.

30. Zhu Xi, *Zhouyi benyi* (1177; rpt. Taibei: Hualian, 1978). To my knowledge, this has not been translated into a Western language.

31. *Xici* B.2, in Zhu Xi, *Zhouyi benyi*, 3:18a. In addition to Zhu Xi's frequent references to this story, its importance to him is suggested by the fact that sometime between 1174 and 1183 he composed a series of "big character posters" (*dazibao*) quoting this passage and one other from the *Xici* (A.11.5). The set of fourteen sheets, each about fourteen inches high, is in the collection of the National Palace Museum in Taipei. See *China at the Inception of the Second Millennium: Art and Culture of the Sung Dynasty, 960–1279* (Taipei: National Palace Museum, 2000), pp. 86–87. Six of the sheets were on display at the museum during summer 2000.

32. After quoting the story of Fuxi in his *Yixue qimeng* (Introduction to the Study of the *Yi*), Zhu comments: "In the fullness of Heaven and Earth there is nothing that is not the wonder of *taiji* [Supreme Polarity, which Zhu identifies with *li*] and *yin-yang*. It was to this that the Sage looked up in contemplation and looked down in examination, seeking from afar and taking from the near at hand. Of course, he could register things in his mind silently and transcendentally [i.e., seeing things not immediately apparent]" (Chu Hsi, *Introduction to the Study of the Classic of Change*, p. 15).

33. *Zhongyong*, chap. 22, trans. Irene Bloom, in de Bary and Bloom, eds., *Sources of Chinese Tradition*, p. 2:338, with "authentic" substituted for "sincere" (*cheng*). Zhou Dunyi, in his *Taijitu shuo*, also develops the notion of the uniqueness of human beings, but grounds it in the cosmology of *qi* (the psychophysical substance of which all existing things are composed). In Zhou's other major work, the *Tongshu* (Comprehensive Writing), which draws largely from the *Yi* and the *Zhongyong*, he further develops this idea, defining sagehood in terms of *cheng* or "authenticity."

34. This had been questioned by Confucian scholars since the early Song and is not given any credence today.

35. The other two earliest figures are Shennong, the Divine Farmer, who invented agriculture, and Huangdi, the Yellow Emperor, who invented the institutions of government. These three are called the Three Sovereigns (*San huang*) and are still worshipped today.

36. I have explored this more thoroughly in *Divination and Philosophy: Chu Hsi's Understanding of the I-ching* (Ph.D. diss., University of California at Santa Barbara, 1984), and in Smith, Bol, Adler, and Wyatt, *Sung Dynasty Uses of the I Ching*, chaps. 6–7.

37. See Adler, "Zhou Dunyi."

38. These are some of the formulaic responses that probably constitute one of the earliest textual layers of the *Yijing*.

39. Chu Hsi, *Introduction to the Study of the Classic of Change*, p. 1.

40. Zhu stressed that divination was only to be used when one was unable to decide the correct course of behavior on one's own. See Smith, Bol, Adler, and Wyatt, *Sung Uses of the I Ching*, pp. 202–204.

41. *Zhouyi benyi*, 1:33a.

42. The conversations, compiled in 1270 from several sets of verbatim notes taken by his students over the last twenty years of his life, are found in the *Zhuzi yulei* (Master Zhu's Classified Conversations), noted earlier. The essays are found in the *Huian xiansheng Zhu wengong wenji* (Zhu Xi's Collected Papers), compiled in 1532 (Sibu beiyao ed., titled *Zhuzi daquan*, and several other editions).

43. See, for example, *Analects* 6:30.

44. *Huainanzi*, 6:6a, trans. Charles Le Blanc, *Huai Nan Tzu: Philosophical Synthesis in Early Han Thought* (Hong Kong: Hong Kong University Press, 1985), p. 133. See my discussion of *ying* in Neo-Confucian thought in Joseph A. Adler, "Response and Responsibility: Chou Tun-i and Confucian Resources for Environmental Ethics," in Mary Evelyn Tucker and John Berthrong, eds., *Confucianism and Ecology: The Interrelation of Heaven, Earth, and Humans* (Cambridge, Mass.: Harvard University Center for the Study of World Religions, 1998), pp. 123–49.

45. *Huainanzi*, 6:6b, trans. Le Blanc, *Huai Nan Tzu*, p. 135, echoing the earlier Daoist classic *Zhuangzi* (chap. 7).

46. Leblanc, *Huai Nan Tzu*, p. 208.

47. Quoting the *Yijing*, *Xici* A.10.4 (*Zhouyi benyi*, 3:12b).

48. Ibid.

49. This is section 4 of the *Tongshu*, titled "The Sage." Zhang Boxing, comp., *Zhou Lianxi xiansheng quanji* (Complete Collection of Master Zhou Lianxi [Zhou Dunyi]; 1708), in *Zhengyi tang quanshu* (Baibu congshu jicheng ed.), 5:17b–18a.

50. Zhu Xi, *Sishu jizhu* (Collected Commentaries on the Four Books) (Sibu beiyao ed.), 7:1a.

51. *Huian xiansheng Zhu wengong wenji* (Zhu Xi's Collected Papers) (Sibu beiyao ed., titled *Zhuzi daquan*), 67:19b.

52. *Tongshu*, section 2.

53. See Zhu's comments on sections 2–4 of Zhou's *Tongshu*, in *Zhou Lianxi quanji*, 5:9a–11a, 17b.

54. This depiction of the sage is an example of how the Neo-Confucians used the newer terminology of *li* and *qi* to interpret Confucius's notion of becoming "ritually proper" (*li*) by learning and internalizing the models of the ancient sages.

55. *Yijing*, *Xici* A.5.6 (*Zhouyi benyi*, 3:6a).

56. Actually, because there is no single/plural distinction in classical Chinese, we cannot say for sure which was originally intended, but the plural form seems to work best in English in this construction. But the later term *Yijing* could be either "Scripture of Change" or "Scripture of Changes."

57. These are different from the three meanings of *yi* proposed by Zheng Xuan (127–200) in his commentary on the *Yiwei Qian zuo du* (Aprocryphal treatise on the *Yi*: Penetrating the measure of Qian), which are ease, change, and constancy. See Hellmut Wilhelm, *Change: Eight Lectures on the I Ching* (Princeton, N.J.: Princeton University Press, 1960), pp. 15–16. For more on this text see Fung Yu-lan, *A History of Chinese Philosophy*, trans. Derk Bodde (Princeton, N.J.: Princeton University Press, 1953), pp. 2:96–105.

58. *Yijing*, *Xici* A.9.3. Note that *bian* and *yi* are used synonymously here. *Bianyi* is the colloquial word for "change."

59. Chu Hsi, *Introduction to the Study of the Classic of Change*, p. 20. "Change" (*yi*) in this and the previous phrase could also be interpreted as "Scripture of Change," for example, "the way of the *Changes*."

60. *Yijing*, *Xici* A.11.5.

61. Ibid., A.11.3, A.11.8.

62. The figure at right depicts the *yin-yang* cycle mapped as a day. The four types of lines correspond to the four stages of the cycle:

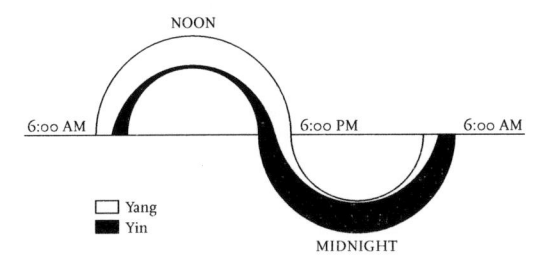

(1) young *yang* (in this case midnight to 6 A.M.): unchanging *yang* line;
(2) mature *yang* (6 A.M. to noon): changing *yang*;
(3) young *yin* (noon to 6 P.M.): unchanging *yin*;
(4) mature *yin* (6 P.M. to midnight): changing *yin*.

63. This procedure, of course, can easily be done in class. A convenient set of instructions is found in the Wilhelm/Baynes translation of the *Yi* (pp. 721–23), as already noted. If a set of fifty yarrow stalks cannot be found, the simpler method using three coins can be followed. I find it useful to discuss how this process can be interpreted as a way of suggesting to the questioner a range of responses to the present situation, one of which may strike him or her as personally meaningful. If such a responsive chord is not struck, one can conclude that the divination did not work.

64. *Xici*, A.11.2.

65. *Zhouyi benyi*, 3:13b.

66. Readers might recognize in this picture the notion of *wu-wei*, or effortless action, which is typically identified with the *Laozi*. But as Edward Slingerland has shown for the Warring States period, various forms of this spiritual ideal were held by all the classical Confucians as well as the authors of the *Laozi* and *Zhuangzi* (see Slingerland, *Effortless Action: Wu-wei as Conceptual Metaphor and Spiritual Ideal in*

*Early China* [New York: Oxford University Press, 2003]). It is also clearly evident in Chan Buddhism and Neo-Confucianism.

67. In 1962 Wilfrid Cantwell Smith proposed that the terms *religion* and *religions* be dropped, for the same reason. Although I think he overstated his case, his argument is still cogent and prescient. See Smith, *The Meaning and End of Religion* (1962; rpt. San Francisco: Harper and Row, 1978).

68. Adler, "Varieties of Spiritual Experience," pp. 141–42.

69. This too is quite close to what Wilfrid Cantwell Smith meant by "faith," which, along with "cumulative tradition," he proposed to replace the terminology of "religion" and "religions." For example, he refers to faith as human beings' "involvement . . . with something greater than they" (Smith, *The Meaning and End of Religion*, p. 171).

70. *Analects*, 6:20. The full statement is, "Be reverent towards ghosts and gods (or spirits), but keep them at a distance." Although there is good reason to emphasize the second part (Confucius was indeed saying that success or failure in social and political affairs was due to human action, not ghosts and spirits), it should not negate the first part.

My reason for including the worship of ghosts and gods under the category of community is that both ghosts and gods are considered extensions of or spiritual parallels to elements of society. Ghosts are traditionally regarded as the spirits of people who, after death, have no family members to worship and nourish them—they are the spiritual parallel of the socially unconnected, or marginal, typified by beggars (when relatively harmless) and bandits (when they haunt or otherwise prey on the living). Gods are those spiritual beings whose numinous power (*ling*) is great enough to affect groups larger than a single family; they are worshipped very much as ancestors are by families but in community shrines or temples. They are traditionally compared to government officials—in fact many of them carry the title *gong*, which means "duke" or official. So both ghosts and gods belong, in a sense, to communities.

71. *Mencius*, 7B.14.

72. See Rodney L. Taylor, *The Cultivation of Sagehood as a Religious Goal in Neo-Confucianism: A Study of Selected Writings of Kao P'an-lung (1562–1626)* (Missoula, Mont.: Scholars Press, 1978), and *The Religious Dimensions of Confucianism* (Albany: State University of New York Press, 1990).

73. This is in Cheng Yi's commentary on hexagram 24 (*Fu*, Return) of the *Yijing* (p. 16). See Smith, Bol, Adler, and Wyatt, *Sung Dynasty Uses of the I Ching*, p. 247.

74. According to Mencius, "The sage and I are of the same kind" (6A.7), and "Even Yao and Shun were the same as anyone else" (4B.32). D. C. Lau, trans., *Mencius* (Harmondsworth: Penguin, 1970), pp. 164, 136.

PART II

# Teaching Confucianism in History

# The Mencius-Xunzi Debate in Early Confucian Ethics

*Aaron Stalnaker*

Intimate familiarity can bring joy and satisfaction, but it can also provoke spiteful and destructive fights. It is no accident that Han dynasty bibliographers settled on the term *jia* 家 family, when describing the different schools of thought and teaching lineages in the Warring States period—no other metaphor could capture the intensity of disputes both between and within different groups such as the *Ru* or Confucians, the followers of Mozi, and numerous other less well-defined tendencies, movements, and lineages.

Like members of a single family, Mencius (i.e., Mengzi 孟子, fourth century B.C.E.) and Xunzi 荀子 (third century B.C.E.) share a great deal, perhaps more than their later interpreters would care to admit. They both agree that there is only one solution to the upheaval and chaos of their times: a return to the tradition of rule by virtuous leaders that had been articulated so compellingly by their intellectual ancestor Confucius (i.e., Kongzi 孔子, sixth to fifth century B.C.E.). Both recognize that good government requires wise and beneficent policies that promote all the people's welfare, as well as public-spirited ministers to faithfully pursue such policies. They share a vision of society as a harmonious community of interdependent members, capable of great flourishing only when all work together according to just norms and beautiful, respectful rituals—rather like an orchestra composed of many players that can make the most beautiful music only when all play together in tune and in time. Furthermore, they agree on a list of both primary and secondary virtues, such as *ren* 仁, humaneness; *yi* 義, righteousness or justice; *li* 禮, ritual propriety; *zhi* 智, wisdom; *xin* 信, trustworthiness; and *gong* 恭, loyalty or doing one's best. They are also both committed to the traditional Confucian practices of ritual and music, although perhaps not equally so. Thus, when teaching about early Confucianism, one should not succumb to the temptation to radically oppose their visions of life; instead, their differences should always be contextualized within their shared *Ru* commitments.

Nevertheless, Mencius and Xunzi certainly do disagree. Although they share much the same vision of a beautifully harmonious society guided by a "moral vanguard" of good Confucian leaders, they differ sharply about how this moral elite ought to be cultivated.[1] In particular, Xunzi attacks Mencius's contention that "human nature is good," arguing instead that it is "bad." This disagreement turns out to concern first the character of inborn human impulses and intuitions but most deeply the proper methods of ethico-religious self-cultivation. Mencius favors introspection, the careful tending of moral intuitions and impulses as if they were crops, and courageous practical engagement in affairs, whereas Xunzi favors careful study of classical Confucian texts, combined with assiduous practice of traditional ritual and music under the guidance of a wise and good teacher. This chapter outlines their disagreement and the deeper ethical issues these thinkers confront under this organizing principle as they articulate some of the most powerful and influential visions of personal formation ever produced.

The Ambiguities of "Human Nature"

The traditional opening in essays contrasting Xunzi and Mencius begins with their widely known disagreement over *xing* 性, generally translated as "human nature." Xunzi himself chose xing as the point where he would attack Mencius, perhaps because he saw it as a useful key for unlocking what he took to be Mencius's erroneous development of Confucian thought.

In debate with his contemporary, Gaozi, Mencius goes so far as to say that "Human *xing*'s goodness is like water's tending downward. There is no human who does not tend toward goodness. There is no water that does not flow downward" (6A2). Although this is stronger than his most careful formulations, it does provide a ready target for Xunzi, who argues famously that "Human *xing* is bad; human goodness is artificial [i.e., the result of conscious effort]" (e.g., 23/113/3).[2]

One might think that Mencius sees the glass of human nature as half full, and Xunzi sees it as half empty; thus, their views would be compatible. This reading is inadequate, for reasons to be discussed. A more subtle version of this position, held by Chen Daqi and Xu Fuguan, is that because Xunzi and Mencius disagree about the definition of *xing*, they end up arguing at crosspurposes; on such a reading, Mencius and Xunzi describe different elements of our selves as *xing* and in the end are separated by no genuinely significant disagreements.[3] Xunzi does disagree with Mencius about the proper meaning of *xing*, and although he sometimes fails to see how this deforms his antagonistic reading of Mencius, this divergence does point to substantive differences in their understanding of human beings and the moral life.

Given that Mencius and Xunzi do not seem to be using *xing* 性 in exactly the same sense, accurately representing the precise character of their respective claims is a crucial task. But few Western writers have recognized the import of a related comparative philosophical problem: analyzing our own preconceptions about what human nature might mean. Without a clearly articulated and delimited framing of at least the areas that human nature could include and exclude, it is deceptively easy to import ideas into Mencius and especially Xunzi that they did not intend, and which distort their respective accounts of the Confucian *Dao* 道 or "Way."

"Nature" is hardly a univocal concept. Even putting aside all use of the term to refer to the natural world or environment as a whole, speaking of the "nature" of humans, or cats, or chairs, is not as straightforward as it might seem. For the purposes of this chapter, at least four distinct sorts of issues may be implied by talk of human nature, and they do not in any obvious way cohere into a single core concept.[4] First, nature can be a way of talking about what is common to all members of a given class—this could take the form of universal or nearly universal characteristics or even relatively strong accounts of a metaphysical essence or essential characteristic. But here ambiguity looms.

A second aspect of nature concerns what is distinctive to (not just commonly shared by) a class or group. Thus we might say that reason or a capacity for language use is what "makes us human," precisely because we have it but nothing else does. It is worth noting that although judgments of uniqueness may be empirical (e.g., we once thought only humans used tools and then found out that other species do, too), judgments about what is essentially and distinctively human, without which we would be subhuman, are always normative and never merely empirical or descriptive. Here "human" becomes a moral status, not merely a species name, and nature is a way of specifying humanity.

A third aspect of nature is opposed to such evaluations of the distinctively human. Speaking of "human nature" may instead be a way of focusing on our continuity with other animals, by marking out those desires, feelings, and actions that are widely shared precisely because they are so necessary to our biological life: impulses such as hunger, thirst, and the urges to sleep and breathe, as well as less immediate desires for things like activity, companionship, touch, sex, dominance, and even learning, exploration, and recognition. What is natural in this sense is frequent, often spontaneous, and hard to avoid or thwart. Needless to say, what counts as natural in this third sense may have little or no overlap with what we judge to be distinctively human.

A fourth aspect of nature concerns a natural course of organismic development. This might be construed as what will happen to an animal without any outside intervention, or any atypical or harmful intervention, or more positively as what will happen over the course of a lifespan if generally suitable conditions obtain. How this aspect is construed will derive to some extent from other elements of a particular anthropology (especially how one evaluates the second and third aspects of human nature), but the focus on development and change over time is distinctive and pertains especially to self-cultivation, a subject of great interest in early Chinese thought and culture.

Having disentangled these different and partially conflicting strands of the idea of human nature, it should be clear that (1) any thinker who intends to give a reasonably full account of human beings will need to develop a position on each of these four topics, but (2) there is no intrinsic necessity to treating them together, or to seeing these four topics as aspects of a single issue more specific than "what humans are like."

It should therefore come as no surprise that Mencius and Xunzi both have articulate accounts of each of these four anthropological topics, but that neither of them bundle them all together into one conceptual package. Even *xing* 性, so often called on to play this role, does not tie all of these issues together, not even for Mencius, who comes the closest to possessing a precise analogue to human nature as already laid out.

In the next section I work through their respective views of *xing* 性, as well as their sometimes unrelated accounts of other aspects of human nature, to give a concise but sufficient account of what divides them, and why Xunzi feels compelled to attack Mencius at this precise point.

Xing and Nature in Early Confucianism

The classical Chinese word usually translated as human nature is *xing* 性. *Xing* became a problem for admirers of Confucius in the fourth century B.C.E. when other groups challenged the value and justification of their ethical and political prescriptions. In this case Yang Zhu, a shadowy figure who left no surviving writings, was the posthumous figurehead for a critical tendency that advocated "keeping one's nature whole, protecting one's genuineness, and not letting the body be tied by other things" (*Huainanzi* 13/123/21).⁵ One's *xing*, for a Yangist, is the natural tendency of a human being to live a full term of life unless thwarted by outside influences, such as disease, violence, or anxiety. For Yangists, it was crucial to use things to nourish one's own *xing*, and not the other way around, which would be to endanger one's person foolishly, even for the sake of something as apparently grand as ruling a large territory. "Protecting the genuine" means rejecting ceremony and rituals, not allowing one's natural spontaneity to be deformed by custom or training.⁶

Together, these ideas were a direct attack on Confucian ritual practice and political commitment. If, as most took for granted, one's *xing* was endowed by Heaven, the same Heaven that mandated the ritual order of the Confucian-venerated Zhou dynasty, then one should presumably not damage or deform it.⁷ But Yangists contended that Confucian ritual practices themselves, along with their attempts to exercise political power, were harmful and dangerous.

The most prominent response to this challenge that survives comes from Mencius, a Confucian of the second half of the fourth century B.C.E. In response to this and other critiques of Confucius's vision of the Way, Mencius aimed to defend the Confucian Way and make it as compelling as possible (3B9). He chose to justify this Way by taking the Yangist idea of *xing* and redescribing it for his own purposes. Mencius sees human *xing* as consisting essentially of the spontaneous sociable inclinations, distinctive of humans, that are initially small and fragile but tend to grow naturally when properly nourished and nurtured, developing into full-fledged moral inclinations (6A7). In other words, Mencius argues that Confucianism is the best Way possible because it perfectly suits our *xing*—Confucian moral culture is itself the fullest expression of our *xing* and perfectly supports and develops it.

Mencius's primary metaphors for human psychology and moral development are agricultural, expressed in terms of the growth of barley or trees (e.g., 6A7, 6A8). His technical term for our incipient moral dispositions is *duan* 端, "beginnings" or "sprouts." He writes:

> Humans all have hearts that will not bear [the suffering of]
> others.... Suppose someone all of a sudden saw a child about to fall
> into a well: anyone [in such a situation] would have a feeling [lit.
> "heart"] of alarm and compassion—although not because one sought
> to get in good with the child's parents, nor because one wanted to be
> acclaimed by neighbors and friends, nor because one disliked the
> sound of the child's cries. From this we see that if one lacks the heart
> of compassion, one is not human. If one lacks the heart of shame, one

is not human. If one lacks the heart of deference, one is not human. If one lacks the heart of approval and disapproval, one is not human. The heart of compassion is the sprout (*duan*) of benevolence. The heart of shame is the sprout of righteousness. The heart of deference is the sprout of ritual propriety. The heart of approval and disapproval is the sprout of wisdom. People having these four sprouts is like their having four limbs. To have these four sprouts but say that one cannot [become virtuous] is to harm oneself. To say that one's lord cannot [become virtuous] is to harm one's lord. In general, having these four sprouts within oneself, if one knows to fill them all out (*kuo er chong zhi* 擴而充之), it will be like a fire starting up, or a spring breaking through! If one can fill them out (*chong*), they will be enough to care for [all within] the Four Seas. But if one fails to fill them out, they will not be enough to serve even one's own parents. (2A6)[8]

For Mencius, our *xing* consists primarily in four such sprouts, which all people have from birth (6A7): the feelings of compassion, shame, deference, and approval and disapproval. These sprouts have an inherent developmental trajectory toward becoming the full moral virtues of benevolence, righteousness, ritual propriety, and wisdom (2A6). They begin as weak emotional promptings that are revealed in certain situations by our spontaneous moral reactions, which, depending on our degree of cultivation, may or may not result in action.

Mencius's thought experiment about seeing a toddler about to fall into a well is supposed to suggest that an observer (or listener to Mencius) would feel at least a twinge of compassion for the endangered child. They might be so emotionally hardened by life that they would ignore this feeling and fail to respond, but as Mencius says, this would not be the fault of their *xing* (2A2). Thus his most basic claim is quite precise and largely believable: People in general have certain spontaneous, prosocial emotional tendencies; whether these lead to action is another matter, but having compassionate feelings for other people (at least sometimes) is quite typical of our species. All those people who are not badly damaged in an emotional and moral sense will possess such impulses, according to Mencius; this will be the vast majority, but as with unfortunate and rare accidents that might deprive someone of one or more of their limbs, it would seem possible for a damaged human being to lack such sprouts without calling Mencius's generic claim about humans into question.[9] Moreover, it is clear from this metaphor that Mencius thinks possessing and taking proper care of these beginnings of morality is extremely important to living a human life.

If nurtured properly, these sprouts will follow what we might call their genetic pathways and "fill out" into virtues. If started well, this process appears to become increasingly powerful and self-reinforcing, "like a fire starting up, or a spring breaking through." Failure to arrive at virtuous, flourishing personhood can for Mencius only be the result of failure to nourish these sprouts or outright damage to or destruction of them through consciously thwarting their motivational promptings (6A8).

For Mencius, our *xing* ties us to the great sages of the past (6A7), but for Xunzi, by contrast, it links us to the "petty person" (4/15/14). Xunzi redefines *xing* as follows: "That which is so from birth is called *xing*. What the *xing*'s harmonious operation generates, the vital essence effortlessly and spontaneously uniting arousal and response, this is [also] called *xing*" (22/107/22–23). Thus, what for Mencius had an intrinsic teleology that defined people as human has become for Xunzi merely what is "innate," done easily and spontaneously, without effort or thought.

So far, this definition does not seem to carry any evaluative judgment, either positive or negative. But Xunzi makes his substantive views quite clear at the beginning of an essay titled "*Xing* is bad":

> Human *xing* is bad; our goodness is artifice. Now, human *xing* is such that from birth it has a love of profit. Following this will produce wrangling and strife, and courtesy and deference will perish. From birth there is envy and hatred in it; following these will produce violence and crime, and loyalty and trust will perish. From birth it has the desires of the ears and eyes, and a love of sounds and colors. Following these will produce wantonness and chaos, and ritual, social obligations, proper form, and good order will all perish. (23/113/3–5)

For Xunzi, our innate endowment contains nothing moral; everything higher in human life is produced out of (and to a certain extent in spite of) our innate feelings and desires, which in themselves lead predominantly to horrifyingly destructive social conflict.

Despite this critical view of our spontaneous impulses, Xunzi, like Mencius, is deeply concerned with the process of moral development and self-cultivation. However, where Mencius favors agricultural metaphors of spontaneous growth and maturation, Xunzi turns to tougher craft metaphors, such as a blacksmith sharpening metal or a carpenter straightening crooked timber on a steam press (23/113/9–14).[10]

Xunzi tends to pair *xing* 性, the innate, with *wei* 偽, literally meaning "artifice" but implying something like conscious thought and effort, as in his repeated statements that "Human innate impulses (*xing*) are bad; human goodness is artificial." For Xunzi, the *xing* does not exhaust our capabilities and potentials; in particular it has little to do with the human heart/mind (*xin* 心) and its capacities to respond to the world and direct action while remaining empty, unified, and tranquil.

With this preliminary sketch in place, let us dig deeper into their differences by taking stock of how Mencius and Xunzi compare with respect to the fourfold conception of human nature sketched previously. Both agree that all people are born possessing a *xing* of essentially common character (e.g., 6A7, 23/115/22–25), but as noted they immediately diverge over its character and parameters.

With regard to what is common to all human beings, the first aspect of human nature as discussed here, it is somewhat unclear whether Mencius intends to refer to all such commonalities as *xing* (e.g., 7B24). He does believe that there is an intrinsic hierarchy ordering the various parts of human beings, with some things (such as the heart/mind) much more important than others (6A14). Regardless of how one reads Mencius on this point, it is clear that Xunzi thinks human *xing*, as the set of our spontaneous inclinations, is only a subset of the things that humans all share. We have other abilities and potentials that are common to all, even "a person in the street"—these tend to concern purposeful activities of our heart/mind, such as deliberation and reflection. Put another way, Xunzi carefully delimits the scope of what is innate to claim greater space and importance for what he calls artifice, which is broadly speaking the work of culture, which he repeatedly highlights and celebrates. Mencius recognizes a distinction between the spontaneous beginnings of virtue (i.e., the sprouts) and fully developed virtue, but he conceives of culture as being much more in harmony with human *xing*, at least so long as that culture is Confucian (e.g., 3A5).

The contrast between Mencius's expansive treatment of *xing* and Xunzi's more restrictive treatment becomes clearer when we examine their accounts of what is distinctively human about human beings. For Mencius, it is precisely our *xing* that makes us human: if we fail to attend to and nurture our proto-moral emotional tendencies, we will rapidly descend into a bestial existence (3A4, 6A7–15). For Xunzi, by contrast, what makes us human has nothing to do with *xing*. He writes, "What makes human beings human? I say it is because we make distinctions" (5/18/13). He goes on to explicitly contrast our bodily form and innate inclinations, which are essentially similar to those of a great ape, with the human capacity to form, recognize, and live in accordance with distinctions, which Xunzi interprets rather broadly as the basis for human social life in complex, differentiated communities. "Therefore among human ways of life none lack distinctions. Of distinctions, none is more important than those concerning social hierarchy, and of the ways to distinguish social hierarchy, none is more important than ritual. Of rituals, none is more important than those of the sage kings" (5/18/13–18). As he makes clear in another passage on the same issue, what makes Confucian hierarchical relationships and their associated rituals so effective at knitting together community is that these hierarchical divisions are just and right, not merely expedient or beneficial. "Thus if people use just norms to divide themselves then they will be harmonious; if harmonious, they will be unified, if unified they will have greater strength, with greater strength they will be powerful, when powerful they will triumph over things" (9/39/9–13). We can draw complex webs of distinctions between ourselves, Xunzi thinks, precisely to constitute subtle and humane relationships. We can thereby form large and differentiated communities that are nevertheless cohesive and powerful, and "obtain" much more than could be gotten through our feeble capacities for strength and speed. It should be noted that for Xunzi this distinctive human feature is hardly innate; justice is something we need to obtain, and Xunzi cautions us not to let go of it for an instant (9/39/16).[11]

This fundamental disagreement about the role of human *xing* within the moral life reappears when we examine the third aspect of human nature: our largely animalistic shared inclinations, such as thirst and hunger. As noted, this is practically the entirety of human xing for Xunzi, although he does occasionally recognize some positive and more or less neutral innate tendencies, such as the basic fondness for other members of the same species that all animals share (19/96/10–13), as well as innate sense capacities that make life possible (23/113/19–22). For his part, Mencius does not deny that human beings have typical, often physical desires, nor that these make us close to the beasts (4B19); he even thinks satisfying these impulses is important, as long as this is understood to be categorically subordinate to the demands of justice and ritual propriety (3A4, 6A15). Mencius tends to contrast these "lesser parts" of human existence, such as desires for food, money, and sex, with the "greater part," that is, the sprouts of virtue within our hearts (6A14–15).

It might seem that Mencius insists strongly on what is distinctively human as the core of our *xing*, whereas Xunzi insists equally strongly that our spontaneous, biologically based inclinations form this core. This is true enough, but the common inference that they are simply talking past each other should not be drawn. Xunzi explicitly denies that human beings have anything like "sprouts of virtue" as part of their various innate inclinations (23/114/18–24). For Xunzi, unlike for Mencius, moral understanding and habits are *completely* acquired, through learning and practice; as we will explore below, Mencius too insists on the importance of practice and learning, but he conceives of these processes very differently than Xunzi (e.g., 6A9).

Mencius might respond to Xunzi's critique much as he did to Gaozi: justice and ritual propriety are not external impositions on our xing, but rather its "natural" fulfillment (3A5, 6A1, 6A6). Mencius, then, puts great emphasis not only on the existence and importance of the emotions that are sprouts of virtue but also on what might be called a natural teleology within the human heart/mind: if human beings grow up and live in a supportive environment, they will naturally develop virtue over time, in the same way that barley sprouts, if given enough light and water and not choked by weeds, will grow up to become mature barley plants (6A7). Mencius is thus equally committed to a strong reading of the fourth aspect of human nature, a natural course of development, which he reads quite positively as a natural tendency toward virtue (as long as we properly tend ourselves over time).

As with the question of the existence of the sprouts of virtue, Xunzi adamantly rejects this Mencian developmental hypothesis. For Xunzi, human *xing* includes only what is thoughtless, spontaneous, and innate. Although Xunzi shies away from the Mencian emphasis on the *xing* having a genetic developmental trajectory, at times we get a glimmer at least of his sense of the general drift of our instincts as an active force. We are like warped wood rather than straight, like dull metal instead of a sharp sword. What is at first a set of selfish, biologically based needs, drives, and capacities will, if free of the influence of education, good government, and the threat of punishment, become "wicked" and "rebellious," actively recalcitrant to the aims of social harmony and peace. Thus not only are the consequences of following such an innate endowment bad, the endowment itself is deeply problematic. Nevertheless, our *xing* is neither thoroughly bad in the sense that every element of it is contemptible, nor truly evil in the sense that we would take any innate delight in destructive or cruel actions for their own sake. Although Xunzi thought many engaged in such crimes in his day, he saw this as deriving from a larger struggle for political dominance and personal aggrandizement carried on by leaders with undisciplined dispositions and desires. He argues that even brothers, if they have valuable goods to apportion among themselves, will fight and rob each other, if they have not worked to transform their spontaneous, innate dispositions. In contrast to this, Xunzi suggests that even fellow countrymen will treat each other with deference in a similar situation if they have undertaken the Confucian program of ritual reformation (23/114/16–18).[12]

As should be clear by now, Xunzi attacks Mencius over his account of human xing because of what he takes to be its unwarranted and even dangerous implications for moral education and self-cultivation. Xunzi is hardly less optimistic than Mencius about human potential for virtue, and the possibility of just and harmonious community life, but his sense of *how* such goods are to be achieved is very different from Mencius's. To sort out this deeper disagreement, and Mencius's likely response to Xunzi's critique, we turn to their diverging accounts of Confucian moral self-cultivation.

## The Moral Psychology of Pursuing Virtue

Mencius's theory that we have sprouts tending toward virtue grounds his whole picture of moral deliberation, action, and self-cultivation. In the context of a discussion of human nature Mencius criticizes "clever people," saying: "'If they could act like [the sage-king] Yu did when he guided the flood waters [e.g., through dredging rivers], then there would be nothing to dislike in them. Yu guided the water by going along with its natural tendency. If clever people too go along with their natural tendency, then great indeed will their cleverness be.'" (4B26). The problem with cleverness is when it is employed to "bore through" things, ignoring our natural tendencies; if one can cleverly help our natural tendencies to roll forward like water flowing downhill (see 6A2), one acts like a sage.

What might this consist in, for Mencius, in a typical person's life? As noted, for Mencius "having these four sprouts [of virtue] within oneself, if one knows to fill them all out, it will be like a fire starting up, a spring breaking through" (2A6)! By attending (*si* 思) to the sprouts and the motivational/emotional responses they produce, one can nourish and fill out these incipient moral dispositions. By acting according to these promptings and then reflecting on this, one will feel a distinctive moral joy, the satisfaction of the sprouts' intrinsically good desires (6A7). By cultivating this feeling over time, one is able to enter an increasingly gratifying feedback loop that only accelerates moral development.

This is what Mencius calls the development of "floodlike vital energy" (*haoran zhi qi* 浩然之氣). He writes of this *qi*:

> It is the greatest and most unyielding of vital energies. If one
> nourishes it with integrity and does it no harm, it will fill the space
> between Heaven and Earth. This energy unites righteousness and
> the Way. Without them, it starves. It is generated by [gradually]
> accumulating righteousness, not carried off after a sudden seizure of
> righteousness. If one's actions do not sit well with one's heart/mind,
> then [this energy] starves. That is why I say Gaozi never understood

> righteousness—because he viewed it as something external. You must pay attention to the task, but do not rectify the heart/mind. Do not forget about [the heart/mind]; [but] do not [try to] help it grow.... There are few in the world who can resist [trying to] help their grain to grow. Some think there is nothing they can do to help, and so abandon their grain, not even bothering to weed. Others [try to] help their grain to grow by pulling at the shoots. Not only does this fail to help; it harms it even more. (2A2)

We are to "pay attention to the task" by remaining alert to our moral promptings, and acting on them whenever we feel their pull (3B8). However, we should not strain ourselves to perform actions that our heart/minds do not genuinely recognize as right; as the passage makes clear, this sort of hypocritical feigning of goodness is as perilous to our character as tugging on young shoots is to grain. We must also "weed," by attending to the promptings of the sprouts in our heart/mind rather than to our senses and basic appetites alone, and allowing the first to have precedence over the latter as the "greater" over the "smaller" part of our being (6A15).

Self-cultivation continues through a process of moral deliberation and action that has two main facets. First, one models oneself on the conduct of the sages of antiquity (4A2, 4A7); in this way one has a target to aim for to help one keep improving and developing. Second, one "extends" (*tui* 推, *da* 達, *ji* 及, or *zhi* 至) or "fills out" (*chong* 充) the reactions of the sprouts until they grow into full virtues. This has two equally important senses. Mencius writes:

> People all have things that they will not bear. To extend (*da*) this reaction to what they will bear is benevolence. People all have things that they will not do. To extend this reaction to what they will do is righteousness. If people can fill out (*chong*) the heart that does not desire to harm others, their benevolence will be inexhaustible. If people can fill out the heart that will not trespass, their righteousness will be inexhaustible. (7B31)

Here Mencius speaks of extending the moral reactions of the heart/mind through attention to them and action on their basis; in this way the heart/mind may be filled out so that these reactions are strong, dependable, and predominant.

In an exemplary case, after discussing the king's pity on an ox that was to be sacrificed, Mencius admonishes King Xuan of Qi.

Treat your elders as elders, and extend (*ji*) this to the elders of others; treat your young as young, and extend this to the young of others, and you can turn the whole world in the palm of your hand. The *Odes* say, "He set an example for his wife, it extended (*zhi*) to his brothers, and so he controlled his family and state." This means that he simply took this heart and applied it to that. Hence, if one extends (*tui*) one's kindness, it will be enough to care for [all within] the Four Seas. If one does not extend (*tui*) one's kindness, in will not be enough to care for one's wife and children. That in which the ancients greatly exceeded others was exactly this. They were simply good at extending (*tui*) what they did. In the present case your kindness is sufficient to reach (*ji*) birds and beasts, but your achievements do not reach (*zhi*) the commoners." (1A7)

Here "extension" refers to the process of analogical reasoning and deepening perceptiveness whereby similar cases are recognized by the heart/mind as calling for action based on the same natural moral promptings. In this way, the scope of one's ethical action will expand as one's moral dispositions grow, and Mencius's "virtuous circle" of ethical cultivation will begin to cycle, leading to the development of "flood-like vital energy" and eventually true sagehood.

In sum, Mencius's account of moral development places great emphasis on three things: awareness of one's own heartfelt impulses toward goodness, as well as their momentous import; patient attentiveness to these inborn moral intuitions and impulses; and repeated action in accordance with these innate intuitions and feelings in the context of one's everyday life. Working locally, one might say, is the only way to make progress toward the sort of heroic goodness that could be called sagely; trying to act like a sage before we have grown into the right frame of mind is a recipe for despair and collapse, according to Mencius.

In opposition to this view, Xunzi sees a dangerous cleavage in Mencius's recommendations to model oneself on the ancient sages and *also* extend one's innate moral promptings according to their natural pattern of growth. After several criticisms of Mencius's theory, Xunzi points out the crux of his worries: "Hence, if our *xing* is good, then we can dispense with the sage kings and put aside ritual and just norms (*liyi* 禮義); if our *xing* is bad then we must adhere to the sage kings and esteem ritual and justice." It is certainly true that modeling oneself on the sage kings is not well integrated into Mencius's account of moral psychology. Xunzi sees that if human beings have the basis for morality within them, then it is not such a long way to a position like that of the Ming dynasty Neo-Confucian Wang Yangming; Wang saw himself as a Mencian but counseled that one could ignore the writings by and about the ancient sages and rely wholly on one's own moral insight.

For Xunzi, our *xing* includes various desires and emotional responses that can be stirred up by external things (stimulus and response) according to unconscious mechanisms. Without conscious attention and rehabilitation, these desires and emotional responses are foolishly selfish, leading to chaos and destructive consequences. For Xunzi it is essential that the heart/mind take up its office as the "Heavenly lord" (17/80/10) of the body and direct these various responses so that over time they might be remade according to the Confucian Way. The engines of this transformation are "conscious effort" and "accumulation" guided by "deliberation" based on correct "knowledge" of the Dao (22/107/22–22/108/2). Put another way, Xunzi articulates a moral psychology that sharply distinguishes between spontaneous desires and feelings on the one hand and conscious abilities to reflect, deliberate about action, and choose on the other hand. He sees no hope for virtue in the pursuit of spontaneous impulses, and so turns instead to the moral possibilities created by enculturation, education, and conscious practice.

According to Xunzi, in the process of personal formation we start "in a state of complete moral blindness."[13] We need a teacher to present to us the model of past exemplars and the Way they followed. Xunzi writes:

> From birth human beings are certainly petty people. If they are without a teacher and the model, they will see things only in terms of personal benefit. Since human beings are certainly petty from birth, if they should moreover meet with a chaotic age they will gain chaotic customs; this is using the petty to deepen the petty, using the chaotic to attain chaos.... Now as for a person's mouth and stomach: How can they know ritual and justice? How can they know declining and yielding? How can they know honesty and shame, and accumulate [all] the corners [i.e., the different aspects of the Way]? They merely suck and chew away, feast and enjoy until full. If a person lacks a teacher and the model then his heart/mind will be just like his mouth and stomach. (4/15/14–17)

For Xunzi, morality is not an outgrowth of our innate impulses but something learned and practiced. Without thorough education people act in all areas as if they were thinking with their stomachs: in a vulgar, short-sighted, selfish, and ultimately destructive manner.

Instead of speaking of watering plants and weeding one's garden, Xunzi favors tougher metaphors when describing personal formation.

> A warped piece of wood must wait until it has been laid against the straightening board, steamed, and forced into shape before it can become straight; a piece of blunt metal must wait until it has been whetted on a grindstone before it can become sharp. Similarly, since humanity's innate endowment is bad it must wait for the instructions of a teacher and the model before it can become upright, and for the guidance of ritual and just norms before it can become well-ordered. (23/113/9–10)

For Xunzi, becoming moral is a process of being "transformed by a teacher and the model, guided by ritual and social roles" (23/113/6) until one completely reshapes one's innate impulses and responses, learns the necessary ritual skills, and develops the discernment necessary to be a Confucian gentleman. For Mencius moral development is a process of gradual cultivation of what is already there according to its natural tendencies, but for Xunzi it is the imprinting of a new set of patterns onto a disruptive but malleable set of impulses so that they are transformed into something new, and a new "acquired character" is developed through sustained "conscious exertion," that is, through what he calls "artifice" (*wei* 偽).

Xunzi analyzes the psychological mechanisms of this gradual change as follows (note the contrast between what one has and receives on the one hand, and what one does and makes on the other):

> If a person lacks a teacher and model then he will exalt innate impulses; if he has a teacher and model then he will exalt accumulation. Now, teaching and modeling are what are gained via accumulation, but not what is received from innate impulses, which are insufficient to allow you to establish yourself alone and be well-ordered. Innate impulses are what you cannot make, and yet they can be transformed. Accumulation is not what you have, and yet you can do it. Focus attention and plan in order to practice [the right] customs; this is the means by which to transform innate promptings. Uniting into one so that you have no division: this is the means to perfect accumulation. Practicing [the right] customs shifts your intent; maintain this for a long time and it shifts the substance [of your heart/mind]. If you unify [yourself] so that you have no [internal] division, then you will comprehend with spiritual clarity and form a triad with Heaven and Earth. Thus if you accumulate earth you will make a mountain; accumulate water and you will make an ocean. . . . If a man on the street, a commoner, accumulates goodness [in this way] and completely exhausts it, call him a sage. (8/33/18–8/34/5)

Uniting one's heart/mind and focusing it on following the Confucian Way are the means to perfect one's accumulation of goodness. Through this conscious, goal-oriented self-cultivation one can gradually shift the orientation of one's heart/mind and even shift its very "substance," that is, its spontaneous tendencies. In this way one consciously remakes one's innate impulses and effectively acquires new and better desires, emotions, and habits, which are virtuous and productive of genuine flourishing. Yet this self-cultivation cannot possibly get off the ground without a teacher and the model (the examples of the sage kings), which introduce a qualitatively higher new form of life and thus give one something to aim at and imitate.

The final goal of Xunzian moral education is sagehood. An essential part of this involves honing the heart/mind's capacities to be open to new impressions, focused and integrated, and calm while remaining active and discerning (21/103/25ff.). Despite our myopic and destructive innate impulses, Xunzi thinks moral perfection is possible for everyone (in theory if not in practice), because of these potentials of the heart/mind. Xunzi's ideal sage has developed a perfected spontaneous responsiveness that allows him to "comprehend with spiritual clarity and form a triad with Heaven and Earth" through his universal understanding. This is possible because the Confucian Way that he teaches accords with the underlying patterns (*li* 理) of Heaven, Earth, and humanity, ordering human society in harmony with the natural world so that all have enough and have an appropriate, merited, and satisfactory position in the social and cosmic whole.

To explain some of the fundamental differences between their positions, one could say that Mencius pursues an inside-out model of personal formation, and Xunzi advocates an outside-in model.[14] As Mencius explicitly states, morality only has "one source," the developing sprouts within one's own heart/mind, not two sources (i.e., the heart/mind and some external teaching) (3A5). For him it is crucial to look within, examine oneself, and remain constantly attentive and responsive to the moral stirrings within one's own heart and mind. As these sprouts grow into full-fledged moral virtues, they radiate outward from their source within, benevolently ordering our families, communities, and even states as our capacities come to full flower. In contrast, Xunzi denies the existence of innate, internal moral guides, finding within the untutored heart/mind only rather ugly impulses like hunger and greed. For him, becoming moral is rather like learning to read or becoming an excellent musician: we must learn everything we need to know, practice certain "unnatural" but beautiful and meaningful activities assiduously, and in the process awaken and develop new desires, perceptions, and skills that reorder everything that came before, ushering us into a new and far superior form of life, both individually and collectively. In this way, civilization built up over many generations can permeate and transform us from the outside in, and when we are transformed we can uphold and even develop it further as time rolls on.

## Two Kinds of Confucian Religiosity

One final difference between Mencius and Xunzi is discussed less often than their well-known disagreements over human nature and the best practices of self-cultivation but may be of particular interest to scholars and teachers in religious studies. This concerns how their disagreement over *xing* 性 relates to their conceptions of *tian* 天, usually translated as "Heaven," the main deity revered by the Zhou dynasty and thus by Confucians as well. Intriguingly, both accept without question that Heaven gives humans their *xing* and is in some sense responsible for its character.

For Mencius, the connection between our moral *xing* and the character of Heaven is relatively straightforward. He writes, "To fully realize one's heart is to understand one's nature (*xing*). To understand one's heart is to understand Heaven. One serves Heaven by preserving one's heart and nurturing one's nature" (7A1). For Mencius, Heaven is dedicated to moral purposes, although sometimes its dictates are inscrutable (2B13). For human beings, the surest way to know and serve Heaven is to cultivate one's own heart/mind and become truly virtuous. Achieving virtue is within our power, even if political or worldly success is not (7A3). Indeed, Heaven-sent sufferings and difficulties tend to befall those who are being groomed for greatness and help propel their ethical and religious development (6B15).

When Mencius reaches for a mystical register to convey his highest hopes, he speaks in terms of personal integrity and authenticity, understood of course with objective reference to our shared *xing*: "The myriad things are all complete within me. There is no greater joy than to reflect and see that I have been sincere. There is no shorter path to benevolence than to strive earnestly to act with reciprocity" (7A4). And again: "Making no distinction between dying young or living long, cultivating oneself with expectancy, these are the ways to establish one's destiny" (7A1). When we "pay attention to the task" of self-cultivation, we become more deeply aligned with the purposes of Heaven and come to understand and care for the wider cosmos as something much greater than but still intimately connected to our deepest self. For Mencius, the Confucian Way entails a courageous effort to focus on one's own heart as a way to engage with the world, knowing all the while that whether striving for goodness will actually result in success is beyond one's control, and is instead subject to Heaven's decree (*ming* 命).[15]

Perhaps surprisingly, Xunzi agrees that Heaven gives us our *xing*, including our innate dispositions and desires. For Xunzi, Heaven stands for spontaneous and effortless natural processes of generation and completion, both in the cosmos and human life, which are generally constant and inevitable; it does not pursue moral purposes nor intervene meaningfully in human affairs.[16] In one passage, he speaks of our Heaven-given dispositions and describes the heart/mind and sense abilities as the Heaven-given "lord" and "officials" of the body (17/80/9–13). Xunzi uses extended bureaucratic metaphors to illuminate the relation of Heaven and human beings and to argue for a particular vision of the interior psychological "government" of persons.

The key to understanding this passage is recognizing that for Xunzi, the cosmic order is a ritual order, and the human ritual order is continuous with (although not identical to) the cosmic order.[17] However, this is not to say that for Xunzi tian and people have the same Way to follow or roles to play in the cosmos; they most certainly do not. For Xunzi, the traditional Zhou deity tian occupies the apex of the cosmic hierarchy, the most honored position. On his account, its duties or "official responsibilities," *zhi* 職, are the mostly constant movements of the various celestial bodies, and in addition those natural processes of generation and development that "develop without [people] acting purposefully, and are attained without seeking [the results]" (17/80/1). These heavenly powers Xunzi calls *shen* 神, "spiritual," meaning that they are mysteriously productive without human effort or visible activity, producing "Heaven's accomplishments," such as the changing but orderly sequence of the seasons (17/80/5–7). For Xunzi, Heaven is like the sage ruler, who takes no apparent action yet governs and orders the entire realm. In this aspect of the metaphor, however, human beings must act as the faithful ministers, implementing policies and following their own Way, which is to actively order the cosmos. "Heaven has its seasons, Earth its resources, and humanity its ordering government; this is called 'being able to form a triad' [with Heaven and Earth]" (17/80/2–3). The cosmic order is a ritual order in that each element has its proper role and place in the hierarchy, with its due honors and deserts, and its own tasks; Xunzi cautions that we must not "compete with Heaven over responsibilities," but accept our own distinctive role and Way (17/80/2).

For Xunzi, we reform ourselves and order the larger natural world for the greater good of human beings and the entire range of the myriad things. The central trope that he uses to evoke this transformative Confucian civilizing process is the image of human ritual. Indeed, as noted, Xunzi even conceives of the cosmos in ritualized terms. He writes:

> Through [ritual] Heaven and Earth come together, the sun and moon shine, the four seasons follow each other, the stars and planets move, the great rivers flow, the myriad things all thrive, love and hate are moderated, and delight and anger made appropriate. If through ritual one is below, then one will be compliant; if through ritual one is above, then one will be enlightened. [Through it] the myriad things change but do not become chaotic. (19/92/4–6)

Because ritual for Xunzi is the key to harmonious and flourishing life, both human and nonhuman, he feels it deserves the most evocative and poetic descriptions (the quotation is in rhymed verse in the original). Ritual is thus his general prescription for the misrule, unrest, and chaos of his age. Different elements of the universe each have their appropriate roles, which the heavenly bodies fill with admirable if not perfect regularity. The human role is to order both the human and natural worlds so that inevitable ebbs and flows, as well as occasional strange events like eclipses, do not result in chaos. This can be accomplished both through agriculture that magnifies and orders natural fecundity, and through what might be called public works projects, such as the dredging and diking of the Yellow and Yangzi Rivers, traditionally credited to the sage king Yu, to stop destructive flooding.

Instead of "knowing Heaven" from the inside as with Mencius, Xunzi counsels us to "form a triad" with Heaven and Earth to take our proper, very important place within the broader cosmos. We are to work with and indeed govern natural processes and materials, to craft a way of life in which all parts of the ecosystem coexist harmoniously. Xunzi thinks that without the ordering governance of wise human beings, both the natural world and the human heart are trackless wilderness. Our *xing* may thus be "bad," but for Xunzi it is still sufficiently pliable to serve as the raw material that artifice remolds into gentlemen and sages. Our dispositions and desires are reformed but not exchanged; they are ordered and ornamented, not demolished and replaced (19/95/1–4). Providing this transformative ordering is our proper role in the cosmos, as followers of the human Way.

In conclusion, seeing the disputes between Mencius and Xunzi as family quarrels can help us teach about their philosophical and religious visions with insight. Although they disagree deeply about the proper methods of moral self-cultivation, about the moral psychology of those aspiring to goodness, and the character of Heaven in relation to human striving, these disagreements should still be understood in relation to their unmistakable similarities as thoughtful interpreters of the *Dao* of Confucius. Mencius accentuates the dignity and potential of innate moral impulses and intuitions, which, if cultivated in accord with their natural tendencies of growth, will come to properly govern the whole of the human organism, family, and community. For his part, Xunzi emphasizes the insufficiency and destructiveness of human instincts, which must be mastered and reshaped over time through the civilizing Confucian disciplines of learning, ritual, and music. Nevertheless, both thinkers aim to cultivate wise and benevolent elites who use their talents for the common good, rather than personal enrichment, and will do so through the cultivation of a harmonious, justly ordered society that is made beautiful and compelling through its ritualized culture and the inspiring virtue of its leaders.

NOTES

1. The phrase "moral vanguard" applied to Confucianism comes from Benjamin Schwartz, *The World of Thought in Ancient China* (Cambridge, Mass.: Harvard University Press, 1985).

2. Citations to the *Mencius* follow the common section breaks; these are marked in D. C. Lau's standard translation (New York: Penguin, 1970) as well as Bryan Van Norden's more philosophically precise partial translation, in Philip J. Ivanhoe and Bryan W. Van Norden, eds., *Readings in Classical Chinese Philosophy*, 2nd ed. (Indianapolis: Hackett, 2005). Citations to the *Xunzi* are to D. C. Lau, *A Concordance to the Xunzi* (Hong Kong: Commercial Press, 1996), in the form chapter/page/line. Translations are my own unless otherwise noted. The standard translation of the *Xunzi* is Burton Watson, trans., *Hsün Tzu: Basic Writings* (New York: Columbia University Press, 1963). An unabridged, copiously annotated translation by John Knoblock is also available: *Xunzi: A Translation and Study of the Complete Works*, 3 vols. (Stanford, Calif.: Stanford University Press, 1988–1994).

3. For analytical discussion of their views, as well as other Chinese scholars' interpretations, see Kwong-Loi Shun, *Mencius and Early Chinese Thought* (Stanford, Calif.: Stanford University Press, 1997), pp. 226–31.

4. On human nature, see Mary Midgley, *Beast and Man: The Roots of Human Nature*, rev. ed. (London: Routledge, 1995); Elliott Sober and David Sloan Wilson, *Unto Others: The Evolution and Psychology of Unselfish Behavior* (Cambridge, Mass.: Harvard University Press, 1998); Alasdair MacIntyre, *Dependent Rational Animals: Why Human Beings Need the Virtues* (Chicago: Open Court, 1999); and Leonard D. Katz, ed., *Evolutionary Origins of Morality: Cross-Disciplinary Perspectives* (Bowling Green, Ohio: Imprint Academic, 2000). I have previously developed versions of this fourfold schema in Stalnaker, "Comparative Religious Ethics and the Problem of 'Human Nature,'" *Journal of Religious Ethics* 33, no. 2 (June 2005): 187–224; and Stalnaker, *Overcoming Our Evil: Human Nature and Spiritual Exercises in Xunzi and Augustine* (Washington, D.C.: Georgetown University Press, 2006).

5. Lau, *Concordance to the Huainanzi*.

6. A. C. Graham, *Disputers of the Tao: Philosophical Argument in Ancient China* (La Salle, Ill.: Open Court, 1989), pp. 53–64, esp. 56–58.

7. Heaven (*tian* 天) was the traditional deity of the Zhou, the dynasty most

admired by Confucians. *Tian* or *tiandi* 天地 (heaven and Earth), was also the closest early Chinese analog to the idea of Nature as the whole natural world.

8. This and my other translations of the *Mencius* owe much to the translations of D. C. Lau, Philip Ivanhoe, and Bryan Van Norden. For Lau and Van Norden, see note 2. For Ivanhoe, see his *Ethics in the Confucian Tradition: The Thought of Mengzi and Wang Yangming*, 2nd ed. (Indianapolis: Hackett, 2002).

9. I owe this way of framing the issue, in terms of generic claims, to P. J. Ivanhoe and Julius Moravcsik.

10. On Xunzi's use of craft metaphors for self-cultivation, see T. C. Kline, "Ethics and Tradition in the Xunzi" (Ph.D. diss., Stanford University, 1998), 215ff.

11. This passage is at the center of an ongoing controversy about the proper interpretation of the *Xunzi*. Note Donald Munro, "A Villain in the *Xunzi*," in P. J. Ivanhoe, ed., *Chinese Language, Thought and Culture: Nivison and His Critics* (Chicago.: Open Court, 1996), pp. 193–201; David Nivison, "Xunzi on 'Human Nature,'" in Bryan Van Norden, ed., *The Ways of Confucianism: Investigations in Chinese Philosophy* (Chicago: Open Court, 1996), pp. 203–13; and Eric Hutton's decisive rejoinder, "On the Meaning of *Yi* (義) in Xunzi" (master's thesis, Harvard University, 1996).

12. Jonathan Schofer argues that Xunzi propounds a "ritual reformation" model of ethical development in "Virtues in Xunzi's Thought," *Journal of Religious Ethics* 21, no. 4 (1993): 501–21; reprinted in T. C. Kline III and Philip J. Ivanhoe, eds., *Virtue, Nature, and Moral Agency in the Xunzi* (Indianapolis: Hackett, 2000).

13. Philip J. Ivanhoe, "Human Nature and Moral Understanding in Xunzi," *International Philosophical Quarterly* 34 (1994): 173.

14. I draw these terms and the general contrast from Kline, "Ethics and Tradition in the Xunzi," pp. 51–52. Note also Edward Slingerland's developed contrast between self-cultivation "internalism" and "externalism," in his *Effortless Action: Wu-Wei as Conceptual Metaphor and Spiritual Ideal in Early China* (New York: Oxford University Press, 2003), 12ff. and passim; as well as my own extended discussion of these issues in Stalnaker, *Overcoming Our Evil*, chap. 8.

15. For a fuller discussion, see Irene Bloom, "Practicality and Spirituality in the Mencius," in Tu Weiming and Mary Evelyn Tucker, eds., *Confucian Spirituality* (New York: Crossroad, 2003), pp. 233–51.

16. *Xunzi*, chap. 17; on Heaven's constancy, see 17/79/16, 17/81/1. For longer discussions of Xunzi's account of *tian* 天, Heaven, see Edward Machle, *Nature and Heaven in the "Xunzi": A Study of the "Tian Lun"* (Albany: State University of New York Press, 1993); and Paul Goldin, *Rituals of the Way: The Philosophy of Xunzi* (Chicago: Open Court, 1999), esp. chap. 2.

17. On these points I have gained from Machle, *Nature and Heaven in the "Xunzi,"* esp. pp. 147–78.

# Understanding the Ethical Universe of Neo-Confucianism

*Robert W. Foster*

During the May Fourth Movement of the early twentieth century, Chinese intellectuals exhorted their countrymen to break free from traditions that inhibited China in the increasingly competitive international scene. One of the main targets of the May Fourth Movement was Neo-Confucianism. Intellectuals from across the spectrum of political views characterized Neo-Confucianism as a reactionary, hierarchical system that prevented the Chinese from entering the modern age. Lu Xun's "A Madman's Diary" went so far as to describe the Neo-Confucian system as one that encouraged the protagonist to "eat people." The extent of the antipathy of the May Fourth leaders toward Neo-Confucianism illustrates how strongly associated it was with China's imperial past.

Neo-Confucianism is the standard translation for the synonymous Chinese terms *daoxue* 道學 (learning of the Way) and *lixue* 理學 (learning of Principle). It refers to the Confucian revival that began in the eighth century and developed into the dominant worldview that held sway in China until the seventeenth century. Even when other modes of thought began to challenge Neo-Confucianism's grip on literati interests, it was still linked with the imperial government through use of Neo-Confucian texts in the examination system that recruited capable men into the imperial bureaucracy. Consequently, Neo-Confucianism was associated with a worldview, a social hierarchy, and a political system. Though focused on the secular world, Neo-Confucianism asked and answered questions dealing with the ultimate concerns of human beings: What is good, how does one live a meaningful life, how are humans connected with the rest of the cosmos, and what role do we play? That Neo-Confucianism was so vigorously opposed by the May Fourth Movement shows how persuasively it had answered those questions for many Chinese into the twentieth century and beyond. Mou Zongsan has described Confucianism as a "religion of ethics," in which the central issue is not seeking separation from this world (as in Buddhism) or salvation through the intervention of the divine (as in Christianity). To embody ethical principles and translate them into ethical action is to become "a sage within." Humans are capable of doing so by developing the internal resources within our minds and human nature. Mou wrote, "It goes without saying that being a sage or not being a sage depends upon self-consciously engaging in ethical practice, upon taking one's original heart-and-mind and human nature as the foundation for thoroughly clarifying one's life. This means that the full ethico-religious deep meaning is completely in this unceasing, inexhaustible effort, that the full morality of learning to be a sage within stems completely from this unceasing, inexhaustible effort."[1] Individuals make the conscious choice to engage in moral action, and morality is universal and ever-lasting.

However, becoming a "sage within" does not connote a purely selfish goal. The Neo-Confucians were intensely concerned with bringing order to a disorderly world. They were social activists who built schools, drafted community compacts that set local standards, and petitioned government officials on behalf of the local populace. Their ideals and actions were shaped by a key passage from the classical text titled the *Great Learning* (大學):

> The ancients who wished to illustrate illustrious virtue throughout the world, first ordered well their own states. Wishing to order well their own states, they first regulated their families. Wishing to regulate their families, they first cultivated their persons. Wishing to cultivate their persons, they first rectified their hearts. Wishing to rectify their hearts, they first sought to be sincere in their thoughts. Wishing to be sincere in their thoughts, they first extended to the utmost their knowledge. Such extension of knowledge lay in the investigation of things.[2]

In this continuum, the development of the individual lies at the beginning of a sequence of steps leading to social and political order and to a virtuous world. The idea also resonates with Confucius's dictum that "the man of perfect virtue, wishing to be established himself, seeks also to establish others; wishing to be enlarged himself, he seeks also to enlarge others."[3] Beginning with the self, the Neo-Confucian worldview argues that human beings have a vital role to play in this world as the agents of order. Through the choices we make, we can develop our innate sense of order into ethical action that results in harmony, or we can ignore our innate sense of order and foment disorder through selfish action. The highest goal for Confucians is an orderly human realm that interacts flawlessly with the orderly cosmos in which it sits.

Like all great traditions whose influence spans centuries, Neo-Confucianism was and continues to be a multifaceted and contested worldview. There have always been competing schools of interpretation within Neo-Confucianism. For the purpose of clarity, this chapter simplifies the discussion of Neo-Confucianism by focusing on Cheng-Zhu Neo-Confucianism, which formed the core of orthodox Neo-Confucianism. This core owes most of its content to Cheng Yi (1033–1107) of the Northern Song dynasty and to Zhu Xi (1130–1200) of the Southern Song, who integrated preceding Confucian works into a streamlined system that linked cosmology to human nature and ethical action. Zhu Xi's system was challenged in his own day and after; however, his arrangement of prior Confucian thinkers into a chronological "Transmission of the Way" (*daotong* 道通) became the standard interpretation of the Neo-Confucian tradition in later periods. In this chapter it has been necessary to overlook many of the competing schools that flourished in the Song. The tradition presented here lay at the heart of Neo-Confucian identity, as recognized in later periods by its selection as the orthodoxy for the examination system and imperial patronage. This chapter focuses on the origins of Neo-Confucianism in the Tang dynasty (618–906) and its development in the Song dynasty.[4]

Scholars point to the later part of the Tang dynasty as the beginning of the Neo-Confucian movement. The early Tang is considered one of the high points of Chinese civilization. It was a time when Chinese power projected into central Asia, while people from other Asian areas came to study Chinese civilization for its applicability to their home regions. Tang was the center for East Asian Buddhism, with numerous international schools and imperially sponsored translations and publications of the Buddhist canon. The Tang political and legal systems were exported to neighboring cultures, such as Korea and Japan. Many point to the Tang as apex of Chinese poetry, noting especially the works of Tu Fu and Li Bai. The latter's life story illustrates Tang's cultural magnetism, as Li was a native of what is now Afghanistan who traveled to the Tang capital, learned Chinese, and mastered its poetic styles.

The Tang emperors ruled from the city of Chang'an (Eternal Peace). They were drawn from the Li family, a mixed Chinese-Turkic clan from the northwestern region of China, who had been swept to power in the early seventh century. The Li family built on the foundations of the short-lived Sui dynasty (581–618) that had begun the process of bringing the Chinese heartland under unified political authority after nearly four hundred years of disunity. The Li family established an imperial system that relied on other powerful families, frequently referred to as the great clans. These clans were long-standing elites who controlled large estates, dominated the economy, and monopolized political appointments within the imperial government. The symbiotic relationship of the Li family with the great clans was solidified in officially maintained records of service for clan members within the government. A clan's status in the hierarchy of great clans was dependent on how many members were chosen for official service. The clans in turn developed traditions of cultural education to aid their self-perceived role as continuators of Chinese civilization. At the heart of this civilization was literary culture, both in terms of the textual traditions stemming back to antiquity and in terms of production of literature that contributed to the development of the culture.

Therefore, the imperial bureaucracy was staffed by literate men steeped in classical and contemporary learning that stressed the centrality of Chinese culture to the well-being of their civilization. These men were recommended by other elite families and officials to fill vacancies in the bureaucracy. At the same time, some few men chose to sit a series of examinations that gave them special status among their peers. These examinations tested the classical knowledge and literary skills of the candidates. Although few within the bureaucracy chose to take these examinations, those who succeeded—comprising about 5 percent of all bureaucrats—usually rose to high positions.[5] This social-political-cultural system helped the Tang develop into one of the largest and wealthiest empires in the world at the time.

This stable, successful society was rocked by the rebellion of An Lushan, one of its most powerful generals, in 755. An Lushan, another Western Asian in the employ of Tang, had gained the trust of the emperor and his favorite consort and had amassed political and military power in the northeast. The imperial court, unprepared for such a crisis, was forced to flee the capital. In the meantime, An Lushan's army had swept through the Central Plains that was the center of the empire's power and wealth and home to the great clans. The estates of the clans were destroyed, the families dispersed, and in the capital, the records of clan service to the empire were deliberately burned.

To regain power, the Li family had to call in non-Chinese allies, the Tibetans and Turks, from the west; they also needed to ensure the support of the other generals in charge of Tang forces. To do so, they granted the generals extraordinary powers. In return for their support, the generals gained broader political powers in the areas under their charge, combining both military generalship with civil governorship, hence, these positions were referred to as governors-general. This compromise was successful in bringing the generals into the fight on the Li family's side. However, the cost of their loyalty was decentralization. Beyond their political power, the governors-general gained economic control over their regions. This created fiscal problems for the imperial government, because the governors-general did not contribute to the central government the tax revenues that had flowed to Chang'an prior to the An Lushan rebellion. It is estimated that the imperial revenues dropped by 25 to 30 percent.[6] Consequently, the imperial government did not have the resources to maintain the costs of a centrally run empire. The regions grew in power while the center declined.

As the great clans had been effectively wiped out, a further problem for not only the central government but also for the regional governments of the governors-general was finding a reliable pool of literate men to serve in the bureaucracies and keep the records. These conditions led to the rise of a social group known as the *shidafu* 士大夫, usually translated as literati. The literati, at least in their initial form, came from families in the lower levels of the pre-An Lushan rebellion social elite. Though literate, they did not have large land holdings, nor were they from families that had supplied men to the imperial central bureaucracy. Yet with the disappearance of a strong central bureaucracy and the rise of local governments in need of staff, the literati found employment.[7]

At the same time as the governors-general were depending more on literati to staff their regional governments, the central government drew not only on literati but also an increasingly powerful coterie of eunuchs. Used as the personal servants of the imperial family, trusted with palace finances and special projects of emperors, the eunuchs grew into a powerful bloc who sought to expand imperial (and personal) prestige in relation to the regional governments and the civil bureaucrats. Thus, the late Tang is characterized by competition between five groups: the imperial family, eunuchs, remnants of the great clans, literati, and governors-general.[8]

In light of the situation, many wondered what had gone wrong. Why had the Tang fallen? Why was the center being eclipsed by the peripheries? One of the most powerful voices of these concerns was a literatus named Han Yu (786–824). Since the Song dynasty, his answers to the origin of this social and political chaos have been seen as the roots of Neo-Confucianism. In the eleventh century, Cheng Yi said, "Since Mencius there has been nothing of value except the single essay [Han Yu's] *The Original Way* (*Yuan dao* 元道). In it there are certainly many erroneous statements, but the essential point is that the general idea is more or less right."[9] Han Yu was, according to one modern commentator, the "most eloquent spokesman for a fundamental renewal of Confucian moral values, for a comprehensive reform that was to affect all spheres of Confucian public and private life."[10] Han believed that one major reason for the decline of the Tang's power was the disinterest in Confucian values and the superabundant interest in Buddhism and Daoism. As mentioned, Buddhism flourished in the Tang and received imperial support. At the same time, Daoism was also patronized by the imperial family. One tradition regarding the central Daoist text *Laozi* holds that the author was a librarian named Li Er. Li is the surname of the Tang imperial family, and they lent their support to the Daoists as much as the Buddhists.

In *The Original Way*, Han attacked both Buddhists and Daoists as being at the core of Tang problems. These two schools had come to dominate the Chinese worldview after the fall of the idealized Zhou dynasty (ca. 1056–249 B.C.E). The Zhou had created the classical canon at its inception and produced Confucius in its decline. However, as Han wrote,

> When the Zhou dynasty's Way declined and Confucius died, the books were burned in the Qin [dynasty], Huang-Lao Taoism dominated the Han [dynasty], and Buddhism the Jin, Wei, Liang, and Sui dynasties. Those who spoke of The Way and virtue, and humaneness and righteousness either accepted the teachings of Yang Zhu or Mozi,[11] Laozi or Buddhism. Those who believe in one school, necessarily rejected the other. What they accepted, they glorified like a ruler. What they rejected, they treated like a slave.[12]

The problem is that the two schools were persuasive to the point where people who would be Confucians were cowed into thinking that Confucian thought was derivative of either Buddhism, Daoism, or both.

> Alas! If a person in later generations wants to hear theories of humaneness and righteousness, the Way and virtue, from whom will he hear them? The Taoists say, "Confucius was our teacher's disciple." The Buddhists say, "Confucius was our teacher's disciple." Those who would be Confucians were accustomed to hearing these statements and were happy with these absurdities. They belittled themselves, saying "our teacher once said this, too." Not only do they say this, they also write it in their books. Alas! Even if a person in later generations wants to hear theories of humaneness and righteousness, the Way and virtue, from whom will he seek them? Indeed, people delight in the strange, so they neither seek their origins, nor do they question their consequences; they only want to hear of the strange.[13]

The Confucian retreat from the intellectual high ground allowed Buddhist and Daoist ideas to predominate with serious consequences for Chinese society. Han Yu initiated two of the major themes of the Neo-Confucian movement: first, the necessary return to Confucian moral categories, and second, the need for each individual to contribute to society. Han Yu's polemical attacks on Buddhism and Daoism set the tone for later Neo-Confucians. Although Han's characterization of the two rival schools is based on a simple reading of their ideas, it is nonetheless a literal reading. Turning to the central Daoist text, the *Daode jing* 道德經, we begin to understand Han's choice of words. "Way" (*dao* 道) and "virtue" (*de* 德) are combined in the title of the work; yet as Han Yu pointed out, they are "empty categories," they have no concrete meaning without further definition; hence, one could have the Way of Laozi, the Way of Buddha, or the Way of Confucius. Each Way could then contain its own set or ethical precepts, or virtues: is it virtuous to be weak or strong, socially active or withdrawn from society, family oriented or universally minded? Han Yu vigorously attacked Daoism on this ground, because the *Daode jing* explicitly rejected moral terminology as part of its Way and Virtue.

In chapter 18 of that work, Laozi wrote that in fact, ethical terminology only develops once a natural uncategorizable moral sensibility (his virtue) has declined. Only then do the Confucian terms *humaneness* and *righteousness* arise. In other words, ethical terminology only appears when people ignore their innate ethical impulses. Terminology defines what ethics are and how they are to be applied. For Laozi, this was a huge issue. In his critique of Confucianism, he argued that Confucian attempts to create ethical categories and prescribe moral action forced people to follow codes that might not apply to every situation. Laozi encouraged people to abandon moral categories, see each situation as it arose, and respond to it spontaneously. Consequently he saw the rise of Confucian ethical categories as a step away from a natural morality that responded appropriately to each issue.[14]

Laozi preferred to speak of human action in terms of *wuwei*, often translated as nonaction. The import of the term was not simple quietism, but instead spontaneous action without a predetermined purpose. The *Daode jing* is replete with language celebrating *wu*, emptiness or nothingness, encouraging us not to view the world in terms of predetermined categories of good and bad, ethical and unethical. Being able to see the world in this nondifferentiated way meant that the practitioner of Laozi's Daoism did not hold to a set of principles that automatically split the world into oppositional categories. If, as related in chapter 3, one valued wealth, then wealth became equated with goodness. It became a goal for all; which in turn could lead the poor to steal to acquire what everyone values. Laozi's response was to "abandon skill and cast away profit"[15] in favor of a simple life that did not differentiate based on preconceived standards of values and ethics but responded to each situation spontaneously.

For Han Yu, this situational ethic was anathema. It created moral relativity at best and social turmoil at worst. He sought to reassert Confucian control of the terms Way and Virtue by connecting them with Confucian ethical categories. "Now there are those who say, 'If the sages do not die, great thieves will not cease. Smash the measures and break the scales and the people will not struggle.' Alas! These people simply are not thinking. If there had been no sages in antiquity, people would have died out long ago. Why? Because we lack feathers, fur, scales, or shells to live in the heat and cold; because we lack claws and fangs to struggle for food."[16] To lift humans from the life of animals, the sages created categories and divisions to organize society. For only in society could humans survive. In place of Laozi's naturalistic optimism, Han Yu espoused a rather grim view of people left to their own devices. The sage-kings, he wrote, "set up government to guide the people's indolence. They created punishments to eradicate their rude obstinacy. Because the people cheated each other, they created tallies, weights, and scales to keep them honest. Because the people stole from each other, they created walls and armed soldiers to protect them. When harm came, they made preparations; when trouble arose they made defenses."[17] For Han Yu, humans needed direction from above and ethical categories to prevent them from falling into a life that was solitary, poor, nasty, brutish, and short. Perhaps we can see his dismissal of Daoism as a direct response to the difficulties besetting late Tang society: decentralized government, competing elites, lack of central purpose, and what seemed a pervasive desire to better one's own lot at the expense of others.

Buddhism fared no better under Han Yu's scrutiny. Having come to China in the Han dynasty (206 B.C.E–220 C.E.), Buddhism flourished in the tumult of the Period of Disunity, when competing states fought for control of China over three centuries. After reunification of China under the Sui (581–618) and consolidation of order in the Tang, Buddhism continued to strongly influence China. As noted, Buddhism received lavish patronage from the court and all levels of society.[18] However, in the aftermath of the An Lushan rebellion, the late Tang might seem a perfect example of the Buddhist beliefs enunciated in the Four Noble Truths: Life is suffering, suffering is caused by desire, desire can be terminated, and that this termination depends on following Buddhist teaching. At its most basic level, Buddhism taught that this world was *samsara*, a world of suffering because of human desire to succeed. The problem, as posed in early Buddhist thought, was that this world is not permanent. Nothing we see before us is ever-lasting. Mountains wear away, trees are cut down, people die, happiness and wealth may be had one day but lost the next. For humans to fix their hopes on gaining some sense of permanent satisfaction in an impermanent world was misguided. Therefore, the Buddhists advocated casting aside worldly attachments to achieve enlightenment.

The best means of doing so was to join religious orders; but this required severing the familial bonds that were central to Confucian thought. The Chinese term for becoming a monk or nun is literally "to leave the family" (*chujia* 出家). Furthermore, Buddhists argued that the bonds of subject to ruler also did not hold for those who renounced their worldly ties. This case was clearly stated by Hui Yuan (334–417) in his piece, "A Monk Does Not Bow Before a King."[19] From Hui Yuan's perspective, a monk removed himself from the politics of the world and so was not under the authority of the ruler in spiritual matters. In contrast, Han Yu believed an all-powerful ruler was central to the stability of the Chinese world:

> Therefore the ruler gives commands. The minister implements the commands and extends them to the people. The people produce grain and cloth, make implements and utensils, and engage in commerce to serve their superiors. If the ruler does not give commands, then he loses that which makes him a ruler. If the minister neither implements the ruler's commands nor extends them to the people, then he loses that which makes him a minister. If the people do not produce grain and cloth, nor make implements and utensils, nor engage in commerce to serve their superiors, then they are executed.[20]

Order needed to flow from above, and all needed to know their place in the imperial continuum. Yet this was precisely what the Buddhist rejection of worldly ties undermined.

> Now the Buddhists' "*dharma*" says, you must cast aside your rulers and ministers, abandon your fathers and sons, repress the way of living together and supporting each other in order to seek so-called purity and *nirvana*. Alas! They are fortunate to have been born after the Three Dynasties [Xia, Shang, and Zhou] so they were not rebuked by Emperor Yu, King Tang, King Wen, King Wu, the Duke of Zhou, or Confucius. They are also unfortunate not to have been born before the Three Dynasties so they were not corrected by Emperor Yu, King Tang, King Wen, King Wu, the Duke of Zhou, or Confucius.[21]

Han Yu's vision did not allow for anyone to sit outside of imperial authority. All would be subject to the moral teachings of the emperor. Here Han Yu is voicing a major concern of the Neo-Confucians, that the individual lies at the center of a series of ever-expanding relationships that link the individual to the cosmos at a number of different levels. Han Yu was reviving the sociopolitical continuum enunciated so clearly in the classical text titled *Great Learning*:

> The tradition says, "Those in antiquity who wanted to illuminate their illustrious virtue in the world first ordered their countries. Those who wanted to order their countries first regulated their families. Those who wanted to regulate their families first cultivated themselves. Those who wanted to cultivate themselves first rectified their hearts-and-minds. Those who wanted to rectify their hearts-and-minds first made their intentions sincere." However, what the ancients referred to as rectifying the mind and making the will sincere was to act with purpose. Now those who want to rectify their hearts-and-minds go beyond the world and the country, eliminating the Heavenly Constants of society: the son accordingly does not treat his father like a father; the minister does not treat his ruler as a ruler; and the people do not treat their service as service.[22]

World order depended on moral cultivation that led to appropriate action in this world. The Buddhists, on the other hand, advocated moral cultivation outside of this socially engaged world, denigrating (if not destroying) the relationships on which Confucian social harmony depended.

The purpose of *The Original Way* was to reemphasize the appropriate moral code. By first attacking Daoism and Buddhism for the harm they did to the social order and by showing that their Way was based in negation and rejection of that social order, Han Yu reclaimed the original Way for Confucianism as the tradition passed down from sage to sage through the ancient and classical periods. But as noted, Han Yu believed that this transmission was interrupted with the fall of the Zhou. This idea of cultural transmission was not new. The great clans of the early Tang also believed in the generational bequest of tradition; however, for the clans the tradition was based in literary culture, not necessarily in moral cultivation. Han Yu posited that with the rise of Buddhism and Daoism there was a break in the Confucian tradition of moral cultivation, and he argued this break was harming the whole of society. Han Yu's source of inspiration lay in the classical tradition.

> What do I call the teachings of the former kings? Universal love is called humaneness. When practiced appropriately it is called righteousness. What stems from these is called the Way. What is sufficient in oneself and does not depend upon externals is called virtue.

Their writings are *The Book of Odes, The Book of Documents, The Book of Change,* and *The Spring and Autumn Annals.* Their regulations are ritual, music, punishment and government. Their people are the literati, the farmers, the artisans, and the merchants. Their roles are ruler and minister, father and son, teacher and friend, guest and host, elder and younger brothers, and husband and wife.[23]

The reason one could reclaim this tradition was that humans are inherently, biologically moral, hence, Han Yu's statement that virtue "is sufficient in oneself and does not depend upon externals." Consequently, Han Yu's Way is what flows from this innate morality. This idea became central to Neo-Confucian identity, for it suggested that the traditions were not irrevocably harmed by the destruction of the great clans. In fact, any individual could reclaim and reinvigorate those traditions if he knew where to look. This notion of individual moral development became the cornerstone of the Neo-Confucian vision.

What distinguishes Han Yu's sense of innate morality from the Daoists' is that the latter claimed that the Way was something prior to this world or beyond it. Human morality, for the Daoists, was a natural response to the world generated by this Way, and any attempt to categorize ethics through definitions would create artificial rather than natural responses. The Daoists argued that Confucian ethics are a secondary creation that removes us from this prior Way by setting up false categories that cause us to focus on the secondary human creation rather than the primary nonhuman Way. In contradistinction, Han Yu's Confucian Way derives from human moral sensibilities. The Way is not a naturalistic Way of the Daoists but a human Way created by sage-kings to help people survive. True, Han Yu believed humans had natural moral sensibilities, but he believed the sensibilities would not translate into actions unless properly defined and incorporated into an ethical system, which he calls the Way of the sages.

With Han Yu we see the rearticulation of Confucianism as an activist worldview. He proposed the central place of Confucianism in the fragmented late Tang. He stressed that the morally cultivated and ethically aware individual is the cornerstone of a stable social-political continuum. The major themes of Neo-Confucianism are also forged in Han Yu's writings: inherent human morality, the ultimate value of living and engaging in this world, ethical knowledge derived from study of the classical tradition, and transmission of those ideals through a line of sages. Although these ideals appealed to a segment of the literati, they did not save the Tang from disintegration. Ultimately, the dynasty disappeared as local governors-general declared their own imperiums and China entered the brief decades of the Five Dynasties period (906–960).

The Five Dynasties period was characterized by political fragmentation of the Chinese heartland and frequent coups d'état. Reunification under the Song dynasty began with just such a coup. Zhao Kuangyin, a general in the army of the Later Zhou dynasty (951–960), overthrew his emperor and was proclaimed emperor of a new dynasty he named Song (960–1279). While the first emperor, Taizu (r. 960–976) went about consolidating the political boundaries of the reunified empire, the second emperor, Taizong (r. 976–998), solidified the imperial bureaucratic system that lasted until 1902. These early Song emperors recognized the dangers of allowing military men to dominate the government, because that was how they had come to power; they also acknowledged the utility of recruiting educated men to serve as officials. This was a modification of the relationship of military men to literati that had emerged in the governments of the governors-general after the An Lushan rebellion: the military men had the power and relied on the literati to administer and keep records.

The Song emperors understood the need to recruit officials who had no personal military power base. By doing so, the emperors controlled the careers of those they appointed, while those literati appointed to civil office had little possibility of raising a rebellion. The governors-general were abolished as the Zhao family centralized control. Military allies found themselves "kicked upstairs" and removed from contact with their troops through promotion within the Song court.

For recruiting literati into government, Taizong decided to expand the use of the examination system that had been used in the Tang. Candidates in this system engaged in three rounds of examinations: provincial, departmental, and palace. This last round was overseen by the emperor himself to ensure that the candidates knew on whom their passing depended. As the emperor himself wrote, "I wish to search broadly for the superior and accomplished within the examination halls. I dare not aspire to select five out of ten, but if only one or two [out of ten] are chosen, even that may be considered preparation for the utmost governance."[24] Despite his self-professed low expectations, Taizong radically increased the number of men who passed the examination. Whereas in Taizu's reign an average of 19 men were granted degrees per year, during the first round overseen by Taizong in 977, he granted a total of 498 degrees.[25] The literati responded to the stimulus. In 977, about 5,300 men took the departmental examination; 10,260 did so in 983; and 17,300 did so in 992.[26]

Candidates could choose to sit one of several examinations that emphasized different knowledge and skills. Although the content of the examinations changed throughout the dynasty, it is fair to say that the core of a candidate's knowledge was facility with the classical tradition that Han Yu alluded to in *The Original Way*. Echoing Han Yu's specifications, the Confucian tradition stemming from the classical tradition was seen as the ideal content for shaping the literati for political service. Confucianism stressed morality, social action, service to the benevolent ruler, and hierarchy. By encouraging the literati to engage in the examination system, Taizong linked literati education to not only literacy and literary skill but also memorizing Confucian classics. Confucianism became the core content of state-sponsored schools and private academies throughout the Song.[27] Thus, the development of the examination system is intimately linked to the development of Neo-Confucianism in the Song dynasty as the hopes of educated men were pinned to examination success that led to appointment as one of the "stars of heaven" in the bureaucracy.

This is not to say that Neo-Confucianism was a creation of the state that was disseminated to the literati. Far from it. Confucianism, like any religious tradition, lends itself to a plurality of interpretations. Neo-Confucian thinkers often found themselves at the margins of official Confucian interpretation, even to the extent of having their works proscribed and themselves black-listed from government service.[28] Some Neo-Confucians avoided official service to continue their quest for becoming the sage within. What the examination system created, though, was a common Confucian cultural education that allowed literati to interpret, discuss, and debate the meaning of Confucianism in their world. In fact, Neo-Confucianism was just one approach to the Confucian tradition that flourished in the Northern Song. We can discern four distinct approaches to the tradition during this period.

The first approach emphasized the role of government directing the livelihood and development of the people. Wang Anshi (1021–1086) articulated this approach in his memorial to Song emperor Renzong (r. 1023–1064). He noted that during antiquity,

> the Two Emperors [Yao and Shun] were separated from the Three Kings [of the Zhou dynasty] by more than a thousand years. There were periods of order and disorder, and there were periods of prosperity and decay. Each of them likewise encountered different changes and faced different circumstances, and each differed also in the way they set up their government. Yet they never differed as to their underlying aims in the government of the empire, the state and the family, nor in their sense of the relative importance and priority of things. Therefore, your servant contends that we should follow only their general intent. If we follow their intent, then the changes and reforms introduced by us would not startle the ears and shock the eyes of the people, nor cause them to murmur. And yet our government would be in accord with that of the ancient kings.[29]

Renzong was so impressed with the memorial and Wang's ideas for thoroughgoing reforms in government and society that he appointed Wang Grand Councilor. Wang developed a series of reforms known as the New Policies (*xinfa* 新法) that stressed economic growth and restructuring the interaction of government and local society. The debate over the New Policies had a deep impact on Song society. Beyond the political fall-out of factionalism and shifting imperial support, the conflict shaped the way people thought about society and how they interpreted the Confucian social-political continuum as outlined in the *Great Learning*. If we briefly examine various positions in the debate concerning the program of education and bureaucratic recruitment in the New Policies, we see very different views of how people who considered themselves Confucians envisioned the relationship of the individual to the state.

Wang Anshi argued that developing men of talent to implement the reforms would be key to the success of the New Policies. He wrote, "The most urgent need of the present time is to secure men of talent. Only when we can produce a large number of talented men in the empire, will it be possible to selected a sufficient number of persons qualified to serve in the government." Furthermore, he wrote that in the past "men not qualified to govern the empire and states would not be given an education, while those who could be so used in government never failed to receive an education. This is the way to conduct the training of men."[30] Wang's view of what constituted appropriate training was more clearly stated later in the memorial when he wrote,

> The affairs of the court, rites, music, punishment, and correction have no place in the schools, and the students pay no attention to them, considering that rites and music, punishment and correction are the business of officials, not something they ought to know about. What is taught to the students consists merely of textual exegesis [of the classics]. That, however, was not the way men were taught in ancient times. In recent years, teaching has been based on the essays required for the civil service examinations. . . . Such proficiency as they attain is at best of no use in the government of the empire, and at most the empire can make no use of them.[31]

Wang's concern was clearly utilitarian. He wanted a pool of literati trained to enact a reform program that would solidify national durability through economic stability, military preparedness, a fair and well-defined legal code, and ideological unity that would be ensured through prescribed examination material. Note that Wang does not mention the development of moral awareness or a positive role for the classical Confucian texts in the schools.

One of the most outspoken opponents of the New Policies, and the man who later dismantled many of them during his brief time as grand councilor, was Sima Guang (1019–1086). He has been characterized as a conservative whose guiding principle for governance was to preserve what good there was, because it was difficult to create good and too easy to lose it.[32] Sima's memorial refuting Wang Anshi's ideas on education does agree with Wang's position that the examinations had become too heavily graded on literary composition to be of real use. He wrote that the candidates for "the 'Advanced Scholar' examination (*jinshi* 進士) esteem contemporary literary vogue, and are not rooted in Classical studies; while the [candidates for the] 'Classical Studies' (*mingjing* 明經) only memorize the texts and do not understand the moral principles. Virtuous conduct (*dexing* 德行) does not make any difference to them."[33] Sima Guang's ideal system of recruitment focused on finding men who had both classical education and virtuous conduct. It is precisely this "virtue" that Sima felt had been neglected in contemporary selection methods. His use of this term also needs to be contrasted with Wang Anshi's use of "talent." The term *virtue* does not appear in Wang's memorial. Virtue is a moral quality, whereas talent is a morally neutral term implying skill or facility at accomplishing a task. Talent clearly fits with Wang's emphasis on literati being "of use to the state." Though Sima Guang was also concerned with literati becoming successful bureaucratic officials, his vision embraced both talent and morality, with the latter given priority.

A third view of the examinations as a tool of recruitment was expressed by Su Shi (1037–1101). In many ways, Su Shi continued the literary/cultural tradition that looked to the past for models and saw the value of an evolving tradition. He wrote, "Policies adapt to changes in custom. It is like channeling a river. If you organize it according to where it wants to flow, then success is easy; but if you dam it and force it where it does not want to go, then it is difficult to work."[34] Although he agreed with Wang and Sima that policies need to change to meet the times, his recommendation was to maintain the examinations as they were. He reasoned that no matter what the government decided to focus on as the criteria for recruiting officials, there was bound to be perversion of the government's intent by those who simply wanted to succeed. He wrote to the emperor,

> If you want to establish fields and categories to select people, then you will teach the world how to fit the criteria and act artificially. If those above use filiality to select people, then the brave will be cut from the submissive, and the cowardly will dwell in a hut by their parents'

> graves. If those above use sincerity to select people, then [the people] will use broken-down carts and mangy nags, [and have] poor clothing and meagre food. In general if one can hit upon the desires of those above, there is no height to which one cannot rise. In one leap the perversion of virtue and proper conduct will reach this extreme! If [those above] talk about essays, then essays in the examinations will be considered useful, and the poetry sections will be considered useless. If [those above] talk about government affairs, then poetry and essay sections will all be considered to be useless. Even though we know they are useless, from the time of the ancestors to the present no one has done away with them, since they considered establishing new policies to select literati was not as good as this system.[35]

Su Shi's point was that if the government were to announce that filial piety was to be the main characteristic sought for in a candidate for office, then the brave, who probably did not always submit to their parents' will, would be excluded, whereas cowards would adopt the outward trappings of being a loving son so as to be recruited. If sincerity were chosen, then people would adopt the appearance of being sincere (living frugally and shunning ostentation) though they might not actually be sincere. Similarly, if the government chose to emphasize essay writing, people would produce good essays, or good poetry, if that was what was desired, or they would eschew literary composition for public policy positions, if that was desired. Su Shi concluded that quality officials had never been in short supply through the examination system, so why change it? Flawed though it was, it still worked. In his view, it was better to maintain a functional system than to replace it with something untested.

The Neo-Confucian response was articulated by Cheng Hao (1032–1085), one of the leaders of the movement. For Cheng Hao, good government depended on the moral development of the individual. His concern was not developing men of talent, nor was he willing to accept the status quo of the examination system. Unlike Su Shi, but similar to Sima Guang, he believed that ethical training was the cornerstone on which a harmonious society was built. He wrote to the emperor, "I believe we are long separated from the sages, that the way of teacher's is not established, and that the learning of Confucians is on the verge of disappearing. Only if the court promotes teaching these can they be restored in no time. The ancients unified morality and customs, but if the learning of the teachers' is not correct, then how can morality be practiced and unified?"[36]

Regarding recruiting literati, Cheng Hao wrote,

> Their Way must be rooted in the Human Relationships,[37] and understood by the *li* of things;[38] their education should proceed from

the lesser learning of scattering water, sweeping, receiving, and responding, to fulfilling their filial piety, fraternity, loyalty, and honesty, being well-rounded in rites and music; this is the Way by which they should be enticed, pulled in, gradually polished, and completed. All this has sequenced order. *The main point is choosing good and improving the self, to arrive at transforming the whole world. This is the Way by which villagers can become sages.* When their learning and conduct all [accord] perfectly with these [preceding injunctions] their virtue may be considered complete.[39]

In this vision, people would be trained in stages from simple etiquette to completed moral development. Cheng Hao introduced the radically new idea that through such training *anyone* could become a sage. The goal was not simply stability and economic development through recruiting men of talent, as Wang Anshi would have it; nor was the goal preserving what good existed through choosing well-educated ethical men, as Sima Guang proposed; nor was it simply to make the best of a flawed system, as Su Shi argued. Instead, what the Northern Song Neo-Confucians proposed was that each individual achieve moral perfection. The perfected individual would then engage in transforming the world. This was to be "learning for the self" rather than "learning for others," the latter having been so well satirized by Su Shi. However, the promise of learning for the self was no less than a penetrating understanding of the cosmos and one's ability to harmonize human action with cosmic processes.

The fundamental building blocks of learning for the self were created by the "masters" of the Northern Song: Zhou Dunyi (1017–1073), Zhang Zai (1020–1077), and Cheng Hao and his brother Cheng Yi (1033–1107). Through the work of Zhou Dunyi and Zhang Zai, the Confucian moral concepts central to Han Yu's *The Original Way* were given cosmological grounding. Han Yu and others argued against Daoist and Buddhist rejection of the reality of this world. For Neo-Confucians, this was the only reality with which human beings could deal. The Neo-Confucians rejected any argument that the world around us is illusory because it is impermanent. Instead, they argued that change was part of a universal pattern that could be understood, and understanding could lead to transformation of the self and the world. However, prior to the Northern Song masters, Neo-Confucians did not offer clear cosmological arguments to support their assertions that this world is fundamentally real, that human ethics are an integral part of human life, and that social action was instrumental to creating a harmonious world. When we talk about the religious dimensions of Confucianism, these issues stand out. Through articulating clear positions in these areas, Neo-Confucians gave shape to a

Confucian worldview that answered ultimate questions about the meaning of life and the means by which individuals become participants in the larger project of human fulfillment. Hence, the vision is more than human-centered- it required understanding of how humans fit into the cosmos. The blueprint for the project was encapsulated in the concept of the investigation of things from the *Great Learning*. The path to world order began with the individual investigating things to extend his knowledge. By doing so he would make his intentions sincere and ultimately illuminate his illustrious virtue throughout the world. This goal is also described as creating harmony throughout the world. In classical Confucian thought, humans were viewed as the intermediaries between Heaven and Earth. It is the duty of humans to bring their world into order and create a harmonious convergence between the order of earthly nature, human society, and heavenly patterns. Two pieces set the general outline for later Neo-Confucians to develop: Zhou Dunyi's "Explanation of the Diagram of the Great Ultimate" (*Taijitu shuo* 太極圖說) and Zhang Zai's *Western Inscription* (*Xi ming* 西銘).

Zhou developed ideas about the interconnected nature of all things and argued that all things are inherently linked to the cosmic processes that give shape and order to the universe. Zhou Dunyi's *Explanation of the Diagram of the Great Ultimate* is an interesting piece that explains a Daoist cosmological chart in light of a Confucian interpretation of the *Book of Change* (*Yijing* 易經).[40] Zhou's *Explanation* is a top-down reading beginning with the blank circle. Given that the *Explanation* lies at the heart of Neo-Confucian cosmological thinking, it is fitting to quote it in full.

> The Ultimate of Non-being and the Great Ultimate. The Great Ultimate moves and gives birth to *yang*. Its movement reaches its maximum and it becomes still. In stillness it gives birth to *yin*. Its stillness reaches its maximum and returns to movement. At one point it is active, at one point it is still, it is the root of both. The two complementary categories are established when it separates *yin* and *yang*. *Yang* changes, *yin* harmonizes and they give birth to water, fire, wood, metal, and earth;[41] these five types of *qi* manifest in order and the four seasons flow within. The five agents are from the same *yin* and *yang*. *Yin* and *yang* are from the same Great Ultimate. The Great Ultimate is originally the Ultimate of Non-being. At the birth of the five agents, each has its unique nature. The true character of the Ultimate of Non-being is the essence of the two [yin-yang] and the five [water, fire, wood, metal, and earth]. They subtly harmonize and coalesce. The Way of *qian* is male; the Way of *kun* is female.[42] These

two types of *qi* interact and resonate giving birth to all things. All things give birth and transform without ceasing. Humans receive their most refined [*qi*] and are the most divine. When born with a body, we extend our knowledge, the five natures respond and move, distinguishing good and bad, and all human affairs arise. The sage settles them with centrality, rectitude, humaneness, and rightness, and being guided by stillness establishes the ultimate of humans. Therefore the sage harmonizes his virtue with heaven and earth, harmonizes his brilliance with the sun and moon, harmonizes his standards with the four seasons, and harmonizes his fortune and misfortune with the spirits. The gentleman's cultivation [of these virtues] leads to fortune; the petty man's ignoring them leads to misfortune. Therefore it is said, "*Yin* and *yang* are said to establish the Way of heaven. Weak and strong are said to establish the Way of earth. Humaneness and righteousness are said to establish the Way of man."[43] It is also said, "If you trace back to the origin and reflect upon the end, then you will understand the meaning of life and death."[44] Magnificent! This is the point of the *Book of Change*!

Zhou's *Explanation* provided future Neo-Confucians with the basis of their cosmology that linked not only human existence but also human morality to the processes of creation and destruction in the natural world. As Zhou noted at the very end of this brief piece, his inspiration was drawn from the *Book of Change*. The *Book of Change* is one of the earliest and most venerated Chinese texts. Confucius once noted that if he could add more years to his life he would spend them studying the *Book of Change*.[45] By turning to the oldest Chinese text—one held in high regard not only by Confucians but also by Daoists and even some Buddhists—Zhou Dunyi was reclaiming this early cosmological tradition as the roots of Confucianism and Chinese civilization. He was not trying to show that Confucianism was similar to Daoism and Buddhism, or that Confucius was a disciple of Daoist and Buddhist teachers. Instead, by emphasizing the link between cosmology and ethics, Zhou stressed that ethics are a natural part of human nature—they are inherent, and consciously developing them leads to good fortune. Zhou's position, like Han Yu's, counters the Buddhist and Daoist positions that regarded ethics as a human creation. His position also underscored the Confucian belief that this world, despite the constant changes, has ultimate reality and that the meaning of life is for human beings to create a harmonious order in this world, in this life. The focus is not on individual immortality (as in Daoism) or on the individual's fate after death (as in Buddhism).

Given that the world is constantly changing due to the creative processes of the cosmos, using the *Book of Change* to understand the changes of the universe and its current state in relation to one's aspirations was of vital importance. The text was central to Neo-Confucian cosmological thinking because of the emphasis they placed on harmonizing human action with the natural world. Zhou Dunyi's *Explanation* gave a clear rationale for how humans are part of the natural processes and pointed the way to greater understanding with his use of the *Book of Change* to explain cosmology in Neo-Confucian terms. Numerous Song dynasty thinkers, not just the Neo-Confucians, wrote commentaries on the *Book of Change*'s description of cosmic processes as fluctuating combinations of *yin* and *yang*.[46] These combinations were symbolized in sixty-four hexagrams, diagrams of six lines each.[47] Appendices to the *Book of Change* explained the means by which one could use stalks of milfoil grass to determine which hexagram described the state of the cosmos at a specific moment in terms of a specific question. The appendices also explained why understanding the meaning of the *Book of Change* was important. Zhou selected two passages from the appendices to underscore this point. For humans to flourish and to be fortunate, we have to understand the processes of nature, how we fit into them, and accordingly arrange our society. Note, too, that the sage's activities and his moral guidelines are established by harmonizing with various nonhuman phenomena: Heaven and Earth, the sun and moon, the seasons, and the spirits. One example of how such harmonization was enacted was setting the imperial calendar to ensure that everyone in the agrarian empire knew when to plant and harvest. It is somewhat commonsensical to recognize that one is inviting disaster if one attempted to plant corn, wheat, or rice in the late fall or winter, but much of what the Neo-Confucians argued for human harmonization with the natural order came from such commonsensical observation. Yet for them adapting to natural patterns was imbued with a deeper cosmic meaning. Therefore, clear correspondences with planting in spring (the season of growth) are extrapolated to the emperor wearing green in spring and pardoning criminals during that season of life, whereas in the autumn (the season of harvest and decline) he wears white and punishes.[48] Harmonization meant fulfilling the human component of existence, which was an important task given that human beings were considered the most divine of things in the cosmos. Again drawing on the *Book of Change*, "Humaneness and rightness are said to establish the Way of man." Further, the "sage settles [human affairs] with centrality, rectitude, humaneness, and rightness, and being guided by stillness establishes the ultimate of humans." What Zhou Dunyi suggested was not simply that humans needed to harmonize with the cosmos but that Confucian moral activity was the means to do so. The sage did not simply plant at the correct time of year, he also understood that human order is created through ethical action.

Although there has been some debate about any connection between Zhou Dunyi's thought and the line of Neo-Confucian thinking developed by the Cheng brothers and their uncle, Zhang Zai, the connection was inferred by Zhu Xi a hundred years later, when he claimed both Zhou's work and Zhang Zai's *Western Inscription* as the cosmological underpinnings of Neo-Confucianism. Cheng Hao, the older of the two Cheng brothers, said the language of the *Western Inscription* "is truly refined and without confusion, something never achieved by scholars since the Qin and Han dynasties. The ideas are truly complete; they are the embodiment of humaneness."[49] Cheng Yi, the younger brother, believed Zhang's piece developed ideas in Han Yu's earlier piece *The Original Way*: "As for the *Western Inscription*, it contains the whole doctrine on which *The Original Way* is based. *The Original Way* only deals with the Way, and the thought of the *Western Inscription* is altogether beyond its scope.... No such writing has been seen since Mencius."[50] Zhou Dunyi's *Explanation* outlined the human connection with the rest of the universe, and Zhang's *Inscription* developed the cosmological connection into a clearer sense of shared humanity. Confucius rejected the life of a hermit, telling his students that if he was to accomplish anything, he had to live as a man among other men.[51] Zhang's *Inscription*, carved onto the western wall of his study, draws on a similar sentiment, making clear his sense of interconnection with other humans. It begins,

> *Qian* is my father; *kun* is my mother. We small things live in their midst. Therefore, what fills the gap between heaven and earth is my body; what directs heaven and earth is my human nature. All people are my siblings, all things and I are the same. The great ruler is the head of my clan; his great ministers are my clan head's stewards. Acknowledging the elderly, I respect their age. Acknowledging the young, I am benevolent due to their weakness. I treat as sages those with harmonious virtue. I treat as worthies those with talent.[52]

Zhang opens his inscription with the primal forces of the universe, *qian* and *kun*, which Zhou Dunyi had described as the form taken by *yang* and *yin*, respectively, once the processes of creation begins. As the creative forces of the universe, Zhang Zai regards them as ultimately responsible for his own creation and, by analogy, considers them his mother and father. Extrapolating from this, he reasoned that all other things are also creations of yang and yin and are therefore related to him. "All the hunchbacks, the cripples, the orphans, and the widowers are my brothers who suffer without complaint. Protecting them when necessary is this son's assistance [to his father and mother]."[53] Moreover, the enlightened individual becomes a co-participant in ordering the cosmos. "Those who understand the [cosmic] transformations will be good at continuing their affairs; those who plumb the divine will be good at continuing its will."[54]

An important thread running through both Zhou Dunyi's *Explanation* and Zhang Zai's *Inscription* is that there is a natural imperative for social action. Because we are born into this world, because we are created of the same stuff as every other thing, and because we are the most divine of these things, we must act in ways that promote the harmony of the human world and the wider cosmos. By using the analogy of a family, probably the fundamental analogy on which all Confucians based social and political thought, Zhang Zai seems to acknowledge, like Han Yu, that the imperial system itself is a natural part of human creation. The emperor and his ministers are considered to be the "clan head" and his "stewards" for the clan of human beings among the other clans of created things. Zhang Zai also argues that there are clear reasons for treating different people differently. One treats older and younger people differently not because of an unnaturally developed system of ethics but because their ages mean they have different needs and capacities. Similarly, one respects the sage because he has achieved a certain level of moral development, whereas a worthy is respected for his talents, which differ from his level of moral development. The importance of this distinction is clearer when we couch it in light of the debate surrounding the New Policies, when Wang Anshi advocated seeking men of talent and Cheng Hao encouraged the quest for sagehood. Talent was worthy of respect, but it was not the ultimate fulfillment of human potential. Without ethical awareness, one could not achieve the highest level of development.

The path of moral development for Zhang Zai continues the familial metaphor and also hinges on cardinal Confucian virtues.

> One who is purely filial is happy and without cares. One who acts to the contrary ignores virtue, while one who harms humaneness is a criminal. One who abets evil is not using his abilities, so his use of his natural endowment is merely that of a decadent. If one understands the [natural] transformations, then he will be good at promoting their affairs; if one fully comprehends the divine, then he will be good at continuing their intentions. Be unashamed in the depths of your house by doing nothing shameful. Preserve your heart-and-mind and cultivate your human nature by being diligent.[55]

Because human beings are creations of the natural processes that create everything, Zhang argued that we all have the potential to be good and to do good.

There is no sense of inherent sin or a proclivity to do evil. Instead, those who do wrong are those who have not engaged in the self-cultivation that lies at the heart of the Confucian continuum of self-society-cosmos as expounded in the *Great Learning*.

Zhou Dunyi and Zhang Zai in particular laid the foundations for the cosmological ideas of Neo-Confucianism, but the movement's development as a coherent school of thought is credited to the Cheng brothers. Zhou Dunyi and Zhang Zai gave justification for a Neo-Confucian cosmology, but not a full explanation of how it worked. The Chengs created a vocabulary to explain how all the pieces fit together, to describe why people can be ethical or unethical, and why ethics are natural. The brothers had studied briefly with Zhou Dunyi when they were teenagers but do not clearly credit him as the source of their ideas. The Chengs met Zhang Zai when all three were taking the imperial examinations in the capital. Cheng Hao and Zhang Zai both passed, while Cheng Yi did not. The three became friends and, probably due to differences in age and the Confucian proclivity to honor elders, Zhang is often credited with influencing the Chengs. However, as with Zhou Dunyi, this assertion of influence on the Chengs seems to be a later addition to the story of Neo-Confucianism's early development. In fact, it is more likely that the Chengs, Cheng Hao in particular, influenced the thinking of Zhang Zai. Cheng Yi said of his older brother,

> After the death of the Duke of Zhou the way of the sages was not applied; after the death of Mencius the learning of the sages was not transmitted. Since the way was not applied, for a hundred generations there was no good government; since the learning was not transmitted, for a thousand years there was no true Confucian.... [Cheng Hao], born fourteen hundred years afterward, found the untransmitted learning in the remaining classics, and made it his object to use this Way to awaken this people.[56]

Cheng Yi's praise for his brother points out three key ideas. First, that the "true" Confucian Way was lost after Mencius. Second, Cheng Hao was able to revive the Way, despite the gap of fourteen centuries. Third, the key to the Way lies in the classical texts. Cheng Yi rejected the work of all between Mencius and Cheng Hao, although he did praise aspects of others' work, such as Han Yu's *The Original Way*. Cheng Yi was clearly breaking with the cultural tradition that flourished in the Tang, which stressed literary accomplishment and one's connection with cultural traditions as the mark of an accomplished individual. Cheng Yi, stating a classic Neo-Confucian position, argued that this tradition of cultural studies had led people away from true Confucianism and, consequently, hadpromoted poor governance. Here it is important to remember that for Neo-Confucians good governance would result in a stable eternal government modeled on the ideals of the sage-emperors of antiquity. Although we now point to the Tang as a high point in Chinese political and cultural power, Cheng Yi rejected its legacy because the Tang had also witnessed the An Lushan rebellion and collapse. The Neo-Confucians sought the perfect social-political system and, as we shall see, regarded the morally aware and socially active individual as the cornerstone of this system.

Consequently, the Chengs continued to oppose Buddhism and Daoism as well as cultural studies. Their critiques were grounded in their own knowledge of these religions. Like many of the Neo-Confucians, Cheng Hao had studied Buddhism for a number of years, from his late teens into his mid-twenties. Both brothers knew the attractions of Buddhism and worried that their students might find themselves persuaded by its doctrines. "Even when a friend sinks into this doctrine one cannot turn him back; now my only hope is in you gentlemen. You must simply put it aside without discussing it; do not say 'We must see what it is like,' for if you see what it is like you will yourselves be changed into Buddhists. The essential thing is decisively to reject its arts."[57] Cheng Hao, however, returned to the Confucian canon when he was dissatisfied with the answers Buddhism provided to the questions he asked. Central to this return to Confucianism was the issue of social action. He chastised Buddhists for turning their backs on social relations: "In deserting his father and leaving his family, the Buddha severed all human relationships. It was merely for himself that he lived alone in the forest."[58] Not only did the Buddhists reject their family, they were rejecting their extended social responsibility. Cheng Yi noted, "The doctrine of the Buddhists includes inward correction by composure, but not ordering the external by morality."[59] The focus on the external world was central to the Neo-Confucians because they believed it was unnatural for human beings to ignore the world around them. Consequently,

> The learner's first task is of course to decide on his goal. But if someone says that he wishes to exclude seeing and hearing, knowing and thinking, this is Laozi's "getting rid of the sages and abandoning wisdom"; if he wishes to exclude thoughts, being distressed by their confusion, he will have to "practice Zen and enter into Samadhi" with the Buddhists. Take the mirror as a parallel; it is inevitable that the innumerable things should all be reflected in it, how can one prevent the mirror from reflecting? The human mind is bound to interact with the innumerable things; how can one prevent it from thinking about them?[60]

The image of the mind as mirror is found in the work of Daoist Zhuangzi and was further developed in Zen Buddhism. In this Daoist and Zen use, the mind as mirror meant that the mind had no preconceptions; like a mirror it should reflect things as they are, not as we might want them to be. When the Chengs appropriated the analogy, the mind as mirror illustrated our ability to think about the world and react to each unique situation based on a strongly developed ethical awareness. To facilitate this, the Cheng brothers developed clearer language for explaining the issues confronting human beings as they tried to understand their place in the ethical universe, they developed a curriculum of classical texts to study, and they explained why such study was vital to self-development and social progress.

To understand how the Chengs conceived human beings' relation to the universe, we need to examine the manner in which they organized some key terms. According to their thought, all things in the cosmos are given shape and order by *li* 理 (principle). The actual material from which all things are made and the energy that infuses living things is comprised of varying degrees of *qi* 氣 (psychophysical stuff). All human beings have individual situations into which they are born and have certain obligations to fulfill according to *li*, this is known as *ming* 命 (fate). At the same time, all humans have *xing* 性 (human nature) that contains the pure ordering principles of *li*. However, because we are born with a physical body comprised of *qi*, our lives are constantly shaped by the interaction of our human nature, which strives for harmony and order, and our physical bodies, which have cravings and desires that need fulfillment, such as hunger and thirst. Sometimes our physical desires overpower our human nature, and we act in selfish, antisocial ways that lead to disorder. The task, then, is to engage in a process of self-cultivation that trains us to balance our physical needs (since we need to live to fulfill our social obligations) with the moral imperatives of our human nature (since harmony is only achieved through being public-minded rather than selfish).

At the heart of the Cheng brothers' philosophy are the concepts of *li* and *qi*. Both terms are central to Neo-Confucianism, and both are difficult to translate, so it is best to simply use the Chinese terms rather than attempt to approximate them in English. *Li* is most often translated as "principle." It is the guiding principle that shapes the universe into an ordered whole. Another translation is "pattern," because the original meaning of the Chinese character means the pattern of colored veins in a piece of jade. Perhaps the best translation is "coherence." *Li* is what gives the cosmos structure and order; it is what holds the diverse things of the universe together while allowing different things to function in different ways. The Cheng brothers developed the Neo-Confucian axiom derived from Zhang Zai's *Western Inscription* that *"li* is one, but its manifestations are many," or, in the Chengs' reiteration, "the innumerable principles amount to one principle."[61] *Li* shapes the world both in terms of what there is (people, animals, politics, seasons) and in terms of how all things ought to function (humans ought to be moral, animals ought to live and reproduce, politics ought to provide stability, and the seasons ought to follow the same sequence year after year). When functioning properly, the cosmos falls into harmonious order usually referred to as the Way, or dao. "All things in the world may be understood through *li*. There being a thing, there must also be a pattern for it. Each individual thing must have its individual *li*."[62] Combined, all these manifestations of *li* comprised the Way (*dao*): "The word *dao* is all-embracing; the *li* are so many veins inside the *dao*."[63] Explaining how key terms related to each other, Angus Graham wrote, "In laying down the lines along which everything moves, [*li*] appears as the Way (*dao*); in that the lines are independent of my personal desires, it imposes itself on me as Heaven (*tian*); as a pattern which from my own viewpoint spreads out from the sub-pattern of my own profoundest reactions, it appears as my own basic Nature (*xing*)."[64]

In other words, each thing has its own embodiment of *li*, but accords with *li* in the way suited to that particular thing; yet each individual embodiment of *li* works toward a unified purpose. Just as humans have certain actions to perform according to *li*, so does a cat, so does a desk, so does a cloud. *Li* both makes things what they are (a person versus a cat) and sets the parameters of what each thing ought to do (how a person or cat ought to act to fulfill his or her purpose in the cosmic pattern). "A single tree and a single grass both have *li* which must be investigated."[65] But it is not only concrete objects like humans, cats, desks, and so on that have *li* that makes each what it is. "Whatever is before the eye is a thing, and all things have *li*, for example that by which fire is hot and that by which water is cold. As for the relations between ruler and minister, father and son, all are *li*."[66]

Because *li* gives coherence to the cosmos, it is also something that can be observed and understood by human beings. Cheng Hao noted that everywhere one looks, one finds order and patterning, such as the constellations. This was an important step in developing Neo-Confucianism, for what the Chengs posited was not only that all things are interconnected but that humans can realize this connection by "tracing back," or inferring from the *li* they find in any object. One was to choose something to observe (an event, a moral precept, an object), then study it carefully to figure out how it worked, how it fit the context in which it was situated, and develop a universal principle from that observation.

It is interesting to note, though, that this notion of observation and inference did not lead to a proto-scientific observation of the natural world. Instead, the focus for the Chengs, other Neo-Confucians, and most Chinese intellectuals outside of Buddhists and Daoists fell on action within human society. Although the Confucian continuum from the *Great Learning* begins with individuals "making the will sincere by extending their knowledge," and though "the extension of knowledge lies in the investigation of things," the overriding concern that shaped one's investigations was translating knowledge into moral action. The movement sparked moralistic readings of the classical tradition, which was viewed as a repository of knowledge that could be used to discern what *li* meant in human affairs. History was an easy object lesson in this regard. One could study an event and its consequences to derive meaning and principles. One could, for example, examine the conquest of the Xia dynasty by the Zhou. This was a favorite topic because it highlighted how a selfish, debased ruler (the last emperor of Xia), who treated his people cruelly and lost their support, was overthrown by a virtuous, compassionate vassal from the state of Zhou. The Xia people rallied to Zhou because of its moral actions and deserted their immoral emperor. One could infer a number of *li* from this event: One *li* was that the ruler must always be concerned for the welfare of his people, for they are foundation on which the empire rest; a second is the persuasive power of moral action; a third is the role of virtuous subjects confronted with immoral rulers.[67]

One reason we can infer other *li* is that *li* is also embodied in our human nature (*xing*). Being the most "divine" of creature due to our rarified *qi*, we have the ability to think and become aware of *li*. Our nature enables us to perceive the patterns in the world around us. Given that Confucius's statements about human nature are cryptic at best and enigmatic about whether human nature is good or evil, it was up to later Confucians to settle the question. Mencius and Xunzi presented opposing arguments. Mencius was certain that human nature is good, whereas Xunzi was equally adamant that it was bad. Mencius's debates with Gaozi are classic expositions of his position that humans have within them the "seeds" of moral action, which he called the Four Beginnings. He argued that humans all have a spontaneous natural impulse toward morality. His example was if someone sees a child about to fall into a well, there is an immediate spark of sympathy.[68] For Mencius, this demonstrated that our first impulses—not our learned impulses, but our natural first impulses—are moral. Xunzi, on the other hand, argued that human nature is evil. Xunzi argued that morality is learned, not spontaneous and natural. He pointed to the initial impulses of a child, who demonstrates no moral understanding until he has developed and been taught. The first impulses are the desires for food and comfort for the self. Therefore, Xunzi argued that we cannot view our first impulses as moral. Though Xunzi was pessimistic about our nature, he was overwhelmingly optimistic about the human ability to transform oneself through education.[69]

Because both positions had their adherents, it remained a problem until the Cheng brothers resolved the issue. As we have seen, Han Yu and the Chengs both refer to Mencius as the last true Confucian. They turn to Mencius's view of human nature as a cornerstone of their system. As Cheng Hao said, "Mencius is right when he says that the nature is good; neither Xun[zi] nor Yang [Xiong] knew anything about it. It is because of his ability to understand the nature that Mencius has gained his unique position, exceeding that of other literati."[70] The faith in human transformation through education that played so prominent a role in Xunzi's thought, however, also informs the Neo-Confucian view of the human condition. Within the Neo-Confucian explanation, our human nature is comprised of *li* and is unquestionably good, and our physical bodies still exhibit the cravings and desires noted by Xunzi. Neo-Confucians established that these cravings are natural responses to our physical needs, and although they are not considered evil because they help us survive, if the craving turns to excessive greed, evil arises. As seen in the criticisms of Buddhism, there is an intense concern with avoiding selfishness by acting morally.

Cheng Yi said, "When it comes to such an act as stepping in water or fire, everyone avoids, for they really see why they should; one will stand out naturally from others only when one has a mind which sees evil as like dipping the hand in hot water."[71] The problem is that we don't always know right from wrong. One had to develop certainty regarding ethical activity if one was to be fully human and help shape society and the world. Good intentions are not enough: "Even an action performed without vicious [motive], if it does not agree with correct *li*, is irregular—which is to be vicious."[72] But if we all are endowed with *li* in our human nature, if we all can understand *li*, why is there action that contravenes *li* even by those who are attempting to follow *li*? The answer for the Chengs is that we are not simply made of *li*. Li gives us shape and can direct our actions, but we also have a physical body made of *qi* that can interfere with our ethical aspirations: "There is nothing in the nature itself that is not good; anything that is not good pertains to 'capacity' (*cai* 才). The nature is the same as *li*, which is uniform from [sage emperors] Yao and Shun down to the man of little intelligence. But 'capacity' means the endowment of *qi*, some of which is clear and some turbid. Persons endowed with its clear elements are the worthies, while those endowed with its turbid elements are the stupid people."[73] It is important to note that it is not the endowment of li that creates differences in people but the endowment of qi.

Although Zhou Dunyi's *Explanation* and Zhang Zai's *Inscription* both discuss our link to other creatures in terms of *qi*, the Cheng brothers expanded on the term and used it to explain not only the connections but also differences in human character and ability. It is the combined use of *li* and *qi* that made the Neo-Confucian view of human beings new and convincing to their contemporaries. A. C. Graham has likened the Cheng brothers' explanation of human nature in terms of *li* and *qi* to a "paradigm shift" similar to a scientific breakthrough.[74] By creating a clear set of interrelated concepts, the Chengs solved the riddle of human nature. *Qi* has been translated as breath, ether, matter, substance, material-force, and psychophysical stuff. Like *li*, it is not easily rendered into English, although the last attempt comes closest to capturing the broad ranging conception of *qi*. *Qi* is our breath, our bodies, even our thought processes. It is the vital energy that flows through our body—as in the traditional exercise known as *qigong*, which seeks to control the flow of *qi* and boost health. Although *li* may set the parameters for how each thing in the cosmos is shaped, that shape only comes into being when infused with *qi*. There is a *li* for human beings, both in terms of our physical form and what constitutes our proper ethical action, but the form is not fulfilled until a body is created and brought to life with *qi*. Similarly, there can be no ethical action without people doing the action. *Li* and *qi* are both necessary for the cosmos to exist and morality to flourish.

Returning to the *Diagram of the Supreme Ultimate*, the cosmos is formed when *yin* and *yang* interact through movement and stillness. In the Neo-Confucian understanding of creation, the interactions of *yin* and *yang* produce various gradations of *qi*, some more pure, some less pure. The purer forms are light and heavenly; the less pure forms are heavier and earthly. Humans sit somewhere between. The fact that we have physical bodies means we have physical needs for such things as food and shelter. When we are hungry, we crave food; when cold, we desire shelter. But sometimes those desires become overbearing and turn into greed. We do not simply seek to satisfy our hunger, we want flavorful food, the best cuts of meat, and rare spices. Overbearing desire can lead us to act in ways that are selfish, rather than socially harmonious. It is not that the craving for food when hungry is bad; but if that desire becomes counterproductive to social harmony, it turns to evil. Cheng Yi said, "Since man has a separate body he has the *li* of selfishness; it is natural that it is difficult to unite himself with the Way."[75] Note that Cheng Yi talks about a *li* of selfishness, though *li* is said to be completely good. Cheng Hao sheds a bit more light on the subject: "The good and evil in the world are both heaven's *li*. What is called evil is not fundamentally evil; it is as it is only by going too far or not far enough."[76] The Neo-Confucians recognized that a certain degree of self-interest is necessary for individuals to live and not throw away their lives. To feed oneself when hungry is proper and accords with *li*; starving oneself or becoming a glutton contravenes *li*. Evil is not an active force in the world.

There is no sense of "the devil made me do it," nor are human beings tainted with sin. Evil is done when we fail to maintain a sense of balance between personal needs and social needs. As Cheng Hao wrote, "The *li* of equilibrium is perfect. There is no production by the *yin* alone or by the *yang* alone. That which leans to one side becomes an animal or bird or barbarian, while that which is in equilibrium becomes a man."[77] To be balanced is the mark of a cultivated person: one maintains a balance between self-interest and altruism, between satisfaction of needs and excess.

There is also a recognition that not all things in accord with *li* are good and pleasant. In a passage that echoes the ideas of Zhuangzi's chapter "Equaling things out,"[78] the Chengs posited that the world is full of opposites (*yin* and *yang*, good and evil, hot and cold, night and day, self and other) and that the task for humans is to understand how all things harmonize. "There is a single *li* in outside things and the self; as soon as 'that' is understood 'this' becomes clear. This is the way to unite external and internal. The scholar should understand everything, at one extreme the height of heaven and the thickness of earth, at the other that by which a single thing is as it is."[79] Further, "In activities there is good and there is evil; both are heaven's *li*. Within heaven's *li* some things must be excellent and some bad; for 'it is inherent in things that they are unequal.' We should look into this, but without ourselves entering into evil, degenerating into separate things."[80]

Although the Chengs did say that one could closely observe the *li* of any object and be able to discern cosmic *dao*, for most the process began with a study of the human condition. The purpose of examining *li* in books and the world was to refine one's understanding of moral action: "In general there is one *li* in each thing; it is necessary to comprehend its *li* exhaustively. There are many ways of exhausting the *li*—the study of books, and explanation of the moral principles in them; discussion of prominent figures, past and present, to distinguish what is right and wrong in their actions; experience of practical affairs and of dealing with them appropriately."[81] Though a great deal of scholarship had been done on the classical Confucian texts before the Song, most of it was commentarial and philological, explaining analogies and obscure language to contemporary audiences. The Chengs advocated interpreting the texts for the sake of one's own moral development. One was to turn to the classics and find in them guidelines for correct action or criticism of incorrect action. Cheng Hao has been credited with reviving interest in four classical texts: Confucius's *Analects*, *Mencius*, *Centrality and Commonality* (more commonly translated *The Doctrine of the Mean*), and the *Great Learning*.[82] The last two works are chapters from the *Liji*, or *Record of Rites*, that were held in special regard by Neo-Confucians in the Song. Combined with the *Analects* and

*Mencius*, the texts became collectively known as the Four Books and became the core of Neo-Confucian education. In the Tang, Han Yu's *The Original Way* considered the writings of the sages to be *The Book of Odes, The Book of Documents, The Book of Change,* and *The Spring and Autumn Annals*. He did not include the *Record of Rites*, nor did he include the *Analects* or *Mencius*.

Another change in the reevaluation of the tradition regarded the ideal of Confucius himself. As Mou Zongsan has argued, prior to the Song, people viewed Confucius as the intellectual heir of the sage-kings of high antiquity and of the Duke of Zhou. Note that when Han Yu chastised the Buddhists in the Tang, he lamented that they had been born after the sages and so "they were not rebuked by Emperor Yu, King Tang, King Wen, King Wu, the Duke of Zhou, or Confucius." In the Song, the emphasis shifted from Confucius as the end of the line of sage-kings (albeit an "uncrowned king"), to Confucius as the first exemplary scholar, to be followed by Mencius.[83] Confucius's model was that of the private scholar and teacher who sought his own perfection because he could not find kings who would employ his moral philosophy. This resonated with Song society elite, who based much of their hopes in successfully passing the examinations to join the civil service and thereby gain political position and the benefits that accompanied it. But as the Song went on, more people engaged in the Confucian education on which the examinations were based, and competition became fiercer with higher percentages of candidates failing. These men often spent the first twenty, thirty, forty, or more years of their lives preparing for the examinations with no degree to show for it. The ideal of Confucius as an avid learner who also failed to find political employment gave them some consolation.

Confucius was the model of someone who became a "sage within." Previous heroes—the sage-emperors Yao, Shun, and Yu; the sage-kings Wen and Wu; and the duke of Zhou—were both moral paragons and political leaders. They were both "sagely within and kingly without." Han Yu's piece from the Tang reflected the traditional ideal that the person who wielded political power also wielded moral authority. Hence, Han Yu called on a return to a social-political system where everyone fell under the authority of the emperor, including those in religious orders who had claimed to renounce all worldly ties. With the Cheng brothers' emphasis on everyone having the same human nature ("from Yao and Shun down to the man of little intelligence") and the growing emphasis on Confucius's sage within as the model for men to emulate, Confucians in the Song began to see their personal development through education less in terms of political service and more in terms of self-fulfillment. Zhou Dunyi was asked, "Can one become a sage through learning?" His simple answer was "yes."[84] Confucius was the model because he used the tradition he loved as a means of perfecting himself through learning. This became the goal of Neo-Confucians: one was to focus on individual moral development that would then lead to social transformation. The approach differed both from statecraft thinkers who stressed perfecting systems of government to benefit the people and from literati who maintained the pre-Song cultural traditions.

As the Song period developed, this outlook stressing sagehood gained greater credence as the main focus of literati education within the Neo-Confucian tradition. Though education was still strongly linked to the examinations, examination education's methodology focused on learning to write the requisite poetic and prose styles used in the examinations and memorizing the classics, or at least key passages from them, to be able to complete "fill in the blank" examination sections testing classical knowledge or to put a given classical passage into a larger textual context to answer a thematic essay question. For the Neo-Confucians, this was "learning for others," a utilitarian learning with the goal of an examination degree as its end. In contrast, the Neo-Confucians stressed "learning for oneself." Neo-Confucian educators did not deny that obtaining a degree in the examinations was an important accomplishment, but they argued that it had to be secondary to one's moral development. In a famous passage, Zhu Xi noted that in education a student ought to spend 70 percent of his time in self-cultivation and 30 percent preparing for the examinations.[85] It was fortuitous that both goals could be achieved with the same texts.

To become a sage, however, was no mean feat. Though the Four Books had not been ignored prior to the Song, they did not have the same status as the Five Classics. Furthermore, the way texts were read and interpreted shifted. Prior to the Song, scholars had viewed the classical texts as repositories of knowledge and standards of an idealized antiquity. The notion that later periods suffered a decline (*shuai* 衰) from the antique ideals was long a part of the pre-Song cultural tradition. Within this tradition students were to learn and embody the models of the past. Cheng Yi's statement that the Way had been lost between Mencius and Cheng Hao posited more than a decline. The term that now characterized the present's relationship to antiquity was *rupture* (*jue* 絕). The significance of the shift in terminology is that "'Decline' idealized antiquity, but it nonetheless supposed cultural continuity throughout history (even if the threads were worn and broken); 'rupture' idealized antiquity, but it supposed that later times could not serve as a model because they had not continued the essential qualities of antiquity. Rupture allowed for moral continuity with antiquity . . . but cultural continuity with the historical past was not longer necessary for restoring contact with antiquity."[86] Learning efforts were exerted in understanding the ethical standards of antiquity, which was possible because every human being has the same nature comprised of li. Anyone could become a sage, and anyone could study the ideals of antiquity and resuscitate them in contemporary society. The shift was, in a sense, more forward thinking because it presumed society could return to the high ideals of antiquity in the future.

However, only eighteen years after the death of Cheng Yi, this optimism for moral renewal was shaken in 1125 when the Song experienced a catastrophic invasion by the Jin dynasty of the Jurchen people who lived on the northern borders. The old emperor, Huizong (r. 1101–1125), abdicated in favor of his eldest son, who took the title Qinzong (r. 1126–1127). After successful campaigns in the north, the Jin temporarily withdrew early in 1126, after the Song agreed annually to pay 300,000 taels of silver, 300,000 bolts of cloth, and 1 million strings of cash over a period of 180 years.[87] However, the war was not over. In 1127, two prongs of the renewed Jin attack met at their goal of Kaifeng, the Song capital. There the Jurchens seized Huizong, Qinzong, and around nine hundred members of the imperial family and court, transporting them to the north.[88] This would have spelled the end of the Song, except that an imperial scion, the prince of Kang, was in the field leading the Song forces south of Kaifeng. The prince retreated south and was enthroned as the next emperor, Gaozong (r. 1127–1163). Gaozong reestablished the court in the southern city of Hangzhou, which was renamed Xingzai, or "location of the imperial progress," denoting the hope that it would be a temporary capital until the north was retaken.

Officials in the new southern court were deeply divided over how to proceed. Should they sue for peace to ensure the return of the captives? This would be the filial thing to do, so that Gaozong could rescue his father, mother, and elder brother. On the other hand, it was the duty of the emperor to rescue his subjects to the north and restore the boundaries of the dynasty. The court split into pro-peace and pro-war camps. Neo-Confucians tended to be conservative supporters of the pro-war faction. In their eyes, the north needed to be reclaimed, and Gaozong needed to fulfill his filial obligations to father and elder brother. Despite strong sentiment, others were equally convinced that the Song could not compete militarily with the Jin. In their opinion, it was better to hold the line at the Huai River and maintain a sure grip on the southern remnants of the empire, rather than risk losing everything in all-out confrontation. The factionalism was so intense and Gaozong's position as emperor was so tenuous that a group of generals forced him to abdicate briefly in 1129. Although other generals loyal to him rushed to the capital and restored him to the throne, from this point on, Gaozong became suspicious of both his military and civil officials. Communications between these groups were heavily monitored.[89]

The war dragged on in fits and starts through the 1130s. Although the Song enjoyed some successes north of the Huai, neither side was able to consolidate any gains beyond those achieved in 1129. The Southern Song court was not only concerned with the Jin to the north but also with powerful bandit groups that had arisen in the turmoil following the invasion. Beset with a number of problems, Gaozong decided to sue for peace in 1141. The treaty stipulated that Song would pay an annual tribute of 250,000 taels each of silver and bolts of cloth, and Gaozong accepted lesser status in diplomatic relation to the Jin ruler. The Neo-Confucians were particularly appalled by the emperor's acceptance of lesser status because it signaled his willingness to give up claims to the Chinese heartland in the north and undercut the traditional Confucian belief that Chinese civilization was morally superior to all other cultures and therefore was politically superior as well.

Not surprisingly, there was a great deal of protest from officials who sought to regain the north. The emperor took a dim view of their opposition, and his chief minister, Qin Gui, launched a purge of opponents of the treaty. Many Neo-Confucians were among those purged. To them, it seemed that the government had purchased a humiliating peace, rather than pursuing the morally correct path. With the emperor's full support, though, Qin Gui's purge continued.

When examining the development of Neo-Confucian thought, it is important to understand the social and political context of the Southern Song. Given the military uncertainty (threatened both by the Jin outside the borders and bandits within) and the political factionalism of the time, Neo-Confucians had to reconsider their position in society. Trained to serve as political officials and exhorted by their education to put into action their ethical knowledge, they were in a quandary. On one hand, it was clear that the dynasty was in dire straits; on the other, they were prevented from political participation by Qin Gui's policies. As a result, Neo-Confucians returned to the question of what was the fundamental basis of their civilization and how that basis could be applied to the contemporary context. It has been suggested that the twelfth century marks an "inward turn" for Chinese culture.

> The eleventh century was a time when culture among the elite expanded. It pioneered in new directions and blazed promising trails. With optimism it emphasized prospects. In contrast, the twelfth century saw elite culture paying more attention to consolidating and extending its values throughout society. Turning more retrospective and introspective than before, it became tempered by a circumspect and sometimes pessimistic tone. In short, while the

Northern Sung characteristically reached outward, the Southern Sung essentially looked inward.[90]

Yet we should not think that this meant stagnation. In fact, the Southern Song was a time of great intellectual vitality within the Neo-Confucian movement. Perhaps as more literati became disenchanted with the political climate and as the percentage of successful examination candidates shrank, literati found the message of becoming a sage within more appealing.

Although a number of competing schools of Neo-Confucianism developed, the leading figure and the man who is most associated with giving shape to Neo-Confucianism was Zhu Xi. Without doubt, Zhu Xi is one of the most influential figures in East Asian history. His interpretation and systematization of Confucian texts into a coherent and manageable program of education became the foundation of educational systems throughout East Asia. What made his way of thinking so persuasive? Certainly part of his appeal comes from the fact that he was accomplished in a variety of fields. Shuen-fu Lin has noted that "Zhu was without doubt the epitome of the Song ideal of the cultivated life, being at the same time the most learned man of his age, an editor and commentator of classics, a historian, an accomplished poet and calligrapher, a literary critic, a statesman, and a brilliant leader of the intellectual movement."[91] Zhu's multiple talents enabled him to comment on nearly all facets of culture that concerned the literati in Southern Song. He had successfully gained an examination degree and political office, but his main efforts were in Confucian education. Due to an incredible ability to integrate disparate strands of culture, politics, and social concerns, Zhu produced a cohesive and comprehensive system of education and self-cultivation grounded firmly in the paradigm of the *Great Learning*. This system was based in the moral cultivation of the individual and expanded outward to society and the state. Through this system, Zhu sought to define key concepts and codify core texts to provide a clearly delineated route for those who would follow him.

Drawing on the Northern Song masters for his inspiration, Zhu Xi, along with Lü Zuqian, compiled *Reflections on Things at Hand* (*Jinsi lu* 近思錄). *Reflections* was to serve as a primer for those who wanted to engage in Neo-Confucian self-cultivation. As Zhu wrote in his preface to the work: "Together [Lü Zuqian and I] read the works of Masters Zhou Dunyi, Cheng Hao, Cheng Yi, and Zhang Zai and lamented over the fact that their doctrines are as extensive and broad as a sea without shores. Fearing that a beginner may not know where to start, we have selected passages concerned with fundamentals and closely related to daily application to constitute this volume."[92] The selected passages were then organized under subject headings reflecting the influence of the *Great Learning*, beginning with cosmology, moving to self-cultivation, then applying cultivation to the family and government. *Reflections* also touched on systems and institutions, teaching, dealing with heterodoxy, and finally, reflecting the ultimate goal, the dispositions of sages and worthies. Perhaps reflecting the frustration many literati felt in the political climate, the seventh chapter is titled "On serving or not serving in government, advancing or withdrawing, and accepting and declining office." Indeed, the *Reflections* were to provide the foundation and shape the direction in which literati could develop themselves. But, in Zhu Xi's own words, "The *Reflections* are worth reading. The Four Books are the stairs to the Six Classics. The *Reflections* are the stairway to the Four Books."[93]

Through his exposition on the Four Books and the compilation published as *Reflections on Things at Hand*, Zhu wove a persuasive system out of the disparate strands of classical and Northern Song Confucianism. He explained the purpose of life, how evil arises, how to develop oneself, and ultimately how to become a sage. To further aid the student in his progress, in 1190 Zhu Xi published his commentaries on the Four Books and informed the readers of the sequence in which they ought to read the works: "I want men first to read the *Great Learning* to fix upon the pattern of the Confucian Way; next the *Analects* to establish its foundations; next the *Book of Mencius* to observe its development; next *Centrality and Commonality* to discover the subtle mysteries of the ancients."[94] Given this program, it is not surprising that when Zhu Xi was granted the honor of lecturing to the emperor in 1194, he spent forty-six days on the *Great Learning*, after which he was dismissed because of his repeated attacks on high court officials during those lectures.[95]

This criticism at the court came because Zhu Xi's program of self-cultivation, developed mainly from Cheng Yi, was based in the idea that all people are born with the same human nature but different physical endowments due to varying qualities of qi. Zhu believed these two aspects of human beings were in constant tension. Human nature provided the pure link to underlying cosmic order, *li*. "In discussing human nature, you must first understand what sort of thing human nature is. Master Cheng [Yi said] 'human nature is *li*; this theory is the best.'"[96] Yet it was the physical body that determined whether a person was "biased or correct." Zhu told his students, "When people are born their physical form is either biased or correct. . . . And according to their being biased or correct there are the differences of being clear or murky, ignorant or enlightened."[97] To clarify this view of *qi*, Zhu provided the following analogy.

> Water flowing to the sea without getting dirty is similar to one whose *qi* with which he is endowed is pure and clear and who is good from

childhood. In the case of a sage it is his nature to be so and he preserves his Heavenly endowment complete. Water that flows only a short distance and is already turbid is like one whose *qi* is extremely unbalanced and impure and is evil from childhood. . . . Because of this, man must increase his effort at purification. If one can overcome *qi* through learning, he will know that this [human] nature is harmonious and unified and from the beginning has never been destroyed.[98]

If one's *qi* is turbulent or murky, the pure human nature (which is *li*) cannot shine forth but will become overwhelmed by human desires generated by the physical body. In another analogy, Zhu Xi compared the mind to an "empty thing" akin to a dumpling, the insides of which were composed of human nature.[99] Without a clear mind—the mind being the "dumpling wrapper" of *qi* that surrounds the nature—one cannot perceive the pure human nature within.

The passage quoted at length sets out three major themes in Zhu Xi's work: the interplay of human nature and *qi*, the role of learning in overcoming *qi*, and the necessity of accessing human nature to know what it truly means to be human. Human nature, which is purely ethical, is in constant conflict with human desires generated from the physical body composed of *qi*. Therefore, Zhu Xi described the mind (*xin* 心) as a compound of these two things: the human mind (*renxin* 人心) and the Dao mind (*daoxin* 道心). "The mind's spiritual consciousness," wrote Zhu, "is unified. Yet if we take it to be something that has the differences between the human mind and the Dao mind, then part is born of the material body's self-interest [the human mind], and part is based in the rectitude of the human nature's mandate [the Dao mind]."[100] The purpose of learning was to overcome the self-interested impulses sparked by one's qi and so allow the moral Dao mind to govern one's actions.

The distinction between the human mind and Dao mind became a focal point for Zhu Xi. He argued that the central concept transmitted by the sage-emperors of antiquity was encapsulated in Shun's statement, "The human mind is precarious. The Dao mind is subtle. Refined and unified. Sincerely hold to the mean."[101] Zhu Xi interpreted this ethical framework to be the vital legacy of the sages, surpassing their political achievements. Therefore, he recounted this transmission as the opening to his "Preface to the Redacted *Centrality and Commonality*" in his edition of the Four Books.

After taking this ethical stance, he went on to elucidate the dichotomy of the human mind and Dao mind in terms of his understanding of the relationship between *li* and *qi*. Zhu Xi also used the preface as a vehicle for expressing his idea of the "transmission of the Way" (*daotong* 道通). Echoing Cheng Yi's assertion, Zhu believed that as sage-emperor Yao had passed on his ethical insight to Shun, and Shun to Yu, there was a chain of enlightened rulers who had embodied and transmitted this insight to others. Zhu Xi's "transmission of the Way" solidified the view of Confucius as the role model for literati: "Our Master Confucius, although he did not achieve the political position of the others, his achievements are as worthy as Yao's and Shun's because he continued the [teachings of] past sages and opened the way for future students."[102] Confucius's wisdom was then passed to his disciples Yan Hui and Zengzi, and the latter passed it on to Confucius's grandson, Zi Si, who both compiled *Centrality and Commonality* and taught Mencius. By developing this line of transmission, Zhu Xi once again gave precedence to the Four Books and bypassed the classical canon of the *Book of Documents, Book of Rites, Book of Odes,* and *Book of Change.* Shorter in length and smaller in scope, the Four Books directed the literatus's attention to his personal ethical development, but also held the promise of connecting with the universal truths known to previous and future sages. His program also implied that moral authority rested with the learned individual, not the state. Moral authority flowed from inside the individual; it was not to be imposed from the outside.

Assuming literacy, Zhu wanted to give individuals a means of embarking on a path of self-cultivation that freed them from dependence on state schools, the curriculum of which was directed toward the civil service examinations. He made this clear when explaining his motivation for compiling *Reflections on Things at Hand*: "I believe that the essentials of the student's search for the beginnings of things, exerting effort, conducting himself, and managing others, as well as the gist of understanding the heterodox schools and observing the sages and worthies can be seen in rough outline. Thus if a young man in an isolated village has the will to learn, but no enlightened teacher or good friend to guide him, obtains this volume and explores and broods over its material in his own mind, he will be able to find the gate to enter."[103] Zhu Xi did not reject the civil service examinations in toto,[104] yet he did believe it misguided to think that examinations could select the best people for political office, because his conception of the best people meant the most ethical people, not the most technically qualified. Zhu also took the position that the worth of an individual should be determined by their moral cultivation, not by social standing (one could be in an "isolated village"), nor by political or literary achievement. Moral cultivation did not preclude such success, but, as with the examinations, ethics had to be given priority. Without an ethical basis, such success was illusory at best in Zhu Xi's eyes.

The appeal of Zhu Xi's work becomes clearer when considered in light of the increased social and political competition in the Southern Song. Politically, the southern court was fractured and factionalized, as witnessed by

THE ETHICAL UNIVERSE OF NEO-CONFUCIANISM   145

Zhu Xi's own experience of being among a group of men who were blacklisted and whose works were proscribed.[105] Political service became a less attractive career choice as factions displaced one another.[106] Beneath the troubles for those who actually made it into the privileged minority holding rank and office was increased competition for entrance into this elite via the examination system. The official policy, begun in the Northern Song, of promoting men through the examinations had worked well as a means of encouraging the literati to align their interests with those of the state. Social status had been linked to success in the examinations.[107] Consequently, people used education for material gain rather than moral edification. Zhu Xi and other Neo-Confucians argued that the perception of education as a means of ratifying social status was a perversion of educational ideals. Hence, Neo-Confucians set up academies or took on disciples to transmit the message they drew from the Classics: education was "for the sake of oneself, not others." This was not to imply selfish motivations, because the outcome was to be a morally aware individual, who in the words of Confucius "wishing to be established himself, seeks also to establish others; wishing to be enlarged himself, he seeks also to enlarge others."[108] In the words of another Southern Song Confucian, Lu Jiuyuan, education was the means "to become truly human" (zuoren). Sponsoring or teaching in academies with this educational motivation became a means of translating one's moral awareness into ethical action if one chose not to participate in government.

Education became the mark of someone within the social elite. But were they doing it for themselves or for others? People disillusioned with the examination system may have asked how education justified their status if the end result was not material gain. Zhu Xi provided them the answer: Through education one becomes moral, and morality is the mark of a "true gentleman." One of the most significant messages Neo-Confucianism had was that moral cultivation carries its own weight and authority. Given the historical context, this message brought the Neo-Confucians to the fore. Although they did experience blacklisting and bans on printing their works, eventually their ideas received imperial sponsorship in the closing decades of the Song. Shrines were built to the famous moralists and ethicists of the Song, and such men were officially included in the Confucian Temple maintained in the capital. It would appear than Zhu Xi lived in straitened circumstances,[109] yet his opinion was highly regarded throughout the empire. Furthermore, with expanded participation in education, greater numbers of students came from families without traditions of office-holding or formal education. These men were precisely those Zhu Xi referred to as living in isolated villages. For them Zhu Xi set the path. He provided cross-referenced definitions of key terms; he told them what self-cultivation accomplished; he gave them a clearly ordered curriculum; he offered them textually argued certainty that they could indeed aim for and achieve the highest goals that inspired the worthies of antiquity; he informed them that virtue was its own reward, while his example showed that virtue could bring prestige as well. His message was that sincere effort and concentrated study of the Four Books and the Northern Song masters were the means by which anyone from any background could achieve nothing less than sagehood.

Han Yu had argued that the Chinese needed to revive Confucianism to resuscitate social-political stability in the late Tang. He explicitly criticized Buddhism and Daoism for undermining Confucianism's position in the empire. Yet Buddhism and Daoism owed much of their appeal to persuasive descriptions of how the world works, why good and evil exist, and how the individual can find fulfillment. The Northern Song masters took up this challenge. Zhou Dunyi provided a Confucian-based cosmological explanation for human beings' position in the universe. Zhang Zai articulated the interrelatedness of all beings, most particularly his connection with all other people in terms of a large family led by the emperor and grounded in Confucian morality. The Cheng brothers elaborated on the cosmological connections and more fully articulated how human beings know right from wrong because of our inherently good human nature. By describing the world in terms of the central concepts of *li* and *qi*, they persuasively answered questions concerning how we can know what is good, how we can develop our innate capacity to be good, and how we can then understand our position within the moral universe. One hundred years later, Zhu Xi compiled the works of his predecessors into a program of learning and self-cultivation that based transformation of the world in the ethical individual. Where Han Yu had started the Neo-Confucian movement with a call for greater Confucian moral authority invested in the emperor, by the Southern Song, Zhu Xi argued that moral authority flowed from the individual who understood how Confucian morality intertwined with *li* and *qi*.

The Neo-Confucian vision cannot be seen as an individualistic version of secular humanism, since it is not solely concerned with human beings (anthropocentric). Instead, it begins with what is common to all of us—the mere fact of our existence. Through understanding that existence, through developing our moral understanding, and fulfilling the moral understanding of the *li* of the cosmos by ethical practice, humans fulfill their role as the "most divine of all things." As Tu Wei-ming, a modern Confucian, has written, "the paradigmatic living example is not a mere creature but is in fact a cocreator of the world in which we live, a guardian of the natural process, and, indeed, a participant of the creative transformation of Heaven and Earth. The question of the ultimate meaning of human existence, in light of the age-old belief that 'it is the human that can make the Way great and not the Way that can make the human great,' is thus an anthropocosmic question."[110]

NOTES

1. Mou Zongsan 牟宗三, 心体与性体 Xin Ti Yu Xing Ti [The Mind and Human Nature] (Shanghai: Shanghai gu ji chu ban she, 1999), pp. 5–6.
2. James Legge, *The Chinese Classics*, 5 in 4 vols. (Taipei: SMC Publications, 1991), pp. 1:357–58.
3. Ibid., p. 1:194.
4. For the sake of brevity, discussions of divergent strands of Song Neo-Confucianism and the development of Neo-Confucianism in later periods have been omitted. Following the bibliography are suggested readings covering these topics.
5. Peter K. Bol, "The Sung Examination System and the Shih," *Asia Major (Third Series)* 3, no. 2 (1990): 149.
6. C. A. Peterson, "Court and Province in Mid- and Late T'ang," in Denis Twitchett, ed., *The Cambridge History of China* (Taipei: Caves Books, 1989), p. 485.
7. For a detailed account of this process, see "The Transformation of the Shih," chapter 2 of Peter K. Bol, *This Culture of Ours: Intellectual Transitions in T'ang and Sung China* (Stanford, Calif.: Stanford University Press, 1992).
8. Charles Hartman, *Han Yü and the T'ang Search for Unity* (Princeton, N.J.: Princeton University Press, 1986), pp. 123–24.
9. A. C. Graham, *Two Chinese Philosophers: The Metaphysics of the Brothers Ch'eng* (LaSalle, Ill.: Open Court, 1992), p. 162. Note that Graham's translation of the title of Han Yu's piece is *Inquiry into the Way*. Here it is changed to *The Original Way* for consistency. Both are possible translations for the Chinese title *Yuan dao*.
10. Hartman, *Han Yü and the T'ang Search for Unity*, p. 3.
11. Viewed by the classical Confucian Mencius (371?–289? B.C.E) as the two most popular schools during his lifetime and two opposed to Confucian ideas. Mencius characterized Yang Zhu's thought as selfish, and Mozi's thought failed to make distinctions in social roles, choosing instead to stress "universal love."
12. Han Yu, "The Original Way," trans. Robert W. Foster, in Victor H. Mair, Nancy Shatzman Steinhardt, and Paul Rakita Goldin, eds., *Hawai'i Reader in Traditional Chinese Culture* (Honolulu: University of Hawai'i Press, 2005), p. 360.
13. Ibid.
14. For example, if there is a moral category of chastity that prescribes men and women should not touch hands, how does a man respond if he sees a woman drowning? His sympathetic impulse is to save the woman, but the moral category of chastity may cause him to hesitate.
15. Chapter 19.
16. Han Yu, "The Original Way," p. 360.
17. Ibid.
18. For the history of Buddhism in China, see Arthur F. Wright, *Buddhism in Chinese History* (Stanford, Calif.: Stanford University Press, 1988), and Kenneth K. S.

Ch'en, *Buddhism in China: A Historical Survey* (Princeton, N.J.: Princeton University Press, 1973).

19. William Theodore de Bary et al., eds., *Sources of Chinese Tradition* (New York: Columbia University Press, 1960), pp. 280–86.

20. Han Yu, "The Original Way," p. 360.

21. Ibid., pp. 360–61.

22. Ibid., p. 361.The internal quotation is from the *Great Learning*, cited at the beginning of the chapter.

23. Ibid.

24. John W. Chaffee, *The Thorny Gates of Learning in Sung China: A Social History of Examinations* (Cambridge: Cambridge University Press, 1985), p. 49.

25. Bol, *This Culture of Ours*, p. 54.

26. Thomas H. C. Lee, *Government Education and Examinations in Sung China, 960–1278* (Hong Kong: Chinese University of Hong Kong, 1985), p. 148, table 9.

27. It should be noted that private Buddhist academies also flourished during the Song, but their education was not linked to government office.

28. For an interesting discussion of one such situation, see Conrad Schirokauer, "Neo-Confucians under Attack: The Condemnation of Wei-Hsüeh," in John Winthrop Haeger, ed., *Crisis and Prosperity in Sung China* (Tucson: University of Arizona Press, 1975).

29. Wang Anshi, "Memorial to the Emperor Jen-tsung" in de Bary et al., eds., *Sources of Chinese Tradition*, p. 1:414–15.

30. Ibid., p. 1:415. Changing the translation of *cai* 才 as "capable" in the original to "talented" for consistency with later translations of the term.

31. Ibid., p. 1:416–17.

32. Xiao-bin Ji, *Politics and Conservatism in Northern Song China: The Career and Thought of Sima Guang (A.D. 1019–1086)* (Hong Kong: Chinese University Press, 2005).

33. Sima Guang, "Yi xuexiao gongju zhuang," 議學校貢舉狀 [Memorial Discussing Schools and Examinations], in Sima Guang and Wang Genlin 王根林. Sima Guang 司馬光, 司馬光奏議 /*Sima Guang Zou Yi* (Taiyuan: Shanxi ren min chu ban she: Shanxi sheng xin hua shu dian fa xing, 1986), p. 270.

34. Su Shi, "Yi xuexiao gongju zhuang," 議學校貢舉狀 [Memorial Discussing Schools and Examinations], in Su Shi and Kong Fanli 蘇軾 and 孔凡禮, 蘇軾文集 /*Su Shi Wen Ji* (Beijing: Zhong hua shu ju: Xin hua shu dian Beijing fa xing suo fa xing, 1986), p. 723.

35. Ibid., p. 724.

36. Cheng Hao, "Qing xiu xuexiao zun shiru qu shi zhazi," 請修學校尊師儒取士劄子 [Memorial Requesting the Renovation of schools, the veneration of Confucian teachers, and the selection of literati], in Cheng Hao, Cheng Yi, and Wang Xiaoyu 程顥, 程頤, and 王孝魚, 二程集 /*Er Cheng Ji* (Beijing: Zhonghua shu ju: Xin hua shu dian Beijing fa xing suo fa xing, 1981), p. 448.

37. Father-son, ruler-minister, husband-wife, elder and younger brother, friend-friend.

38. Li 理 is a concept developed by Cheng Hao and his brother Cheng Yi and is central to Neo-Confucianism. It will be discussed in detail shortly.

39. Cheng Hao, "Qing xiu xuexiao zun shiru qu shi zhazi," p. 448; emphasis added.

40. On Zhou Dunyi's position in the development of Neo-Confucianism during the Song dynasty see Graham, *Two Chinese Philosophers*, pp. 152–75.

41. Water, fire, wood, metal, and earth are traditionally considered the five elements from which everything in the cosmos is created.

42. In the *Book of Change*, yang is represented by a solid straight line (———), while yin is represented as a broken line (– –). Thus, the hexagram for *qian* is made of six yang lines (below left), whereas *kun* is composed of six yin lines (below right). Each represents the pure combination of yang and yin, respectively.

43. *Book of Change*, "Shuo gua," see Richard Wilhelm, *The I Ching, or Book of Changes*, trans. Cary F. Baynes (Princeton, N.J.: Princeton University Press, 1984), p. 264.

44. *Book of Change*, "Xici shang," see ibid., p. 294.

45. *Analects*, 7.16; Legge, *The Chinese Classics*, p. 1:200.

46. For the importance of the *Book of Change* to Song dynasty Neo-Confucians see chapter 4 in this book and Kidder Smith Jr., Peter K. Bol, Joseph A. Adler, and Don J. Wyatt, *Sung Dynasty Uses of the I Ching* (Princeton, N.J.: Princeton University Press, 1990).

47. See note 42.

48. A. C. Graham, "What Was New in the Ch'eng-Chu Theory of Human Nature?" in *Studies in Chinese Philosophy and Philosophical Literature* (Albany: State University of New York Press, 1990), p. 425.

49. Huang Zongxi, et al. 全祖望 陳金生 梁運華 黃宗羲, 宋元學案 /*Song Yuan Xue an* [A Record of Song and Yuan Dynasty Scholars] (Beijing: Zhonghua shu ju: Xin hua shu dian Beijing fa xing suo fa xing, 1986), p. 1.17.665. "Humaneness" is a translation of the central Confucian virtue *ren* 仁.

50. Graham, *Two Chinese Philosophers*, p. 162.

51. *Analects*, 18.6. See Legge, *The Chinese Classics*, p. 334.

52. Huang Zongxi et al., *Song Yuan Xue an*, p. 1.17.665. For complete translations see Wing-tsit Chan, *A Source Book in Chinese Philosophy* (Princeton, N.J.: Princeton University Press, 1973), pp. 497–98, or Yu-lan Fung, *A History of Chinese Philosophy*, trans. Derk Bodde, 2 vols. (Princeton, N.J.: Princeton University Press, 1983), pp. 2:493–95.

53. Huang Zongxi, *Song Yuan Xue an*, p. 1.17.665.

54. Ibid.

55. Ibid.

56. Graham, *Two Chinese Philosophers*, p. 158.

57. Ibid., p. 83.

58. William Theodore de Bary et al., *Sources of Chinese Tradition*, 2nd ed. (New York: Columbia University Press, 1999), p. 2:697.

59. Graham, *Two Chinese Philosophers*, p. 69.

60. Ibid., pp. 70–71.

61. Ibid., p. 11.

62. Fung, *A History of Chinese Philosophy*, p. 2:503. Changing "Principle" in the original to li, for the sake of consistency.

63. Graham, *Two Chinese Philosophers*, p. 12.

64. Graham, "What Was New in the Ch'eng-Chu Theory of Human Nature?" p. 426.

65. Graham, *Two Chinese Philosophers*, p. 78.

66. Ibid., p. 75.

67. For the recounting of the overthrow of Xia, see Legge, *The Chinese Classics*, pp. 3:281–319.

68. For the argument with Gaozi, see *Mencius* 6.A.1–7 in ibid., pp. 2:394–407; for the analogy of the child and the well, see *Mencius* 2.A.6 in Legge, *The Chinese Classics*, pp. 2:202–204.

69. See "Man's Nature is Evil," chapter 6 of Xunzi, *Hsün Tzu: Basic Writings*, ed. Burton Watson (New York: Columbia University Press, 1963), pp. 157–71.

70. Fung, *A History of Chinese Philosophy*, p. 2:517.

71. Graham, *Two Chinese Philosophers*, p. 81.

72. Ibid., p. 68.

73. Fung, *A History of Chinese Philosophy*, p. 2:517.

74. Graham, "What Was New in the Ch'eng-Chu Theory of Human Nature?" p. 413.

75. Graham, *Two Chinese Philosophers*, p. 127.

76. Ibid.

77. Ibid., p. 129.

78. Zhuangzi, *The Complete Works of Chuang Tzu*, trans. Burton Watson (New York: Columbia University Press, 1968), pp. 39–40.

79. Graham, *Two Chinese Philosophers*, p. 8.

80. Ibid., p. 127. The internal quotation is from Mencius. See James Legge, ed., *The Analects and Mencius, The Chinese Classics*, 4 vols. (Taipei: SMC Publishing, 1991), p. 2:256.

81. Graham, *Two Chinese Philosophers*, p. 76.

82. Mou Zongsan 牟宗三, "宋明儒學概述/Song-Ming Ruxue Gaishu" [A General Discussion of Song-Ming Confucianism], in 中國哲學十九講/*Zhongguo Zhexue Shijiu Jiang* [Nineteen Lectures on Chinese Philosophy] (Shanghai: Shanghai guji chubanshe, 1997), p. 373.

83. Ibid., p. 376.

84. Wei-ming Tu, "The Sung Confucian Idea of Education: A Background Understanding," in William Theodore de Bary and John W. Chaffee, eds., *Neo-Confucian Education: The Formative Stage, Studies on China* (Berkeley: University of California Press, 1989), p. 149.

85. Zhu Xi, *Learning to Be a Sage: Selections from the Conversations of Master Chu Topically Arranged*, trans. Daniel K. Gardner (Berkeley: University of California Press, 1990), p. 19.

THE ETHICAL UNIVERSE OF NEO-CONFUCIANISM  151

86. Peter K. Bol, "Neo-Confucianism and Local Society, Twelfth to Sixteenth Century: A Case Study," in Paul J. and Richard von Glahn Smith, eds., *The Song-Yuan-Ming Transition in Chinese History*, Harvard East Asian Monographs 221 (Cambridge, Mass.: Harvard University Asia Center, 2003), p. 246.

87. Herbert Franke, "The Chin Dynasty," in Denis Twitchett and Herbert Franke, eds., *The Cambridge History of China* (Cambridge: Cambridge University Press, 1994), p. 229.

88. James T. C. Liu, *China Turning Inward: Intellectual-Political Changes in the Early Twelfth Century* (Cambridge, Mass.: Harvard University Press, 1988), p. 57.

89. For a brief overview of some of the politics of this period, see Robert W. Foster, "Yue Fei, 1103–1141," in Kenneth James Hammond, ed., *The Human Tradition in Premodern China*, Human Tradition around the World, no. 4 (Wilmington, Del.: Scholarly Resources, 2002). For a more detailed account, see Liu, *China Turning Inward*, and Edward Harold Kaplan, "Yueh Fei and the Founding of the Southern Song" (Ph.D. dissertation, University of Iowa, 1970).

90. Liu, *China Turning Inward*, p. 10.

91. Shuen-fu Lin, *The Transformation of a Chinese Lyrical Tradition: Chiang K'uei and Southern Sung Tz'u Poetry* (Princeton, N.J.: Princeton University Press, 1978), p. 43.

92. Zhu Xi and Lü Zuqian, *Reflections on Things at Hand: The Neo-Confucian Anthology*, ed. Wing-tsit Chan (New York: Columbia University Press, 1967).

93. Adapted from ibid., p. xl. Note that Zhu talks of the Six Classics, instead of five. He is adding the lost *Classic of Music*.

94. Zhu, *Learning to Be a Sage: Selections from the Conversations of Master Chu Topically Arranged*, 44.

95. Zhu and Zuqian, *Reflections on Things at Hand*, p. xxxvii.

96. Zhu Xi, Li Jingde, and Wang Xingxian 黎靖德 王星賢 朱熹, 朱子語類/ *Zhuzi Yu Lei* (1986; rpt Beijing : Zhonghua shu ju: Xin hua shu dian Beijing fa xing suo fa xing, 1988 ), p. 1.4.63.

97. Ibid., p. 1.4.56.

98. Zhu Xi, "Mingdao lunxing shuo" 明道論性說 [A Treatise on Cheng Mingdao's Discourse on Nature]. With the exception of substituting qi for "material force," the translation is taken from Chan, *A Source Book in Chinese Philosophy*, pp. 598–99.

99. Zhu Xi, Li Jingde, and Wang Xingxian, *Zhuzi Yu Lei*, p. 4.60.1426.

100. Zhu Xi 朱熹, 四書章句集注/*Si Shu Zhang Ju Ji Zhu* (1983; rpt Beijing: Zhonghua shu ju: Xin hua shu dian Beijing fa xing suo fa xing, 1986), p. 14.

101. Yao's transmission to Shun is found in *Analects*, 20.1, see Legge, *The Chinese Classics*, p. 1:350, while Shun's expanded comment to Yu is found in "The Counsels of the Great Yu," in Legge, *The Chinese Classics*, p. 3:61–62.

102. Mair, Steinhardt, and Goldin, *Hawai'i Reader in Traditional Chinese Culture*, p. 427.

103. Zhu and Zuqian, *Reflections on Things at Hand*, pp. 1–2.

104. Zhu advocated giving 70 percent of one's study to ethical pursuits and 30 percent to examination learning. See Zhu, *Learning to Be a Sage*, p. 191.

105. For a detail analysis of this event, see Schirokauer, "Neo-Confucians under Attack."

106. For a analysis of the early Southern Song situation, see Liu, *China Turning Inward*. For a description of one case that combines political and intellectual factionalism, see John Chaffee, "Chao Ju-Yü, Spurious Learning, and Southern Song Political Culture," *Journal of Sung-Yuan Studies* 22 (1990–92).

107. See Peter K. Bol, "The Transformation of the Shi," chap. 2 of Bol, *This Culture of Ours*, pp. 32–75. See also Robert P. Hymes, "Examinations, Office, and Social Mobility," chap. 1 of Robert P. Hymes, *Statesmen and Gentlemen: The Elite of Fu-Chou, Chiang-Hsi, in Northern and Southern Sung* (Cambridge: Cambridge University Press, 1986), pp. 29–61.

108. *Analects*, 6.30; Legge, *The Chinese Classics*, p. 1:194.

109. Wing-tsit Chan, *Chu Hsi: Life and Thought, The Ch'ien Mu Lectures 1984* (Hong Kong: Chinese University Press, 1987), pp. 12–13.

110. Tu, "The Sung Confucian Idea of Education," pp. 139–40. The internal quotation is from *Analects*, 15.29.

## BIBLIOGRAPHY

Bol, Peter K. "The Sung Examination System and the Shih." *Asia Major* 3, no. 2 (1990): 149–71.

———. *This Culture of Ours: Intellectual Transitions in T'ang and Sung China*. Stanford, Calif.: Stanford University Press, 1992.

———. "Neo-Confucianism and Local Society, Twelfth to Sixteenth Century: A Case Study." In Paul J. and Richard von Glahn Smith, eds., *The Song-Yuan-Ming Transition in Chinese History*. Cambridge, Mass.: Harvard University Asia Center, 2003, pp. 241–83.

Chaffee, John. "Chao Ju-Yü, Spurious Learning, and Southern Song Political Culture." *Journal of Sung-Yuan Studies* 22 (1990–92): 23–62.

Chaffee, John W. *The Thorny Gates of Learning in Sung China: A Social History of Examinations*. Cambridge: Cambridge University Press, 1985.

Chan, Wing-tsit. *A Source Book in Chinese Philosophy*. Princeton, N.J.: Princeton University Press, 1973.

———. *Chu Hsi: Life and Thought, The Ch'ien Mu Lectures 1984*. Hong Kong: Chinese University Press, 1987.

Ch'en, Kenneth K. S. *Buddhism in China: A Historical Survey*. Princeton, N.J.: Princeton University Press, 1973.

Cheng Hao, Cheng Yi and Wang Xiaoyu 程顥, 程頤, and 王孝魚. 二程集/*Er Cheng Ji*. Beijing: Zhonghua shu ju: Xin hua shu dian Beijing fa xing suo fa xing, 1981.

de Bary, William Theodore, Irene Bloom, Wing-tsit Chan, and Joseph Adler. *Sources of Chinese Tradition*, 2nd ed., Introduction to Asian Civilizations. New York: Columbia University Press, 1999.

de Bary, William Theodore, Wing-tsit Chan, Burton Watson, and Chester Tan, eds. *Sources of Chinese Tradition*. New York: Columbia University Press, 1960.

Foster, Robert W. "Yue Fei, 1103–1141." In Kenneth James Hammond, ed., *The Human Tradition in Premodern China*. Wilmington, Del.: Scholarly Resources, 2002.

Franke, Herbert. "The Chin Dynasty." In Denis Twitchett and Herbert Franke, eds., *The Cambridge History of China*. Cambridge: Cambridge University Press, 1994, pp. 215–320.

Fung, Yu-lan. *A History of Chinese Philosophy*, trans. Derk Bodde, 2 vols. Princeton, N.J.: Princeton University Press, 1983.

Graham, A. C. "What Was New in the Ch'eng-Chu Theory of Human Nature?" In *Studies in Chinese Philosophy and Philosophical Literature,*. Albany: State University of New York Press, 1990, pp. 412–35.

———. *Two Chinese Philosophers: The Metaphysics of the Brothers Ch'eng*. LaSalle, Ill.: Open Court, 1992.

Hartman, Charles. *Han Yü and the T'ang Search for Unity*. Princeton, N.J.: Princeton University Press, 1986.

Huang Zongxi, Quan Zuwang, Chen Jinsheng, and Liang Yunhua 黃宗羲, 全祖望, 陳金生, 梁運華. 宋元學案/*Song Yuan Xue an* [A Record of Song and Yuan Dynasty Scholars]. Beijing: Zhonghua shu ju: Xin hua shu dian Beijing fa xing suo fa xing, 1986.

Hymes, Robert P. *Statesmen and Gentlemen: The Elite of Fu-Chou, Chiang-Hsi, in Northern and Southern Sung*. Cambridge: Cambridge University Press, 1986.

Ji, Xiao-bin. *Politics and Conservatism in Northern Song China: The Career and Thought of Sima Guang (A.D. 1019–1086)*. Hong Kong: Chinese University Press, 2005.

Kaplan, Edward Harold. "Yueh Fei and the Founding of the Southern Song." Ph.D. dissertation, University of Iowa, 1970.

Lee, Thomas H. C. *Government Education and Examinations in Sung China, 960–1278*. Hong Kong: Chinese University of Hong Kong, 1985.

Legge, James. *The Chinese Classics*, 4 vols. Taipei: SMC, 1991.

Lin, Shuen-fu. *The Transformation of a Chinese Lyrical Tradition: Chiang K'uei and Southern Sung Tz'u Poetry*. Princeton, N.J.: Princeton University Press, 1978.

Liu, James T. C. *China Turning Inward: Intellectual-Political Changes in the Early Twelfth Century*. Cambridge, Mass.: Harvard University Press, 1988.

Mair, Victor H., Nancy Shatzman Steinhardt, and Paul Rakita Goldin, eds. *Hawai'i Reader in Traditional Chinese Culture*. Honolulu: University of Hawai'i Press, 2005.

Mou Zongsan 牟宗三. "宋明儒學概述/Song-Ming Ruxue Gaishu" [A General Discussion of Song-Ming Confucianism]. In 中國哲學十九講/*Zhongguo Zhexue Shijiu Jiang* [Nineteen Lectures on Chinese Philosophy]. Shanghai: Shanghai guji chubanshe, 1997, pp. 368–98.

———. 心體与性體/*Xin Ti Yu Xing Ti* [The Mind and Human Nature]. Shanghai: Shanghai gu ji chu ban she, 1999.

Peterson, C. A. "Court and Province in Mid- and Late T'ang." In Denis Twitchett, ed., *The Cambridge History of China*. Taipei: Caves Books, 1989, pp. 464–560.

Schirokauer, Conrad. "Neo-Confucians under Attack: The Condemnation of Wei-Hsüeh." In John Winthrop Haeger, ed., *Crisis and Prosperity in Sung China*. Tucson: University of Arizona Press, 1975, pp. 163–98.

Sima Guang and Wang Genlin 司馬光, 王根林. 司馬光奏議/*Sima Guang Zou Yi*. Taiyuan: Shanxi ren min chu ban she: Shanxi sheng xin hua shu dian fa xing, 1986.

Smith, Kidder Jr., Peter K. Bol, Joseph A. Adler, and Don J. Wyatt. *Sung Dynasty Uses of the I Ching*. Princeton, N.J.: Princeton University Press, 1990.

Su Shi and Kong Fanli 蘇軾 and 孔凡禮. 蘇軾文集/*Su Shi Wen Ji*. Beijing: Zhong hua shu ju: Xin hua shu dian Beijing fa xing suo fa xing, 1986.

Tu, Wei-ming. "The Sung Confucian Idea of Education: A Background Understanding." In William Theodore de Bary and John W. Chaffee, eds., *Neo-Confucian Education: The Formative Stage*. Berkeley: University of California Press, 1989, pp. 139–50.

Wilhelm, Richard. *The I Ching, or Book of Changes*, trans. Cary F. Baynes. Princeton. N.J.: Princeton University Press, 1984.

Wright, Arthur F. *Buddhism in Chinese History*. Stanford, Calif.: Stanford University Press, 1988.

Xunzi. "Hsün Tzu: Basic Writings," ed. Burton Watson. New York: Columbia University Press, 1963.

Zhu, Xi. *Learning to Be a Sage: Selections from the Conversations of Master Chu Topically Arranged*, trans. Daniel K. Gardner. Berkeley: University of California Press, 1990.

Zhu, Xi, and Lü Zuqian. *Reflections on Things at Hand: The Neo-Confucian Anthology*, ed. Wing-tsit Chan. New York: Columbia University Press, 1967.

Zhu Xi 朱熹. 四書章句集注/*Si Shu Zhang Ju Ji Zhu*. 1983; rpt. Beijing: Zhonghua shu ju: Xin hua shu dian Beijing fa xing suo fa xing, 1986.

Zhu Xi, Li Jingde, and Wang Xingxian 朱熹, 黎靖德, and 王星賢. 朱子語類/*Zhuzi Yu Lei*. 1986; rpt. Beijing: Zhonghua shu ju: Xin hua shu dian Beijing fa xing suo fa xing, 1988.

Zhuangzi. *The Complete Works of Chuang Tzu*, trans. Burton Watson. New York: Columbia University Press, 1968.

*Suggested Further Readings*

Chan, Wing-tsit. *Chu Hsi and Neo-Confucianism*. Honolulu: University of Hawai'i Press, 1986.

———. *Chu Hsi: New Studies*. Honolulu: University of Hawai'i Press, 1989.

de Bary, William Theodore. *Neo-Confucian Orthodoxy and the Learning of the Mind-and-Heart*. New York: Columbia University Press, 1981.

———, ed. *Self and Society in Ming Thought*. New York: Columbia University Press, 1970.

de Bary, William Theodore, and American Council of Learned Societies, Committee on Studies of Chinese Civilization. *The Unfolding of Neo-Confucianism*, Studies in Oriental Culture, No. 10. New York: Columbia University Press, 1975.

Elman, Benjamin A. *From Philosophy to Philology*. Cambridge, Mass.: Harvard University Press, 1990.

Gardner, Daniel K. *Chu Hsi and the Ta-Hsueh*. Cambridge, Mass.: Harvard University Press, 1986.

Munro, Donald J. *Images of Human Nature: A Sung Portrait*. Princeton, N.J.: Princeton University Press, 1988.

Tillman, Hoyt Cleveland. *Utilitarian Confucianism: Ch'en Liang's Challenge to Chu Hsi*. Cambridge, Mass.: Council on East Asian Studies, Harvard University, 1982.

———. *Confucian Discourse and Chu Hsi's Ascendancy*. Honolulu: University of Hawai'i Press, 1992.

Wang, Yangming, and Wing-tsit Chan. *Instructions for Practical Living and Other Neo-Confucian Writings*, ed. William Theodore de Bary, Records of Civilization: Sources and Studies. New York: Columbia University Press, 1963.

Wilson, Thomas A. *Genealogy of the Way: The Construction and Uses of the Confucian Tradition in Late Imperial China*. Stanford, Calif.: Stanford University Press, 1995.

# Problematizing Contemporary Confucianism in East Asia

*Yiu-ming Fung*

The Rise of Contemporary Confucianism

In premodern China, Confucianism was not only identified as an ethico-political doctrine that constituted the basic value system of Chinese culture and formed some sort of attitude of life in Chinese people's mind and behavior. As an ideology, it also was the "software" of the social and political system of the empire. It is obvious that Confucianism was one of the major constituents of Chinese culture and was useful in maintaining the Chinese society in a stable state for about two thousand years. Nevertheless, the situation changed when Western culture, accompanied by its military power, challenged Chinese society in the nineteenth century. As described by many scholars of Chinese history, the rise of the May Fourth Movement in 1919 was the major response to the Western challenge and indicated a great change in modern China. Many leading Chinese intellectuals joined the movement and blamed Chinese traditional culture in general, and Confucianism in particular, for making China stagnant and backward in comparison with other nations, including Japan. To save the country, they thought the only route was to search for modernization. One possible way was to transplant new elements of culture, such as science and democracy, from modern Western societies. The leaders of the movement argued that obliterating the old culture of feudal China was necessary for modernization. One of their main targets was "the shop of

Confucius's family," which was more or less identified as premodern Confucianism. So for the intellectuals of the May Fourth Movement, Confucianism was nothing but the hurdle of modernization; antitraditionalism (which meant anti-Confucianism) became a necessity.

Although the traditionalists who wanted to promote the values of Confucianism and to defend its contemporary relevance were a minority without great impact on society after the May Fourth Movement, some leading scholars retained faith in Confucianism and raised a strong voice against the tide of anti-Confucianism. One of the pioneers was Liang Shuming, who was labeled by Guy Alitto as "the Last Confucian."[1] Liang's famous book, *Dongxi wenhua jiqi zhexue* (Eastern and Western Cultures and Their Philosophies),[2] gave Hu Shi and other leaders of the May Fourth Movement a real rebuttal to their thesis of anti-Confucianism. As indicated by Chan Wing-tsit, Liang's book "championed Confucian moral values and aroused the Chinese to a degree seldom seen in the contemporary world"[3] by comparing the traditional Chinese worldview with the Indian view on one hand and the Western on the other. Liang's comparative study of cultures and his reaction to anti-Confucianism provided a solid platform for the traditionalists to develop their discourse. Later, Xiong Shili (Hsiung Shi-li), another scholar teaching at Peking University, wrote a book on Confucian metaphysics and thus attracted some outstanding scholars to follow his line of thinking.[4] Through his book, he formed a new approach to Confucianism on the basis of a critique of Yogācāra Buddhist presuppositions on one hand and a reception of Yogācāra Buddhist methodology on the other. His metaphysical reconstruction of Confucianism was recognized as sophisticated and interesting by the standards of Western philosophy. Xiong's students included Tang Junyi (Tang Chun-i), Mou Zongsan (Mou Tsung-san), and Xu Fuguan (Hsu Fu-kwan); collectively, these men produced many solid and outstanding research works in Chinese and comparative philosophy and subsequently developed a school of Confucian study in Hong Kong and Taiwan after 1949. This school was based on the New Asia College in Hong Kong, which was incorporated into the Chinese University of Hong Kong in 1963. Later it spread its influence to Taiwan and the Chinese mainland and aroused international academia's attention. Over the past thirty years, this school's movement has been recognized not only as a shining cultural phenomenon but also as one of the rare philosophical achievements in contemporary China.

During the late 1970s and early 1980s, some intellectuals and scholars in Hong Kong and Taiwan, influenced by Xiang, Mou, and Tang, worked together to set up a sort of academic group. They organized a series of conferences and activities on Confucianism, especially on the thought of these Confucian scholars, and thus attracted both academic and popular attention. In this environment, people with the commitment to Confucian faith and in alignment with Xiong, Mou, and Tang began to identify their group as a school of "contemporary (Neo-) Confucianism" or "New Confucianism" in comparison with the Neo-Confucianism of the Song-Ming Dynasties. The late 1970s was also the period in which mainland China began to promote its "open-door" policy of reform. Under this new policy, academics were gradually released from ideological thinking and tried to search for some kind of spiritual ideal to replace the past ideology. The increasing academic exchange between mainland China, Hong Kong, Taiwan, and other places aroused many people's interest in the study of Confucianism, and the thought of these contemporary Confucian scholars became a hot topic of research. In 1986, some scholars in mainland China began an extensive historical and philosophic research project, titled "Contemporary Confucianism," as a designated national project for a period of ten years. Meanwhile, to give a response to the challenge from local and Western liberals and to rationalize their idea of authoritarian democracy, some political leaders of Southeast Asian countries began to promote so-called Asian values against Western liberal-democratic civilization. They thought that the idea of modernization was pluralistic and that Western liberal-democratic civilization, in contrast to the Oriental communitarian spirit, was too individualistic and thus not the option for Asian people to choose. Some leaders, officials, and scholars also thought that Confucian values were more suitable for East Asian people to live by and saw confirmation of this in the successes of so-called Asian capitalism. At the same time, some Western scholars were aware of the miracle of economic success in Japan and the four little dragons (i.e., South Korea, Taiwan, Hong Kong, and Singapore) and claimed that these economic phenomena indicated a different model of capitalistic modernization. They thought that Confucianism, in terms of how its value system functioned in daily life, was probably the commensurable factor among these different Asian societies and was the functional equivalent to the Protestant ethic in terms of its role in the rise of capitalism, as claimed by Max Weber.

In the 1990s, the study of contemporary Confucianism was not restricted to the academic figures mentioned; some other philosophers with training in Western philosophy similar to Mou and Tang, such as Feng Youlan (Fung Yulan) and He Lin,[5] also were recognized as representatives of this academic-cultural movement. Qian Mu (Chien Mu), an influential historian and one of the key founders of New Asia College, also was identified as a contemporary Confucian, although his student Yu Ying-shih wrote a long essay to clarify that Qian understood the idea of Confucianism and Chinese culture quite differently than

Mou and Tang. However, in the past twenty years, contemporary Confucianism has been recognized as an important trend of thought in the academic arena of Chinese studies. It arose from Hong Kong and Taiwan, and extended to mainland China, spread to other East Asian societies, including Singapore, Malaysia, Vietnam, South Korea, and Japan. Finally, through the effort of promotion made by Tu Weiming and other scholars in the field of Chinese studies and comparative religions, it was well perceived in Western academia as a significant and interesting project of philosophical and cultural thinking.

The Idea of Three Epochs of Confucianism

Based on Shen Youding's idea of "Three Epochs of Chinese Culture and Philosophy," Mou Zongsan made a similar distinction of "Three Epochs of Confucianism" in the 1960s. Later, Tu Weiming followed his teacher Mou's line of thinking to extend the scope of the second epoch of Confucianism to the whole region of East Asia and the scope of the third epoch of Confucianism to so-called Cultural China, which includes regions not restricted to contemporary East Asia.[6] It seems that by making their distinction, these scholars provide a factual description of the history of Chinese thought; actually, what they provide is only a subjective idealization or philosophical appropriation of the historical fact of Chinese thought. This is because Mou and his followers' distinction is based on selective thinking that enables them to include some people but not others as eligible members in one of the three epochs of Confucianism and exclude some periods of Confucianism as outside the scope of the distinction. In addition to this selective thinking, their distinction also presupposes that there is some kind of spiritual essence or *dao* transmitted from the first to the third epoch via the second. Although I consider this idea of transmission a presupposition, Mou and his followers believe that Mengzi's (371–289 B.C.E.) transmission of Kongzi's (551–479 B.C.E.) spiritual essence has effected some kind of correspondence or union between their minds or moral lives. They think that the representatives of the second epoch of Confucianism, such as Lu Xiangshan (1139–1193 C.E.) and Wang Yangming (1472–1529 C.E.), who are understood by Mou as the true successors of Kongzi and Mengzi, also have this kind of mental or mystic transmission from their "spiritual parents." However, this thinking is not grounded on empirical evidence and cannot be objectively verified. If we do not want to follow Mou and Tu's moral-*cum*-metaphysical perspective but interpret Confucianism in history as a family of resemblance, there are probably more than three epochs to be classified. Here, I am not so much interested in the problem of how many epochs of Confucianism can be classified in China and East Asia. In this chapter, I demonstrate that this view of *daotong* (the orthodox line of transmission of *dao*) on the history of Confucianism and Chinese philosophy, together with its essentialist presupposition, is basically wrong.

In 1958, some of the exiled Confucian scholars in Hong Kong, Taiwan, and the United States, including Tang Junyi, Mou Zongsan, Xu Fuguan, and Zhang Junmai (Carsun Chang), co-contributed a declaration of Chinese culture to call people's attention to the essential distinction between Chinese and Western culture and philosophy and to stress the important contribution of the Chinese spiritual tradition to the modern world, especially to the modernization of China. This is the famous declaration known as "A Manifesto on Chinese Culture to the World" (*Wei Zhongguo wenhua jinggao shijie renshi xuanyan*).[7] One of the main points of the declaration is that Song-Ming Neo-Confucianism (i.e., the defined second epoch of Confucianism), especially the School of Lu (Xiangshan)-Wang (Yangming), is the true successor of the ancient Confucianism (i.e., the defined first epoch of Confucianism) in the sense that the Confucians in the main trend of the second epoch (unlike those in the Han dynasty) can grasp and develop the spiritual essence or dao manifested in the moral lives of Kongzi and Mengzi. The declaration also asserts that the politicized ideology of Confucianism established in the Han dynasty deviated from the spirit of ancient Confucianism because the politicized Confucianism cannot transmit the dao from Kongzi and Mengzi. Mou Zongsan elaborated this idea of spiritual essence in more details in his publications after the 1970s. He thinks that the spiritual essence can be expressed in a slogan, "the unity of *tiandao* (the transcendent *dao* of the Heaven) and *xingming* (the moral order or decree in human nature)," which was first mentioned in the *Doctrine of the Mean* (*Zhongyong*) and later explicated in Lu Xiangshan and Wang Yangming's writings. Tu Weiming makes this point clearly by saying that "all major Neo-Confucian thinkers accept the view that human nature, as the ordaining principle, is endowed by heaven. The *raison d'être* of human nature can thus be understood as the manifestation of the 'heavenly principle' (*tianli*) inherent in our nature." In contrast to Plato's Idea and the Christian God, "the heavenly decree can never become the 'wholly other,' on the contrary, it is immanent in the basic structure of being human: if one can fully realise one's mind, one can understand human nature; by understanding human nature, one knows heaven."[8] I think it is one of the main reasons why the contemporary (New) Confucians of the so-called third epoch, including Tu Weiming and Mou Zongsan, describe the Confucian idea of "ultimate reality" (heavenly principle) as "immanent transcendence" or "inner transcendence"—a notion with the color of mysticism—which is essentially different from the concept of "outer transcendence" in the tradition of

Judeo-Christian thought and Plato's metaphysics. For Mou and other contemporary Confucians, this thesis cannot be grasped by rational thinking and is not subject to logical analysis, because they think that it is not a viewpoint from metaphysical speculation. Just like many metaphysical theses in the history of Western philosophy, it is a *wisdom* or *truth* that can only be grasped by some kind of intellectual intuition, a nonsensible or mystical experience. They believe that this kind of intuition or experience is essentially different from rational thinking, because it can only be obtained by each person's mind through a private access. They claim that after a long period of hard work and serious moral practice, each person can be enlightened with this intuition or experience and thus can entertain the wisdom or truth of the transcendental realm. Tang Junyi borrows Hegel's notion to call this experience "pure consciousness" or "pure subjectivity,"[9] while Mou Zongsan borrows Kant's notion to call it "intellectual intuition" or "intuitive understanding."[10]

Obviously this thesis is similar to that about Zen experience and mystical experience in other religious traditions. This kind of thesis obviously cannot be confirmed or disconfirmed by empirical evidence and cannot be justified by logical thinking as correct or incorrect. Most intellectual historians of Confucian studies, such as Yu Ying-shih and his colleagues, do not accept this viewpoint. They regard this kind of thinking as appealing to the authority of some kind of nonempirical or absolute mind that is defined in a transcendental and mystical sense. They think that to appeal to the prestige status of each person's inner nonsensible experience as a private access to the spiritual essence is tantamount to committing a fallacy, called "the pride of *liangzhi*" (i.e., cosmic mind with innate knowledge of the good). However, Mou Zongsan does not agree with this accusation and thinks that the historian's external approach cannot help in reaching the ultimate reality. He also asserts that the spiritual essence can only be approached by some kind of moral metaphysics that is essentially different from the Western speculative metaphysics; the wisdom or truth of the spiritual essence can only be obtained by some kind of intellectual intuition as described by the moral metaphysics. So, he thinks that this nonrational wisdom or transcendental truth cannot be obtained by a historian's positivistic mind.

I have discussed the possibility and validity of the contemporary Confucians' transcendental viewpoint elsewhere; I do not want to repeat it here.[11] But I discuss the question whether there is a spiritual essence that permeates the so-called three epochs of Confucianism. It seems to me that there must be some elements of Kongzi's teachings shared by the later Confucians, although these may not entail an objectively identified core among the ancient and the later Confucians' thoughts; there may simply be a family resemblance between them. Han dynasty Confucians adopted and developed some aspects of the pre-Confucian and early Confucian religious idea of *tian* (Heaven as God or supernatural power) and *ming* (fate or decree), while Song-Ming Confucians relegated these ideas to the periphery of their conceptual scheme. On the other hand, the Song-Ming Confucians provided a moral metaphysics borrowed and reconstructed from Buddhism and Daoism to interpret the moral teachings of ancient Confucianism; Qing dynasty Confucians saw this as a misunderstanding of the original teachings and as a deviation from Kongzi's tradition. So it is obvious that to claim that there is a spiritual essence implicitly running thorough the three epochs of Confucianism is not a historical fact. It also is obvious that to claim that the referent of the so-called spiritual essence is universally functioning in all the things of the world is not a rational fact. Just as is the case with other traditions, there are no essential "drops" in any parts of the "long river" of Confucianism's history.

Kongzi's major ideas, including *ren* (humanity), *yi* (righteousness), *li* (rite or ritual), and *zhong-shu* (loyalty and reciprocity), find their basic meaning in ethical, social, and political contexts. Some of their uses may be of religious implication and of philosophical interest, but clearly there is no explicit metaphysical issue discussed in Kongzi's *Analects*. Most of Kongzi's teachings are concerning people's conduct and self-cultivation, social norms, and political ideals. Although Kongzi himself was well educated in the religious traditions of the Shang and Zhou dynasties and was not an atheist or agnostic, he seems to put the religious element of the traditional ethico-religious culture aside and stress the autonomy and rationality of human's moral behaviors.[12] As indicated by some Chinese scholars in the field of pre-Qin history, the idea of *di* (the Lord) or *shangdi* (the Lord on High) in the Shang dynasty was used as a symbol for the origin of political power on Earth. It means that the legitimacy of an emperor's political power on Earth is coming from the religious power of the "emperor" of Heaven. Sometimes members of the ruling class of Shang dynasty even identified shangdi as their ancestor-god, who was supposed to have absolute power to protect their posterity and support their political enterprise in the human world. In an effort to diminish the effect of this kind of legitimacy, the founding members of the Zhou dynasty used the terms *tian* and *tian-dao* to replace *di* and *shangdi*, respectively, and cried out that "there is no relative of *tian* on earth; only humans' virtuous performance can evoke Heaven's assistance." They declared that the reason why the Zhou dynasty replaced the Shang dynasty was that the leaders of Zhou were virtuous and loved their people, whereas the leaders of Shang were tyrants and thus were deprived of power by tian. Kongzi still accepted the melody of this virtue-oriented reasoning in justifying political power but minimized the role played by *tian* in terms of supernatural power. In this regard, the emergence of the idea of *ren* in Kongzi's thought indicates that he wanted to minimize the political function from the idea of tian and used the concept of ren as a moral ground to establish and justify his ideal of social and political order. As argued by Xu Fuguan and Mou Zongsan,[13] to appeal to *tian* as a religious ground to legitimize a political power was not workable in the later period of the Zhou dynasty (i.e., the Spring and Autumn period and the Warring States period), because the foundation of the feudalism established in the early Zhou had been broken and people no longer recognized the ethico-religious symbolism of the traditional political culture as a valid tool of legitimization. In comparison to the religious heteronomy of tian's function in political culture, to appeal to moral practice and moral autonomy seems to be a feasible alternative for Kongzi to reconstruct an ideal social and political order. Kongzi's main concern, as reported in some Chinese classics, was to rectify and reconstruct the social and political order of the Zhou dynasty; but his social and political theses were grounded on his ideas of moral psychology, action theory, and virtue ethics. In this sense, we can say that Kongzi was a moral humanist, a real founder of Confucianism.

The Song-Ming Confucians had a different agenda from that of Kongzi and Mengzi, although they claimed that they were the true successors of Kongzi and Mengzi. Of course, we can see that Mengzi is much more interested in metaphysical thinking on human nature in a way that seems distinct from Kongzi's concerns. Furthermore, because of interaction with the School of YinYang and "Huang-Lao" Daoism, the author(s) of *The Commentaries of the Book of Change* (*Yichuan*) developed a kind of morally oriented ontocosmology, while the author(s) of *The Doctrine of the Mean* (*Zhongyong*) established some rough idea of moral metaphysics. Yet Kongzi and Mengzi did not have these ideas. Mainly based on these two later pre-Qin classics, the Song-Ming Confucians borrowed some conceptual tools from Buddhism and Daoism to reconstruct Confucianism by reinterpreting the early pre-Qin texts. In confrontation with the popular Buddhism and religious Daoism in these two dynasties, they attacked Buddhism and Daoism as their enemies to attract elites back to a reconstructed Confucianism. Paradoxically, however, the framework of their reconstructive work was basically borrowed from their enemies, although most contents of their theories are different from and even contrary to that of their enemies. For example, the Cheng (brothers)–Zhu (Xi)'s framework of *li* (reason/principle) and *qi* (material or vital force) is actually an amalgamation of the formal characteristic of Buddhism's *li* and the similar idea of sectarian Daoism's *qi*. It is obvious that the basic ideas of Zhou Dunyi (Chou Tun-yi) (1017–1073), Zhang Zai (Chang Tsai) (1020–1077), and Zhu Xi (Chu Hsi) (1130–1200) (especially his *qi*-cosmology) are mainly borrowed from philosophical and sectarian Daoism, and Zhu Xi's idea of *liyi fenshu* (one principle with many manifestations) is nothing but a framework coming from Huayan Buddhism. Besides, Wang Yangming claimed that all things in the world have *xing* (essential nature of things or *li* as exemplified or embodied into things) and that *xing* is identical with *xin* (heart-mind). So his concept of *xin* refers to a cosmic mind that is exemplified or embodied into all the things in the world, even into those without feeling (i.e., what the Buddhists call "plants, trees, tiles and stones"). In terms of *qi*, including *yin* and *yang* and the "five phases" (*wuxing*), the Song-Ming Confucians cosmologically described the world as an organic cycling whole. In addition, based on the ethical-*cum*-mystical meaning of *li*, they added a moral metaphysical meaning to this organic whole. In a loose sense, we may say that there is a paradigm shift from ancient Confucianism to Song-Ming Confucianism whereby some of the basic concepts of the former are locally incommensurable to those of the latter, even though both concepts are used with the same types of words.

If I am right in the foregoing discussion, the hidden essentialist program of the idea of three epochs of Confucianism cannot be sustained. Undoubtedly, the philological movement in the Qing dynasty and the rise of *kogaku* (ancient learning) in Tokugawa Japan can be understood as reactions to this shift or deviation of the original meaning of Confucianism. On the other hand, the emergence of contemporary Confucianism as a cultural phenomenon is definitely a counterreaction to this philological turn, a response to the challenge coming from the West, and perhaps a possible solution to the crisis of meaning that followed the May Fourth Movement. As an important figure of contemporary Confucianism, Mou Zongsan thought that the revival of Confucianism depended on the Chinese people's "coming back to the *ben* (origin or foundation, i.e., the tradition of the spiritual essence) and opening up the *xin* (new things, i.e., the new elements from the Western culture)." In other words, the future development of the third epoch of Confucianism is due to a dialectical amalgamation of the spiritual essence of Chinese tradition and the modern elements of Western culture. But if the so-called spiritual essence only exists in speculation, how can this "chemical engineering" happen?

## The Problematic of Contemporary Confucianism

Whether in ancient or modern times, in China or elsewhere, Confucianism has been perceived as playing a significant role in providing spiritual rationale for cultural construction or political identity as well as providing moral teachings for all kinds of people. For example, as indicated by many intellectual historians of modern China, the emergence of contemporary Confucianism in Hong Kong, Taiwan, and mainland China was a push against the current of Westernization since the May Fourth Movement of 1919. In facing the challenge from Western culture, some intellectuals and scholars—who still believed that traditional Chinese culture and its values can be transformed into vital core elements of a new culture that are useful for building a strong and independent nation—tried to work on a project of disclosing some kind of elegant cultural elements or spiritual source of the tradition. The rise of contemporary Confucianism in Hong Kong, Taiwan, and mainland China was one of the projects done with this background. Although most of the major figures of contemporary Confucianism were well trained in both Western philosophy and Chinese classics from academic institutes and conducted a great deal of academic research in both Chinese and Western philosophy, philosophical investigation for them was not an end in itself. Instead, their main concern was how to disclose the spiritual source that had been swept away by the antitraditionalists and how to reconstruct Chinese culture such that it might be used to overcome the crisis of meaning and the crisis of culture in facing the challenge from the West.

Thus, the main problematic of contemporary Confucianism is how to meet the challenge of the West and how to revive and reconstruct the Chinese culture. In the 1930s, Mou Zongsan's teacher, Xiong Shili, reconstructed the old thesis of *neisheng waiwang* (inner sageliness and outer kingliness) from *The Great Learning* (*Daxue*) by using some constituents of the Buddhist framework. The former was redescribed by him as a goal of moral transformation based on some kind of spiritual ground in terms of ontocosmology, while the latter was presented as a result of the intellectual function (*yong*) of this spiritual ground (*ti*). The spiritual ground can be understood as both a moral mind and a transcendental reality; the function includes science, democracy, and other cultural achievements, that is, the new things from the West, as the result of the moral mind's social practice or as the transcendental reality's realization in the phenomenal world through human activities. In the period of ancient Confucianism, a moral decree or order was thought to be causally related to *tian*'s power, in terms of either natural endowment or divine request.[14] In Song-Ming Neo-Confucianism, this was recognized as mystically related to some kind of metaphysical ground. Although some scholars in the field of intellectual history argue that the term *tian* is mainly used by Kongzi and Mengzi as referring to a supernatural power, some scholars in the field of Confucian philosophy follow the line of Song-Ming Neo-Confucians' thinking to interpret Mengzi's idea of original mind and human nature not as natural endowment from *tian* in its literal sense but as metaphysical manifestation from the ultimate transcendental reality. For example, one Confucian philosopher claims, "Mencius never meant that people do not actually do evils in real life. He only made the assertion that everyone of us has endowment from the Heaven, that is why the original human nature is good, and its great potentiality can be actualized by fully developing the Beginnings present in the original mind. As there is correlation between the microcosm and macrocosm, or immanence and transcendence, there is no need to look for a supreme supernatural power or a transcendent personal God like Christianity."[15] It is obvious that this viewpoint combines the idea of *tianren heyi* (the unity of Heaven and man) with the idea of "inner sageliness and outer kingliness." In other words, the latter is recognized as aiming at building an ideal of social and political order that is grounded on the moral perfection of individual, and the former is understood as a channel of justification that the moral perfection of individual is metaphysically manifested from the transcendental-cum-creative reality. Here they seem to give the ancient Confucianism a new interpretation that is able to link social and political practice to self-cultivation and provide an ontological ascent for self-cultivation.

In regard to the contemporary Confucians' idea of inner sageliness, because they make a claim for disclosing the spiritual essence via true transmission from the past, it seems that there is basically no difference between their idea and those mentioned by the Song-Ming Confucians (although both ideas are different from the original idea in *The Great Learning*). But their idea of outer kingliness is obviously distinct from the Song-Ming Confucians', because the new idea includes science, democracy, and economic success as targets of achievement. So we may call this new function the "new outer kingliness." To explain this new function, Mou Zongsan uses Hegel's idea of self-negation to describe the relation of the transcendental (nonempirical) mind and the cognitive (empirical) mind. He thinks that the transcendental mind, which is identical with the ultimate reality, is the ground of morality, that is, the practical use of reason, but it cannot directly open up the realm of knowledge, including science and democracy, which is based on the theoretical use of reason. To open the realm of knowledge, the transcendental mind has to enter into a state of self-negation. Besides, this dialectical thinking also includes an element coming from the school of "consciousness only" in Buddhism, that is, "one mind with two gates": noumenal and phenomenal. It is clear that Mou does not accept Xiong Shili's idea of *tiyong* in terms of a "go-through" model and proposes a dialectic model as replacement. Still, Mou agrees with Xiong that *ti* is an essential condition or foundation of *yong*.

In other words, without moral transformation and recovering people's transcendental mind, there would be no development of science and democracy in China.

Mou seems to use a Hegelian model of thinking to treat social practice and cultural realization as an objectification of spiritual reality. But this picture from metaphysical speculation is not a map of the actual world; it cannot lead people to modernization. Of course, to claim for recovering and disclosing the lost spiritual tradition may be helpful for building Chinese people's cultural identity; but to claim for recovering and disclosing is not identical with real recovering and disclosing and thus does not really lead to the metaphysical goal of moral transformation. Furthermore, if, for the sake of argument, we accept that the inner sageliness is really the essential condition or foundation of the new outer kingliness, there is still a problem that the contemporary Confucians cannot answer: how can they explain the achievements of science and democracy in the Western world if the Westerners have not yet achieved the goal of the inner sageliness as indicated by the contemporary Confucians? Mou and Xiong did not answer this question. I do not think they ever can do so.

The contemporary Confucians' idea of "coming back to the origin and opening up new things" means that if Chinese people want to develop the new culture that signifies the achievements of the Western civilization, they must search for the spiritual power from the original mind—the ground of Chinese culture. In other words, they believe that Chinese people cannot develop the new culture in terms of scientific achievement, political construction, and economic success just by means of implantation from the West; they can only nurture the Western flowers in the Chinese earth. This kind of belief is not theoretically warranted, but it may be practically significant. Psychologically speaking, emphasizing the Chinese spiritual origin as the ground of cultural development may be a good rationale and driving force for people to make effort in modernization; but this cannot justify in theory any logical or causal relation between the spiritual ground and the cultural construction. This is basically a variant of Zhang Zhidong's (1837–1909) idea of "Chinese learning as ground and Western learning as function" (*zhongxue weiti xixue weiyong*). Even though some scholars do not agree with contemporary Confucianism, because they stress the positive role of Confucian values in the emergence of the economic success in modern East Asia (much like the active function of Protestant ethic in the rise of the Western capitalism), they still more or less have this kind of schematic thinking—*ti* and *yong*—and may have the same kind of Hegelian idea of objectification. These scholars do not agree with Weber's comparative view that the non-Western cultures do not have the equivalent of the Protestant ethic functioning in the rise of capitalism; but they accept the Weberian thesis that mental entities, such as religious ideas or moral values, have modal power in activating or promoting economic events. These scholars and contemporary Confucians actually commit the same fallacy, that is, a false idea of efficacy from ideas to events. Hence, the project of contemporary Confucianism fails and the discourse of Confucian capitalism also is of little avail. (I talk about this issue in detail in the section "The Weberian Thesis and the Asian View of Values.")

## Approaches to Confucianism and Confucian Studies

For contemporary Confucians as well as the Song-Ming Neo-Confucians, Confucianism is more than Confucian studies.[16] They believe that the ultimate Confucian teaching is to search for some kind of inner wisdom and transcendental truth that cannot be understood by objective and logical methods. They stress that there is an essential difference between Chinese philosophy and Western philosophy in the sense that both are incommensurable to each other. They also emphasize that to understand this wisdom and truth is to enter into a transcendental realm that can only be accessed by some kind of intellectual intuition or mystical experience after doing long-term hard and serious work on moral practice and mental transformation. In this sense, one can say that they mystify Confucianism and Chinese philosophy and give the Western philosophers the impression that Confucianism and Chinese philosophy cannot be understood as philosophy because they are basically not recognized with rational thinking.

It seems to me that in comparison to contemporary Confucians' "pride of *liangzhi*," intellectual historians and Sinologists (including those active in Confucian studies), such as Hu Shi and his followers, do have some kind of "prejudice of historical mind." Hu Shi was the godfather of the liberal wing of the May Fourth New Cultural Movement in modern China. He radically criticized the old Chinese culture and passionately embraced Western scientific civilization. Although he was enamored with science, he did not recognize that his idea of science was much more radical and romantic than its Western counterpart. In the late nineteenth and early twentieth centuries, most Western thinkers still recognized a demarcation in methodology between humanities and science, although some of them may have had a very positivist attitude in treating humanities. Nevertheless, Hu Shi adopted a pan-scientific approach to humanities that drifted far away from Westerners' normal target of scientific approach. Because Hu Shi was the "leader of leaders" in terms of administrative power and academic authority, his historical-*cum*-philological approach to humanities, with a very strong positivist mentality, was dominant in Chinese communities for more than half a century and has had a significant influence on Sinological studies in the West. This bias or prejudice not only prevented Hu Shi from writing the second volume of his book on the history of Chinese philosophy after publishing his unsuccessful first volume,[17] it also pushed him into a dead end of "dephilosophizing." Based on this bias or prejudice, unfortunately, Hu Shi and his followers built a powerful thread of Chinese studies that seems by definition to reject any other kinds of approach, especially the philosophical one. Although they claimed that their approach is intellectually oriented, based on objective evidence and equipped with scientific methods, they rarely acknowledged that evidences are theory-laden and philosophical analysis cannot be replaced by sociohistorical explanation. They thought that a solid study of Chinese thought should not be an intellectual play of nonempirical problems or transcendental issues, and all problems or issues should be investigated on empirical ground. In other words, for Hu Shi and his disciples, the only significant research is to define and elaborate a problem in a historical context and then investigate its sociopolitical meaning. If this were correct, all nonhistorical and nonphilological studies of Chinese thought, especially for those of metaphysical import, would be insignificant, and for the same reason, all researches in the Western metaphysics, such as Plato's metaphysics and Kant's transcendental philosophy, would also be nonsensical. I think this bias or prejudice arises from Hu Shi and his followers ignoring the distinction between the problem of how a thought is generated and functions in a historical context and the problem of how a thought is justified and understood in a philosophical theory. It may be one of the reasons why Lao Siguang (Lao Szekwang) criticizes Hu Shi's book on the history of Chinese philosophy by saying that "it is a historical and philological study without philosophy."[18] His studies of *Gongsun Longzi* and the *Mohist Canons* also indicate that he made a great effort in dealing with philological problems but could not enter into the area of logic and the philosophy of language, the problems of which clearly constitute the "main course of the dinner." His ignorance brought disaster on the academic study of Chinese philosophy in general and Confucianism in particular in the sense that it resulted in a study of Chinese thought without philosophy. Though contemporary Confucians mystify philosophy on one hand, the historical Sinologists, like Hu Shi and his followers, nullify philosophy on the other hand. They are two extremes of doing the same thing, and both contribute to the same result: they give Western philosophers the impression that Confucianism and Chinese thought cannot be understood as philosophy.

In between these two extremes, there is an approach to Chinese philosophy and Confucianism that can be fully understood by Western philosophers as a philosophical approach. That is Feng Youlan's approach. Feng identified his approach as "logical analysis," and almost all Chinese and Western scholars agree with this identification. It is obvious that Feng's book on the history of Chinese philosophy is similar in methodology to the writings in the field of the history of idea in the West, because, in addition to historical explanation, he used conceptual and logical analyses to deal with philosophical problems.[19] However, his analysis of Song-Ming Confucianism and his construction of a new system of Confucianism (*A New Learning of Principle* or *Xin Lixue*) in other books seem to use the method of logical analysis, but actually they do not. For example, he asserts that the purpose of building his new metaphysics of Confucianism is to give a logical analysis of human experience. He thinks that, for example, there is a logical implication from the premise that "there is a mountain" to the conclusion that "there is such (other) thing by which a mountain is a mountain" or from "there is a square thing" to "there is such (other) thing by which a square is a square." In general, there also is a logical implication from the premise that "there is a thing" to the conclusion that "there is such (other) thing that makes this thing to be this thing." Based on this seemingly logical relation, he asserts that this "such" is a *li* (reason/principle) that can be understood as the metaphysical ground by which something is something. In other words, the existence of a mountain verified by our experience presupposes the existence of the *li* of the mountain; without the latter, the former cannot exist.[20] Almost all the scholars in China agree with this seemingly logical analysis, and they believe this is a successful case of applying the Western logical method to Confucianism and Chinese philosophy. Nevertheless, the presupposition asserted by Feng is not welcome to any nonrealists who do not accept that the existence of a phenomenal thing is metaphysically grounded on some kind of transcendental object. I think what Feng has done is not a logical analysis but one based on some kind of transcendental argument. In this regard, we can conclude that Feng's approach is not logical but metaphysical.

Hu Shi and his followers complain that contemporary Confucians' approach is mystical and nonempirical. But contemporary Confucians reply that the Confucian enlightenment is not rationally recognizable and that the inner wisdom or transcendental truth can only be obtained from a nonsensible intuition or transcendental experience through long-term hard and serious work on moral practice and mental transformation. Nevertheless, they think that the theoretical analysis as a skillful strategy of preliminary understanding for the entrance to the transcendental realm is helpful. As a matter of fact, although the contemporary Confucians often claim that their ultimate concern is not rationally analyzable, more than 90 percent of their writing is theoretical in nature. Although sometimes they talk about nonsensible intuition and transcendental experience, they have to use the Western metaphysical concepts to explicate and analyze the "unanalyzable." For example, the method of "transcendental reflection" mentioned by Tang Junyi for explaining the concept of absolute consciousness or pure consciousness is basically similar to Descartes's or Kant's "transcendental deduction." Although Mou Zongsan stresses that *liangzhi* is not something hypothetical, as claimed by Feng Youlan, but a "self-presenting" entity, he cannot but demonstrate the self-presenting entity by some kind of "transcendental deduction" similar to what he talks about the Kantian idea of practical necessity. As I have argued elsewhere, his ideas of "transcendental embodiment-justification" (*chaoyue tizheng*) and "inner embodiment-justification" (*neizai tizheng*) cannot be understood as justification by any intuition but only as transcendental deduction.[21] Mou and Tang's appeal to nonsensible intuition or transcendental experience is not different from other religious traditions' appeal to the private experience of the first-person authority, and their theory-constructions are mainly based on "transcendental argument," so I can conclude that their approach to Confucianism is still in the category of metaphysical speculation in the Western sense. If I am right at this point, I can also conclude that although Feng Youlan claims that his approach is logical and conceptual and Mou and Tang stress that their approach is nonanalytic and intuitionistic, actually they are both speculative philosophers and both of their metaphysical theories fail in understanding ancient Confucianism.

In comparison to the internal approach of transcendentalism (i.e., to arrive the transcendental realm from within) of Song-Ming and contemporary Confucians in China, the approach of Japanese Confucians is more or less external and characteristically antitranscendental. The main study of Japanese Confucianism since Itō Jinsai (1627–1705) and Ogyū Sorai (1666–1728) was developed as an "ancient learning" of the original thought of Kongzi—the "true message of the sage." They thought that Song-Ming Confucianism was mixed with Buddhist idealistic thought and thus deviated from Kongzi's practical teaching. They wanted to deconstruct the Song-Ming Confucians' interpretation, especially Zhu Xi's transcendental interpretation on one hand, and return to the original and authentic teaching of Kongzi on the other hand. For example, Ogyū Sorai thinks that the Song-Ming Neo-Confucians' assumption that one might, through the workings of the human intellect, arrive at an interpretation or explication of the original message of the sages was nothing less than arrogance and betrayed a serious lack of reverence for the classical texts. He stresses that "the ceremonial forms were 'external' and complex, existing outside the self and requiring years of disciplined study and cultivation" and that, "the ceremonial forms did not originate within the individual or within the mind, as the Ch'eng-Chu (i.e., Cheng-Zhu) scholars suggested, but rather had been created by the sages and early kings at heaven's request and were preserved in the classical texts."[22] Itō Jinsai disagrees with Zhu Xi's dualism of transcendental *dao* and material (or vital) force (*qi*) by pointing out that "that which enables yin and yang is the Way [*dao*]" and "*yin* and *yang* are material force."[23] Itō Jinsai and Ogyū Sorai both refuse this transcendentalism and its related dualism.

In general, for the Chinese Neo-Confucians, their values transmitted from ancient Confucianism are constituted as an internal (and transcendental) driving force that can guide external behaviors on a right track; whereas for the Japanese Confucians, the values learned from the teachings of the early kings and Kongzi are nothing but some kind of appropriate arrangements of behaviors in a good order. However, the practical characteristics and antitranscendental orientation of Japanese Confucianism are not merely the outcome of objective study; they are basically grounded in and suggested by Japanese local culture. In comparison to the Chinese Neo-Confucians,

> Japanese Confucianists, on the other hand, rejected *en masse* Zhu Xi's leading idea that the ultimate reality is something abstract, immaterial, eternal, and unchanging, existing apart from material *qi* and individual things. If there is anything that is peculiarly Japanese in Japanese Confucianism, or indeed in Japanese philosophy in general, it is surely this preference for what is immediate, immanent, sensuous, changing, material, and naturalistic, along with the correlative suspicion and lack of sympathy for anything exclusively intellectual, transcendental, abstract, immaterial, unchanging, ethereal, and so on. Indeed, throughout their history whenever Japanese have embraced foreign culture, they have taken and interpreted only those parts that were compatible with this preference: despite many extensive borrowings from other culture. They have rarely if ever abandoned any of their own culture. They have simply used the new, foreign culture to buttress and more rationally justify their own uniquely Japanese ways.[24]

Two points should be mentioned here for clarification. The first is that Chinese culture was always adjusted to Japanese sensibilities and needs; Neo-Confucianism is no exception. This implies that some Japanese viewpoints may be based on the misunderstanding of the Chinese texts. The second point is that the idea of Tokugawa Confucians' antitranscendentalism is in accordance with their "ancient learning," and the ancient learning in some aspect is objective studies. This means that some Japanese viewpoints may be well grounded on the Chinese texts. So I think there is an inner tension between their cultural reinterpretation and their objective interpretation as regard to Confucianism. For example, Ogyū Sorai's view on Kongzi's general teaching is right in regard to his nonmetaphysical interpretation. But his understanding of Kongzi's idea of the "*dao* of early kings" is inaccurate, because some of the relevant concepts of moral psychology cannot be explained only by the concepts of external behaviors. However, the external approach is consistent with the mainstream of Japanese culture. This is a characteristic of Tokugawa era and later Confucianism in Japan.

Just like the Song-Ming Confucians, most of the representatives of the first generation of contemporary Confucianism used the Buddhist conceptual scheme to construct their theory. However, because the main figures of the second generation were well trained in Western philosophy, they often borrowed ideas from the Western idealists, such as Kant and Hegel, to reconstruct the ancient teaching. For example, Feng Youlan's *New Learning of Principle* cannot be constructed without the notion of Platonic Idea, and Mou Zongsan's moral metaphysics of Confucianism cannot be elaborated without the Kantian distinction between appearance and thing-in-itself. In contrast to this philosophical or metaphysical approach, the approach of Japanese Confucianism since Itō Jinsai and Ogyū Sorai was basically philological and historical. Nevertheless, their studies mainly are contextually relevant not to the Chinese cultural background but to the Japanese social-political situation.

Today, scholars of Confucianism who do not self-identify as Confucians in the manner of scholars just mentioned, usually treat Confucianism as an objective study. The major trend of Confucian studies both in China and North America is intellectual historical studies; the minor trend is comparative religious and philosophical studies. The approach provided by the former is not philosophical, although the scholars of this trend have made contributions to understanding Confucianism in a historical perspective. For example, Theodore de Bary, Benjamin Schwartz, Chang Hao, and Yu Ying-shih are some of the outstanding scholars of this approach. It is well known that in 1964, de Bary together with Chan Wing-tsit began to establish the University Seminar at Columbia University on Neo-Confucianism and subsequently organized a great project of research and publication in this field.[25] He and his colleagues put Confucianism into a global context and gave Western readers a systematic understanding of the Confucian core of the premodern Chinese civilization. Their sympathetic interpretation of Confucianism seems to help them disclose its modern relevance and its vital force, which is ignored by many scholars, such as Joseph Levenson and Hu Shi. It seems that de Bary has placed more emphasis on the humanistic aspect of Confucianism, whereas Schwartz stressed its religious dimension. Schwartz appealed to Karl Jaspers's idea of axial age to elaborate Kongzi's thinking as a "transcendental" breakthrough in ancient China, whereas de Bary explored a prophetic dimension to the Confucian tradition in comparison with the biblical prophecy in Western tradition. In dealing with the problem of Chinese intellectuals' reaction to the Western challenge in modern China, Chang Hao has done a good job in elaborating a clear historical picture of the meaning crisis in this period. On the other hand, Yu Ying-shih returned to premodern China and located some major figures of Confucianism in a relevant social and political context to discover their true message. His big project on Zhu Xi's thought seems to provide a paradigmatic case study for all intellectual historians in Chinese studies, particularly in Confucian studies.

The approach provided by the latter is comparative and seems to be well perceived by recent scholars in the field of Confucianism. Some of the representatives of this approach, such as David Hall and Roger Ames,[26] have developed an interpretation of Confucianism that is claimed to reflect some characteristics of Chinese philosophy—some elements of "Chinese-ness"—in ancient China. They think that ancient Confucians see the world as an organic whole with an aesthetic sense, such that there are neither transcendental commitments nor dualistic ideas in Kongzi's thought. They believe that the mode of thinking in ancient China is processual rather than analytic. It seems that ancient Confucian thought under their interpretation coincides with postmodern antilogocentrism, anti-Descartes's dualism and antirepresentationalism, and new pragmatism as stated by Richard Rorty. Nevertheless, what they provide seems to be an overinterpretation and a thesis out of the texts. In comparison with Hall and Ames's perspective from comparative philosophy, the perspective of the so-called Boston Confucians, such as Robert Neville and John Berthrong, is from comparative religions. Although they are different from each other, both are interested in using the conceptual apparatus from Whitehead's process ontology and from pragmatism to interpret Confucian texts and to explain the problems of Confucianism. These two projects are not successful; at least, they are not recognized by most Sinologists as accurate understandings of Confucianism. If the contemporary Confucians' approach can be called "mystify Chinese (and Confucian) philosophy" and the philologists and historians like Hu Shi's approach can be called "nullify Chinese (and Confucian) philosophy," then this comparative approach can be labeled as "miscodify Chinese (and Confucian) philosophy."

Although some comparative philosophical studies have been produced recently, most of them are not related to the main current of the Anglo-American philosophy, that is, analytic philosophy.[27] One of the few exceptions is Herbert Fingarette's study of Kongzi.[28] His approach is mainly based on John Austin's theory of speech acts and Gibert Ryle's logical behaviorism. It seems to me that his interpretation of Kongzi's teaching is a glorious failure. It fails because some of the mental concepts in the *Analects* and in the texts before and after Kongzi cannot be explained away by dispositional terms as he claims. Because the commonsense distinction of inner-outer of mental contents embedded in ancient and modern Chinese is not identical with Descartes's dualism, to accuse a mental interpretation of Kongzi's language as misapplying Descartes's dualism to Kongzi's teaching is a straw-man attack. Furthermore, the logical behaviorism as a theory of mind is notoriously unworkable to explain our psychological language; it is quite strange that Kongzi could unconsciously use dispositional terms to replace mental concepts and Mengzi could consciously use mental concepts in Descartes's sense if, for the sake of argument, we accept Fingarette's interpretation.

On the other hand, why do I say Fingarette's failure is glorious? It is because his study is a good try in terms of providing another option to interpret Kongzi's teaching that is free from the cage of metaphysical psychology and opens up a new avenue of comparative study of Chinese and Western ethics and action theories. Besides, I think A. S. Cua and Kwong-loi Shun's studies of Confucianism are two successful cases of using analytic methods to deal with the problems of ethics and moral psychology in Confucianism and Chinese philosophy.[29] As of the time of this writing, these outstanding scholars seem to have increasing influence in the field, not only in North America but also in the Chinese academic communities. Recently, Bo Mou of the United States, Kim-chong Chong of Singapore, and Yiu-ming Fung of Hong Kong have undertaken comparative studies of Confucianism, not only at the level of philosophical theory but also at the level of meta-philosophy.[30] These works may help in changing the prejudice of incommensurability between Chinese and Western philosophy and may take the first step toward building a common discourse between Chinese and Western philosophy, especially in regard to Confucianism.

The Weberian Thesis and the Asian View of Values

Besides disclosing the internal transcendental realm, contemporary Confucians have to deal with the problem in the outside world. The former is what they call by inner sageliness, and the latter is outer kingliness. In other words, in addition to cultivating oneself into an ideal person with the moral experience in the ultimate and transcendental realm, one has to open up a channel from internal to external through which the ideal can be materialized in social practice. Contemporary Confucians think that their ideal functions not only to sustain individual well-being in terms of morality but also to provide good moral order for society.

In regard to the problem of social practice, contemporary Confucians take up the discourse of the new Weberian thesis addressed by sociologists such as Peter Berger and Ambrose King.[31] According to these sociologists' view, Max Weber is wrong in saying that there is no functional equivalent to the Protestant ethic in the non-Western world that can give rise to modern capitalism. They think that the successful economic phenomena that occurred in Japan and the four little dragons (including South Korea, Taiwan, Hong Kong, and Singapore) after World War II are considered as counterexamples of Weber's viewpoint. However, on the other hand, they think that Weber is right in saying that religious (and moral) values are relevant to the rise of modern economic growth. They claim that institutional factors are not crucial to explaining these East Asian phenomena; Confucian values (as described by Berger as "vulgar Confucianism" or by King as "instrumental Confucianism") are common to all these communities and can be considered cultural factors to explain the phenomena with good statistic evidence. To extend this new Weberian thesis, some scholars claim that the Confucian values can be a positive constituent of modernization. They assert that these values play a significant role not only in economic growth but also in social and political construction. In this regard, the so-called Asian view of values has been proclaimed by some scholars and political leaders (for example, the former prime ministers of Singapore and Malaysia) as distinct from and an alternative to the Western counterpart in the sense that Asia can develop a unique modernization in a good shape. This suggests what Tu Weiming and others call the thesis of "multiple modernities."[32]

Let us put aside the problem of whether the proponents of this kind of new Weberian thesis confuse Weber's idea of the rise of capitalism with that of the transmission of capitalism; it is obvious that they do not take their thesis seriously in terms of methodology. The contemporary Confucians, such as Mou Zongsan and his followers, claim that when people achieve the goal of inner sageliness, there will be a driving force in them to open up the result of new outer kingliness. The sociologists of this kind of new Weberian thesis claim that the cultural or ethical factor is much more significant than the institutional factor in explaining the modernized economic achievements in contemporary East Asia. Nevertheless, neither of them provides a persuasive explanation for the relation between mental contents in terms of Confucian values and ideas, on one hand, and behavioral events in terms of modern economic achievements on the other hand. Here, the methodological problem is how to explain the relation between mental factor and physical result. The idea of dialectical transformation from moral mind to social practice is only a philosophical speculation of the contemporary Confucians; they cannot explain how it is possible to have this kind of mystic transformation. The sociologists' functional explanation is also unhelpful because it freezes up too many variables to adapt to the assumed factor for explanation.[33] Weber knows that "functional explanation," "teleological explanation," and "intentional explanation" are either dangerous or trivial; he also knows that we cannot directly apply the concept of physical causality to humanities because we cannot maintain the same kind of physical regularity in the areas beyond physical sciences. So he designs a non-Humean concept of causality for applying to humanities. Hume's idea is that if a previous physical event $c$ causes a consequent physical event $e$, then a similar $c$ event would cause a similar $e$ event. It is clear that this causal law cannot be used in the realm in terms of mental concepts. Weber's new concept of causality is not of Hume's kind that requires its modal power in terms of regularity; his concept's modal power is based on some kind of counterfactual conditional. In this regard, his comparative studies of the non-Western cultures provide "imaginary experiments" as counterfactual condition to justify why they cannot have the Western modernity, including the rise of capitalism. This counterfactual condition makes the explained relation "causally adequate." In addition, if the relation can be rationally explained in a motivational pattern, it also is "adequate on the level of meaning." It seems that he combines the counterfactual model of causality with the motivational rationalization into a new concept that can be used in humanities. However, if, for argument's sake, we accept his new concept, it still cannot be applied to the relation between Protestant ethic and capitalism. This is because the relaters of explanation under this new concept should be individual events; but both of them are ideal types or theoretical constructs of social reality. Both of them are high-level concept-construction from examples that are selected and interpreted by a theorist as ideal cases. In other words, these ideal cases are general ideas that are generalized and constructed from individual events. So it is not clear in what sense these abstract entities can be causally related. Weber sometime uses the concept "elective affinity" to describe the relation. But elective affinity is definitely not a concept with causal efficacy or modal power, and this idea can also be accused of epiphenomenalism.

Werner Sombart does not agree with Weber. He provides a different ideal type for capitalism and considers the Protestant ethic as epiphenomenal to human interest and its behavioral performance as supervenient (or dependent) on economic behavior. Although Sombart also gives an idealistic explanation to the rise of capitalism, he stresses human interest more than Protestant ethic. He thinks that the capitalist spirit was a combination of a spirit of enterprise, which was associated with acquisitiveness and competition, and a bourgeois spirit, which was epitomized by methods of exact rational calculation, careful business planning, and efficiency.[34] For Sombart, it is not people with the Protestant ethic but Jews who embodied all the traits valued most highly by the market—egoism, self-interest, and abstract thinking.

If this methodological problem cannot be solved, how can Weber's thesis or the Weberian thesis that held by the theorists we mentioned survive?[35] As regard to the phenomena of modern economic achievements in contemporary East Asia, there may be some aspect related to Confucian ethic or values; this relation at most can be a rationalization. It is because there is no nomological relation between the Confucian ethic and the economic performance of East Asia. Rationalization is of course helpful in terms of reinforcement. But reinforcement is basically a justifying power, not a causal power. Just like the case that even though one has a right method to justify why he or she can swim so fast as to get the gold medal at the Olympic Games, it may be the behavioral pattern embedded with interest of making money and being famous to cause him or her to swim so fast. Confucianism is just like any other moral or religious doctrines that can be used to rationalize or justify the social reality in one way or the other. Today, I think, Confucian teaching is still alive in the sense that it can make some people feel that their life is reasonable or meaningful.

## The Prospect of Confucian Studies

As a philosopher with training in both Western analytic philosophy and Sinology, I confess that I do not recognize any philosophical views and theories either in the history of Western philosophy or in the history of Chinese philosophy as absolutely right. It seems that some arguments for some of these views and theories are not convincing but other arguments for the others seem persuasive. However, most of the problems related to these views and theories are significant in terms of their generative power of deepening and extending humans' rational thinking. In other words, most of the views and theories are unable to solve problems in a conclusive sense but are able to raise problems in an enlightening way. This is one of the reasons why philosophy in general, and Confucianism in particular, is interesting. Eventually, we may not have as much objective knowledge in philosophy as is found in science. Nevertheless, we can always have significant problems for philosophizing that are suggestive for enriching our rational thinking in dealing with the outside world and our inside world.

Based on this idea of philosophizing, I have made a critical remark on the scholarships of ancient and contemporary Confucianism in the previous sections. I hope readers do not misunderstand me as failing to recognize the academic and cultural contributions of the Confucian scholars. Of course, I consider them the main figures in the field of Confucianism, and they have made important contributions in the sense that their problems and ways of solving problems are stimulating for further step of thinking—that is, philosophizing.

In regard to the future of Confucian studies, I think there are at least two routes for us to go. The first is about the comparative philosophical studies between Confucian and Western ethics, including the comparison of similarity and difference of problems in moral psychology, action theory and practical ethics, and similarities and differences of the ways to solve problems in these areas. The second route is about the comparative religious studies between Confucian and Western religious traditions, including the comparison of similarity and difference on problems such as those in ultimate concern, transcendence and immanence, secularization and the function of culture forming, and similarities and differences of the ways to solve problems in these topics. Of course, the project of how to interpret the Confucian classics is an ongoing job for every generation. The people of each generation cannot free themselves from using their own language to form the old problems and are able to discover some potential insight and wisdom from the open and universal part of the content in the Confucian classics.[36] Living in a pluralistic and globalized world, I believe it is suggestive (if not necessary) for people to open an arena of comparative studies between East and West for learning from each other. If we do not want to live in the world defined by Samuel Huntington's clash of civilizations, we should make the effort to understand other cultures, including Confucianism.

NOTES

1. Guy Alitto, *The Last Confucian: Liang Shu-ming and the Chinese Dilemma of Modernity* (Berkeley: University of California Press, 1979).

2. Liang Shuming, *Dongxi wenhua jiqi zhexue* [Eastern and Western Cultures and Their Philosophies] (Shanghai: Commercial Press, 1921).

3. Chan Wing-tsit, ed., *A Source Book in Chinese Philosophy* (Princeton, N.J.: Princeton University Press, 1969), p. 743.

4. Xiong Shili, *Hsin weishih lun* [New Exposition of the Consciousness-Only Doctrine] (Beijing: Peking University Press, 1933).

5. Because Mou applied the conceptual scheme of German idealism and followed the line of thinking in Wang Yangming's philosophy of *xin* (heart-mind), on one hand, and Feng applied the conceptual scheme of new realism and followed the line of thinking in Zhu Xi's philosophy of *li* (reason/principle), on the other, quite a few scholars in Taiwan and China mainland thus recognized their philosophy as "New *Xin* School" and "New *Li* School," respectively.

6. Tu Weiming, "Confucianism," in Arvind Sharma, ed., *Our Religions* (New York: Harper-Collins, 1993), pp. 141–60.

7. Mou Zongsan, Tang Junyi, Xu Fuguan, and Zhang Junmai, "Wei Zhongguo wenhua jinggao shijie renshi xuanyan" [A Manifest on Chinese Culture to the World], *Minzhu pinglun* [Democracy Review] 9, no. 1 (1958) and *Zaisheng* [Revitalization] 1, no. 1 (1958).

8. Tu Weiming, *Way, Learning, and Politics—Essays on the Confucian Intellectual* (Singapore: Institute of East Asian Philosophies, 1983), pp. 105–106.

9. Tang Junyi, "Liu Tsung-chou's Doctrine of Moral Mind and Practice and His Critique of Wang Yang-ming," in William Theodore de Bary et al. eds., *The Unfolding of Neo-Confucianism* (New York: Columbia University Press, 1975), p. 315.

10. Mou Zongsan, *Zhidizhijue yu zhongguo zhexue* [Intellectual Intuition and Chinese Philosophy] (Taipei: Taiwan Commercial Press, 1971).

11. Yiu-ming Fung, "Three Dogmas of New Confucianism: A Perspective of Analytic Philosophy," in Bo Mou, ed., *Two Roads to Wisdom? Chinese and Analytic Philosophical Traditions* (Chicago: Open Court, 2001), pp. 245–66.

12. In regard to the question of whether Confucianism in general and ancient Confucianism in particular is a religion, I think it depends on how we define the term *religion*. If we define it as referring to a doctrine of external deity, it is clear that this kind of religious element does not play a crucial role in Kongzi's or Mengzi's thought. If we use it to designate a doctrine concerning human's ultimate concern or a doctrine with some kind of transcendent reference, it is obvious that all Confucians in Chinese history do have this sort of religious dimension in their thinking.

13. Xu Fuguan, *Zhongguo renxing lunshi* [A History of Chinese Theories of Human Nature], a volume of the pre-Qin period (Taipei: Taiwan Commercial Press, 1975), chap. 2; Mou Zongsan, *Zhongguo zhexue di tezhi* [The Essential of Chinese Philosophy] (Taipei: Lantai Book, 1973), chaps. 3 and 6.

14. Although for Kongzi and Mengzi, a moral decree or order is thought as causally related to Heaven's power, when the moral decree or order is accepted by people, it can only be decided by people's self as obligatory and justified as rational.

15. Shu-hsien Liu, "An Integral Understanding of Knowledge and Value: A Confucian Perspective," *Journal of Chinese Philosophy* 30, no. 3–4 (September–December 2003): 391.

16. The difference between Confucians and Confucian scholars is not clear-cut. Basically, most Confucians in the past and present are eager to publish their views on the major problems of Confucianism and provide their interpretations of the Confucian

classics. In this sense, they are also Confucian scholars. But today, most Confucian scholars are equipped with the training from modern universities of the Western style; they may not have the same kind of spiritual commitment or faith as the Song-Ming Confucians or the contemporary Confucians had. In other words, they are eager to understand Confucian teachings in terms of modern language accurately and do their research objectively; they need not to have any mission to transmit Confucius's *Dao* or any intention to revive the spiritual tradition of Confucianism.

17. Hu Shi, *Zhongguo zhexueshi dagang* [An Outline of the History of Chinese Philosophy], vol. 1 (Shanghai: Commercial Press, 1919).

18. Lao Siguang, *Xinbian zhongguo zhexueshi* [A History of Chinese Philosophy, new ed.] (Taipei: Sanmin Book, 1982), pp. 1–2.

19. Feng Youlan, *A History of Chinese Philosophy*, trans. Derk Bodde, 2 vols. (Princeton, N.J.: Princeton University Press, 1952).

20. Feng Youlan, *A New Treatise on the Methodology of Metaphysics* (Beijing: Foreign Languages Press, 1997), chap. 6.

21. Yiu-ming Fung, *Chaoyue neizai di misi: Cong fenxi zhexue guandian kan dangdai xinruxue* [The Myth of "Transcendent Immanence": A Perspective of Analytic Philosophy on Contemporary New Confucianism] (Hong Kong: Chinese University Press, 2003), chap. 6.

22. Samuel Hideo Yamashita, "Nature and Artifice in the Writings of Ogyū Sorai (1666–1728)," in Peter Nosco, ed., *Confucianism and Tokugawa Culture* (Princeton, N.J.: Princeton University Press, 1984), p. 147.

23. Ibid., p. 149.

24. H. Gene Blocker and Christopher L. Starling, *Japanese Philosophy* (Albany: State University of New York Press, 2001), p. 71.

25. The four collections of essays edited by William Theodore de Bary were subsequently published under this project. They are: *Self and Society in Ming Thought* (New York: Columbia University Press, 1970), *The Unfolding of Neo-Confucianism* (New York: Columbia University Press, 1975), *Principle and Practicality: Essays in Neo-Confucianism and Practical Learning* (New York: Columbia University Press, 1979), and *Yuan Thought: Chinese Thought and Religion under the Mongols* (New York: Columbia University Press, 1982).

26. David Hall and Roger Ames, *Thinking through Confucius* (Albany: State University of New York Press, 1987).

27. Angus Graham, Donald Munro, and David Nivison are Sinologists who have strong Western philosophical backgrounds. Although their perspective is not totally in line with analytic philosophy, they do make important contributions to the study of Chinese philosophy in general and Confucianism in particular. Graham's *Two Chinese Philosophers: Ch'êng Ming-tao and Ch'êng Yi-ch'uan* (La Salle, IL: Open Court, 1992), Munro's *The Concept of Man in Early China* (Stanford, CA: Stanford University Press, 1969), *The Concept of Man in Contemporary China* (Ann Arbor, MI: University of Michigan Press, 1977), and *Images of Human Nature: A Sung Portrait* (Princeton, NJ: Princeton University Press, 1988), and Nivison's *The Ways of Confucianism: Investigations in Chinese Philosophy*, edited with an introduction by Bryan W. Van Norden (La Salle, IL: Open Court, 1996) are successful cases of a mixture of Sinology and philosophy.

28. Herbert Fingarette, *Confucius—The Secular as Sacred* (New York: Harper & Row, 1972).

29. A. S. Cua, *Ethical Argumentation: A Study in Hsun Tzu's [Xun Zi] Moral Epistemology* (Honolulu: University of Hawai'i Press, 1985); Kwong-loi Shun, *Mencius and Early Chinese Thought* (Stanford, Calif.: Stanford University Press, 1997).

30. Kim-chong Chong, *Early Confucian Ethics* (Chicago: Open Court, forthcoming); Bo Mou, ed., *Two Roads to Wisdoms? Chinese and Analytic Philosophical Traditions* (Chicago: Open Court, 2001) and *Comparative Approaches to Chinese Philosophy* (Ashgate, 2003). Yiu-ming, *Chaoyue neizai di misi*.

31. Peter Berger, *The Capitalist Revolution* (New York: Basic Books, 1986); Ambrose King, *Zhongguo shehui yu wenhua* [Chinese Society and Culture] (Hong Kong: Oxford University Press, 1992).

32. Tu Weiming, "Multiple Modernities—Implications of the Rise of 'Confucian' East Asia," in Karl-Heinz Pohl and Anselm W. Müller, eds., *Chinese Ethics in a Global Context: Moral Bases of Contemporary Societies* (Leiden: Brill, 2002).

33. For example, Berger is aware that the topic is highly complex and we should be cautious methodologically in dealing with this topic, so he thinks that "culture, social institutions and specific policies are interacting variables, with none having the status of invariant determination." However, he also claims that "If there is a special East-Asian secularity, then Confucian morality, whether as causal agent or as theoretical legitimator, must be considered an important part of it." He still uses some poorly-defined phrases like "facilitation factor," "motivating forces," "influence," and "cultural factors" to explain the process of modernization in the regions of East Asia. This point can be found in Peter Berger's "Secularity: West and East," keynote paper for the Cultural Identity and Modernization in Asian Countries: Proceedings of Kokugakuin University Centennial Symposium, 1983.

34. Warwick Funnell, "Distortions of History, Accounting and the Paradox of Werner Sombart," *Abacus* 37, no. 1 (February 2001): 71.

35. I believe we should try to avoid confusing Weber's thesis with the Weberian thesis. Weber's thesis is Weber's own thesis about the Protestant ethic as a unique factor of the emergence of capitalism, and other non-Western civilizations do not have this same factor, whereas the Weberian thesis attacks the aspect of uniqueness in Weber's thesis, on the one hand, and maintains that some sort of instrumental Confucianism can be considered as a functional equivalent to the Protestant ethic in promoting capitalism in East Asia on the other hand.

36. In contrast to the closed and particular part, the open and universal part of the content of the Confucian classics is the ideas or views that are not culturally bound or societally restricted. For example, the idea of *li* (rite or ritual) in the pre-Qin period cannot be understood as context-free from the social and political reality of that period. However, the idea of *ren* (humanity) is about human virtue or moral sensibility that is not restricted by any social and political system in a specific period of history. The historical background may be helpful in understanding the emergence of the idea, but the universal meaning of the idea and the justification of the views on it can be theorized in our philosophical language.

PART III

# Teaching Confucianism in Dialogue

# Reenchanting Confucius: A Western-Trained Philosopher Teaches the *Analects*

*John J. Furlong*

In this chapter, I discuss how I, a Western-trained philosopher, approach the teaching of Confucius in an undergraduate (lower-level) course titled "Ancient Chinese Thought." I have spent most of my career in the interstices between contemporary analytic philosophy of mind and recent continental philosophy. My most recent work involves continental ideology critique, cognitive science, and comparative psychology, though, like most continentalists, I have a strong interest in the history of philosophy and often taught ancient Greek and Roman philosophy before I began—rather late in my career—teaching ancient Chinese thought. I have in no way tired of such inquiries. The lure of Confucius and Laozi and others has been positive and substantial rather than a mere pleasant diversion. In other words, I have gone out of my way and delayed enticing projects to prepare myself to teach this course.

My dissertation director, Antonio S. Cua—a name not unknown in ancient Chinese philosophy circles—guided my study of the ontological status of mental imagery; that is, instead of Confucius or Xunzi, chapters involved analyses of Wittgenstein, Sartre, and Husserl. Yet we often met in the basement office of his home, where volumes of ancient Chinese texts lined one wall. Discussions of experiments in cognitive psychology, intentionality, and language games would infrequently be punctuated by references to his work on Xunzi, and though these observations piqued my interest, I had a dissertation to plow, and I needed, head forward, to keep my rows straight and my interests narrow. Fully a decade later, as part of an external teaching evaluation, I was visited by Michael Nylan and a colleague of hers, Stephen Salkever. They observed a class on Heidegger in a course titled "Recent Continental Philosophy." In response to a question, I made the mistake of observing that I thought ancient Chinese thinkers relied less on written texts and were thus closer to what Heidegger called Being. Nylan set me straight after the class, suggesting that textuality might not be the exclusive preserve of Western cultures! I confessed to her that, post-Cua, I had often been tempted to read more Chinese philosophy but had done so fitfully, having read little Confucius and less Zhuangzi.She not only encouraged my enthusiasm but helped me organize the first version of the current course I teach. Called "Origins of Philosophy in Greece and China," that early course allowed me, through comparisons, to develop a wider and deeper command of the Chinese texts and, to some extent, of the current controversies in the field. In future versions, the course evolved to focus on Warring States texts only, and I am currently finishing the fifth version of this course, continually grateful to Nylan and Salkever for their intellectual and collegial generosity.

I fervently hope that this brief introduction lowers expectations. I am not a scholar of Chinese thought. I have no Mandarin skills to speak of; I limit myself to teaching one course and that at the lower level. What academic competence I have to offer lies in the way my usual research areas—and cultural patterns of my students—have shaped my pedagogical decisions regarding the course I teach. What use I may be in a general discussion about teaching Confucius may rest on a tactic I have employed, owing to that shaping, to entice my students to read the *Analects* "with a new ear," as Jacques Derrida might say.[1]

The Birth of a Title

After discussions with Nylan and Salkever and several exchanges of materials and concerns—their materials and my concerns—I began to discuss how to teach a course on ancient Chinese texts with my colleagues in philosophy, classics, and religion. In a small liberal arts college such as ours, these consultations are natural and expected. After that first, comparative version of the course, discussions ensued with classics and religion colleagues about how to focus the course only on ancient China and then what to call it. As a result of these discussions as well as the occasional exchanges of readings on the matter, all agreed that a course in ancient Chinese classic texts would enrich the curriculum. But where did it fit? Should I continue to teach it as philosophy, or would it more properly settle under the rubric of religion? In the end, we agreed to call the course I now teach "Ancient Chinese Thought" and to cross-list it in the philosophy and religion programs. We realized that this decision was in no way merely administrative. It committed us to a distinct position: ancient Chinese texts arguably bear *both* religious and philosophical significance, even if neither term would be accepted by a Confucius or a Xunzi, nor encapsulate their aims.

One could maintain, of course, that those ancient Chinese texts are *sui generis* and so the business of neither discipline. Fang Zhaohui represents this view when he says that "the process of cutting apart and rearranging classical Chinese learning according to Western systematics is one of the oddest features of Chinese academics in the twentieth century."[2] For Fang, no indigenous Chinese practice or textual category corresponds to philosophy or religion. To the traditional categories of knowledge found in the West—history, philosophy, religion, literature, science, and so on—Fang opposes the traditional Chinese categorization of the Six Arts: history, poetry, ritual, changes, music, and the Springs and Autumns annuals. He claims that the tradition saw these as systematically interacting, just as, in its own way, the Western categories systematically relate. Hence, maintaining that China had a philosophical/religious tradition is tantamount to trying to find a Western discipline or canon called *ritual*. Those who claim to have found philosophy in ancient China have "fallen into a paradoxical position."[3]

Yet especially during the Warring States period, texts emerged that do not fit snugly into any of the Six Arts. Fang, curiously, hardly mentions any of these—the very works I wanted to teach—except in passing. Are the *Analects*, the *Zhuangzi*, or the *Laozi* exhibits of poetry? Ritual? Changes? He quotes the *Zhuangzi* where it praises the Six Arts but doesn't situate that text itself.

On the other hand, I am not entirely persuaded—nor were my colleagues—by Hu Shi and his student, Fung Yu-lan, that texts from *jia* are inherently philosophical to the exclusion of a simultaneous claim of religious import. As Fung states: "Philosophy is originally a Western concept. Now while I want to discuss the history of Chinese philosophy, what I will do is to choose from the various classical Chinese theories of learning and describe the corresponding parts that could be called philosophy in the Western sense."[4] A major advantage of Fung's empiricist approach is the dialogue created between Chinese and Western scholars owing to his neologizing. Confucius could be seen as a "humanist" and Mozi a "utilitarian" *ceteris paribus*.[5] The major disadvantage is the narrowing of what we then must examine in these works. A lot of what Confucius is up to looks like what we in the West would call moral philosophy, but to view it and assess it as such would be like reading Plato's *Republic* as a handbook for rulers.[6]

As a philosopher in the ideology-critique traditions, an ancient Chinese thought enthusiast, and a teacher of that material, I could not—and did not—view *jia* texts as comparable to Western philosophical texts of the same period *without* recognizing equally compelling reverberations of Western religious studies. Nor would my colleagues in our religion program have let me. What both of our traditions had in common as we focused on Confucius, Zhuangzi, and others was a concern (lacking a more exact term) for their *thought* as distinct from their literary, paleographical, philological, social-historical, or material-cultural aspects. My religious studies colleagues were just as focused as I was on what we may call religiophilosophical vocabulary, the play of such terms off one another, their logical trajectories, their *Geistesgeschishtliches* import, and so on. Thanks to that mutual commitment, it has been a hallmark of this course that both religion and philosophy majors can meet on equal footing. In approach, the course is as interdisciplinary and otherwise as anticolonializing as we can make it. Religion majors, in evaluations, have compared Ancient Chinese Thought to courses they have had in non-Western religious traditions, whereas some philosophy majors have noted that the lack of familiar touchstones had made them tentative and a bit uneasy throughout the semester. Precisely so!

## Constructing a Proper Other

Through its debt to hermeneutics, structuralism, and poststructuralism, some scholarship in ancient Chinese thought rings familiar tunes to me. One of the most distinctive (perhaps the key) themes of recent continental philosophy has given me an easier purchase than expected in such exciting controversies. At least since Hegel, continental philosophers have involved themselves in what we might call the project of defamiliarizing or "disenchanting" what we think we know.[7] Sticking only to the details we need for what follows, one can tell a post-Hegelian thinker in the continental tradition from most others by her or his skepticism about what is intuitively philosophical versus everything else. Whether it is Marx's "alienation" or Bultmann's "demythologizing," Adorno's "negative dialectics," Derrida's *differance*, or Lacan's "Big Other," continentalists develop tools to cast a particularly cold eye on judgments we make about cultural Others—especially judgments that come as second nature to us. Richard Rorty crystallizes this intellectual style by distinguishing between scientifically motivated analytic philosophers who talk about solving problems and historically oriented continentalists who worry about problematics.[8] The analytic philosopher strives to solve the problem of other minds, whereas the continental philosopher asks: what makes us think there is a problem of other minds in the first place—just when did we get this itch and why at that particular historical moment?

This twice-told tale of continentalist self-reflection bears the virtues of being true in general and of explaining not only my entré into ancient Chinese thought but the one I offer my students. From the beginning of my attempts to teach ancient Chinese thought and Confucius in particular, I have sought first to distance my young colleagues from their most cherished and comforting beliefs and enthusiasms—to "defamiliarize" the familiar, or to disenchant them from their Orientalized consciousness of things Chinese and then reenchant them in a more authentically situated, much harder to handle, and endlessly disturbing Confucius.

To a first approximation, the universal otherness of virtually all complex texts to my students makes for a pedagogical advantage. Because Plato is as foreign to them as Confucius, the comparativist philosopher does not have to take pains to carefully defamiliarize the Western texts before comparing them to the Asian ones because the Western exhibits are not familiar in the first place (though the concepts are; more on this later). A possible exposure in high school to the name of Plato, even to a passage or two from the *Apology* or the *Republic*, does not make Plato any more accessible, in my experience, than Asian texts of roughly the same time period. "Form" is no better received than "Rites." Both the Greek *arête* and the Chinese *de* could just as well appear on the same page. I do not mean to put my students down but to lament their limited acculturation.

On the other hand, this cultural cumulonimbus surrounding my students presents a further insidious difficulty for ancient Chinese texts: American popular culture always already pre-understands Asian thought and trivializes it, even when it opposes it favorably—and thus equally wrongly—to its less exotic representations of Western culture. On the first day of class, when I ask my students why they are taking the course, a majority complain of the excessively rule-bound, navel-gazing Western tradition and then express their desire to explore an intellectual culture free of petty logical restraints, conceptual bean counting, and bootless self-reflection. Here, both traditions are trivialized, and the impossible burden put on the Other virtually ensures disappointment, frustration, and disengagement. Hearing such comments, I feel hoisted by my own petard: they are but innocent versions of my previous blinkered and pretentious judgment about ancient Chinese freedom from excessive textuality.

How should I teach the gamut of ancient Chinese thought to students coming with such expectations? Particularly, how should I teach the *Analects*?

Perhaps I could slake students' thirst for the exotic and new by first offering them Zhuangzi, Laozi, or even Mozi. Anybody but Confucius, because if students want to get away from what they view as hidebound doctrines and strict moralizing, serious discussion about the importance of rites is likely to be dismissed as a busman's holiday from Western toil.

Ironically, however, as a continentalist trained to problematize the familiar, I have found that explicitly foregrounding and continually emphasizing the *Analects* turns out to be the ideal frame for situating responsibly the more "Californianizable" or Orientalizable texts such as Zhuangzi. Teaching Confucius first and continually returning to the *Analects* to defamiliarize and reframe student expectations has proven to be my most useful tool in reminding my students that they are not in Kansas . . . or in Oz.

It will not surprise the readers of this volume that persuading students they are not in Kansas or Oz is no straightforward geography lesson. Not all teachers of classic texts would agree, however. In the *Closing of the American Mind*, for instance, Allan Bloom urged that students should, in effect, "just read" the classic texts. No contextualizing or critical apparatus should get in the way of the intimate engagement of reader with author.

The one concession that Bloom seems to allow is that provided by discussions with one's peers and an able elder. Why would this model not work with teaching Confucius? It surely has the advantage of simplicity and plausibility. However, the chances of colonizing the text are enormous, and the subtlety of the *Analects* stands to be overlooked, especially when we inspect Bloom's own model—a philosophical tradition of reading Western classics that trains us to ignore the idiosyncrasies of a Plato or a Plotinus.[9] As a feeble counter to this unavoidable objection, Bloom frightens us with the specter of relativism: if we can't, for instance, "just read" important authors as if they wrote for us, then they must be "totally other," impossible ever to get right or to read for the truth of what they say, much less criticize and assimilate.

Would that the theoretical issue were as simple as "just reading" makes it, because its simplicity would solve the pedagogical problem for a Western-trained philosopher. Just read the *Analects*. Take Confucius to be a contemporary, a member of our reading group or journal club. Assume reading him together will yield truth for us today and will purge those suspect student desires for the exotic. We can then add the truth of Confucius to the truth of Augustine and the truth of Leibniz.

As contemporary continental philosophy has become more sophisticated about approaching the Other, the pedagogical questions for those of us influenced by that tradition have become more complex, and thus Bloom's suggestion becomes all the more impossible. But before we take up where this more circumspect tradition leaves us as teachers, we should recognize the kernel of wisdom in the Bloomian approach. If we were to read Confucius as an historical artifact *merely*—that is, if our interests were solely antiquarian—then we would be in a worse position than Bloom, because our own colonialism would be hidden from us as Bloom's was not from him, and we would be able to dismiss important texts as so many baubles. As Haun Saussy has emphasized, just as we may naively make ancient authors our contemporaries, so we may, by a thousand complexities, trivialize them as historical oddities.[10]

Bloom's ethnocentrism, his assumption that one should be able to make sense of a text without the advantage of historico-cultural contextualizing, is matched by the equally unhelpful tactic of reading texts as "totally other," as completely alien. Can this even be done? Philosophy, as Derrida famously points out to us, not only constructs itself but constructs its own proper "other" in the process.[11] To ask, "How does Confucius address *our* issues?" is as impossible a demand as the corresponding "How should we read Confucians as Warring States *shi* did?" Ask a seemingly simple question: who is the audience for the *Analects*? The Bloom answer—the audience is us—requires us to read/teach that text as Shakespeare claimed Satan reads Scripture,[12] for our own purposes. The antiquarian answer—the audience is only Warring States elites—requires us to read/teach the *Analects* through the lens of anthropological and historical apparatus, distancing us from any interesting connection to our own age.

Salkever and Nylan have helpfully cast the problems I'm getting at in terms of a trilemma: texts from other cultures are often read with the distorting lenses of an anthropologist, economist, or missionary.[13] For our purposes, we can reduce the trilemma to a dilemma, because both economist and anthropologist aim to disconnect vestiges of familiarity. According to Salkever and Nylan, the anthropologist wants to defamiliarize texts from other cultures, showing how those cultures from which the authors speak must be seen as radically different from our own. The missionary intends just the opposite; namely, to show how, deep down, we are all saying the same thing . . . only we Westerners say it better. Matteo Ricci and his fellow Jesuits might serve as paradigmatic missionary enchanters with regard to ancient Chinese texts.

Given what I've said about students being equal opportunity misreaders of texts—their own as well as those of ancient Chinese—one might object that the burden of Otherness is surely as hard on the teacher of ancient Greek and Roman philosophy as it is on ancient Chinese thought. But this seeming similarity works the other way. One can, for instance, contextualize Plato or Aristotle without trivializing some of their key ideas because those ideas (or at least echoes of them) can be found in important Western institutions and values.

One can show how Plato's account of soul owes much to mystery cults, that his arguments for its immortality tend to be of merely historical interest and do not translate credibly through the centuries—in other words, one can try as much as possible to *antiquate* Plato. Yet the Platonic concept of the soul has worked itself into the intellectual lives of many Westerners and remains a focal point even today. Hence, I've found that students are quite interested in Platonic soul, and no amount of contextualizing, anthropologizing, or other scholar-squirrel activities diminishes it.

But *ren* does not occur in the Western student ether. In the study of texts from other cultures, ancient China in particular, I have found that the anthropologizing apparatus of philological and historical scholarship does work somewhat better (and with some groups of students, immensely better) to diminish those exaggerated and pedagogically tendentious student desires for an Other of their own making.

I take it as read that the Bloomian, missionary approach to teaching ancient Chinese texts is forlorn, and it doesn't take a hermeneut or a deconstructionist to be able to articulate the reason. The second temptation, a reaction to the missionary, distances, demystifies, and defamiliarizes. It makes the object of study Other and takes care to make sure the Other is, to use Derrida's coinage, its own Other and not *our* Other. The danger of this gesture has most famously been experienced in the current strife between scriptural exegetes and religious fundamentalists, where the latter, using philology and historical revisionist models like *Heilsgeschichte* and *Redaktionsgeschichte*, disconnect the actual meaning of the texts in question from the meanings fervently desired from those texts by biblical inerrantists.

Bryan Van Norden discovers the same stress in the ancient Chinese context over a "sacred" work: "For the last two millennia, most scholars (whether Eastern or Western) have taken all twenty 'books' of the *Analects* as an accurate record of what Confucius and his disciples have said. But scholarship in recent centuries has become more suspicious, investigating such issues as the historical composition of the text of the *Analects* and the sectarian motives behind various conceptions of Confucius."[14] This tension between the exegetes and the adepts mirrors the larger perennialist/missionary/enchanter versus demythologizer/anthropologist/disenchanter controversy. My strategy, in brief, is to use the historicizing disenchanters early in the course to distance my students from their expectations while building up—reenchanting—a more sophisticated appreciation as the course ensues. That appreciation will not—cannot after this approach—be missionary. Indeed, it opens up an *Analects* every bit as polyvalent, morally complex, and puzzling as the *Republic* or the Gospel of John. No mere historical oddity, cultural bling, or pious and ossified tract, the text thinks along with its age and so becomes meaningful to ours.

## The Warring States Project as Means of Reenchantment

In the formal presentation of Confucius and the *Analects*, I draw heavily from the Brookses' *Original Analects,* and I try as much as possible to emphasize the doctrinal differences one finds among the chronological layers. Because I am not a Sinologist, and the aim of the course is not strictly exegetical, my employment of the Brookses' work is instrumental and perhaps a bit casual. I do not worry overmuch about taking a position on all of the disputed dates or, frankly, some nondisputed dates, but rather emphasize the spread of these writings throughout the Warring States period and how this one text changes what it means to be Confucian as it confronts intellectual and political trends. Employing this historicizing, philological approach to the *Analects*, I try to enjoin an attitude that takes textual details seriously, even to the extent of deferring the larger meanings, at least at first. The study of the *Analects*, I hope to convey, must be taken as seriously as the study of any Western text, whether that is the *Republic* in a philosophy class or *Genesis* in a religion class—only in this case the sequence is reversed. Before reading such Western texts with attention to historical and philological details, students will have already become familiar with their meanings and cultural importance, whereas in my course sequence, the *Analects* are first introduced in their *Sitz-im-Leben* and only later will it be apparent how powerful the ideas themselves are.

In a series of seventy-five-minute class periods, we read the text in three phases, organized by their possible authorial concerns and audience contexts: (1) books 4–9; (2) books 10–11, 3, 12–13; and (3) books 2, 14–15, 1, and 16–20. At the beginning of the course, we read about the disintegration of the Zhou and the disenfranchisement of feudal elites. The first audience for the *Analects* is the *shi*, and such early Confucian circles would, for instance, naturally valorize ren (humaneness) and other virtues as elite. With the second set of readings comes the Kong transformation—the influx of *xie* (new men, men of worth) and the influence of Mohism and other schools. Perhaps as a reaction, *li* (rituals) are emphasized in these books, a tone of individualism enters, what might be called Daoist elements appear; thus ren becomes more demotic and personal: "the key to achieving *ren* lies within yourself—how could it come from others?" (12.1).[15] Whereas the second set of books registers a reaction to the other schools, the third set brings in the assimilation of these back into Confucian orthodoxy, thanks largely to influences from Mengzi (Mencius) and Xunzi. *Wuwei* (effortless action), for instance, which students will soon discover to be a major Daoist theme, is now comfortably wearing Confucian garments: "Was not Shun one who ruled by means of *wuwei*? What did he do? He made himself reverent and took his [ritual] position facing south, that is all" (15.5).

Although artificial, this framing of the *Analects* undercuts student attempts to pull the text too quickly into their own orbits or trivialize incongruities. Discontinuities and inconsistencies, they find, now have possible explanations. More important, disappointment at not finding some fantasized novel approach to life is greatly downplayed with the clinical approach to the text. By first refusing to read and "sell" the *Analects* straightforwardly, I thus hope to subvert those prepackaged, commodified student expectations I have mentioned. I emphasize to them that the first reading of the *Analects* should merely inform us of the major themes of Warring States thought as seen through Confucian lenses. The rest of the course will enflesh those themes as they grow in Confucianism as well as in the other schools.

As we encounter the Warring State thinkers in their historical context in the progression of the course, we revisit the *Analects* to see how Confucian thinkers assimilate, redraw, and otherwise finesse their doctrines into the organic and living text. The *Analects* thus becomes a reliable touchstone, eventually a familiar place to compare and contrast, to assess new developments.

For example, perhaps the easiest thinker to contrast with Confucians is Mozi, because he so explicitly criticizes that tradition. Mozi is an easy read for American students, who warm to his themes of activism and equality, and it is easy to take his side against his effigy of Confucius. However, we then turn to passages in the *Analects* that, given their *Sitz-im-Leben*, could be seen as a response to Mozi's one-sided criticisms. We could then, for instance, read 1.9 to be showing how attention to funeral rites—a practice Mozi attacks—could actually benefit the people in general. There, Zengzi says, "Be meticulous in the passing of those close to you and do not fail to continue the sacrifices to your distant ancestors. This will be enough to cause the Virtue of the people to return to fullness." Few students end up siding with Confucius on this issue, but most of them end up appreciating the seriousness of the controversy.

In the latest version of the course, students caught on to this practice and by the time we reached the *Zhuangzi* began pointing out echoes in the *Analects*. Without my help (except in the initial marking of a wuwei citation in our first reading of the *Analects*), students discovered that the both/and strategy of the Confucian response to Mozi could be extended to Zhuangzi. "If you are really *ren*," one student remarked, commenting on book 15, "you can't help but be *wuwei*." Finding Mencius in the text then became a stampede of searching for "nature," as in book 17.2: "By *xing* (nature), people are similar; they diverge as a result of *xi* (practice)."

As the course progresses, we continue to attempt adjustments in students' views of what I call (inspired by Derrida) the resources of the Confucian text. At junctures of introductions to new thinkers, we recall Confucian teachings to see how the new thinker is confronting them. But Warring States dialogues are not the only locales for discussing the *Analects* in the course. At three points, roughly several weeks apart, I stage a conversation between the forms of Confucianism expressed in the *Analects* and the contemporary world. Called "Intercultural Connections," the exercise involves four groups of students reading one item of contemporary secondary research on the role of Confucian thought in a contemporary controversy. Each group, with its own article or chapter, informs the rest of the class about its thesis and content. Hence, feminism, ecology, and the human rights/Asian values debates bring the *Analects* into contemporary focus.

Viewing Warring States intellectual traditions as a complex, nuanced dialogue with the *Analects* aims to provide students a non-Orientalized Other or, more responsibly put, an Other that refuses to be Orientalized in the way *they* expect. This Other takes its texts seriously, it commits to certain intellectual pathways, enriches them, attempts to assimilate small paths into larger ones, re-marks other paths. Whatever this tradition is up to, it is momentous, complex, and not easily assimilatable into our comfortable schemata. If one must make comparisons, one must do so as Nietzsche says one must read, "with delicate eyes and fingers."[16]

## Conclusion

Before I resorted to this tactic, I would read the *Analects* from book 1 to 20, resisting student frustrations by trying to be missionary about the point and meaning of each book; worse, I would have to motivate the great number of students who were frustrated at not finding the mystical Other they anticipated: "This stuff is in no way what I expected from an Asian culture. It's just a bunch of rules about clothing and obeying your parents! Maybe *they* understand how this all fits together and maybe *they* think it's meaningful, but I don't, and I'm not supposed to anyway, since I'm a Westerner." Pulling in Derrida's acute observations about how all texts are grafts and all volumes begin and end arbitrarily did no good here.[17]

What has worked is to show, with the help of the Brookses' project, that the books were written at different stages throughout the period, *and that different audiences were addressed.* In the first reading of the *Analects,* I want to demythologize the authority of a mythic Confucius from whom one will expect apothegms of life-transforming wisdom—an Asian Epictetus or Nietzsche. The audience for these texts, I underscore to my students, is not you, a twenty-first-century Western student. Yes, I urge, this document should be held to your perhaps logo-centric anticipations of consistency and relevance, but you will not find them fulfilled unless you take the large, centuries-long perspective within which the text was actually accreted. As the Brookses state, "the *Analects* does have a rationale, but a developmental rather than an integral one."[18]

Although the historicizing, demystifying phase of our reading of the *Analects* might leave students with the impression that they can take the text as someone else's sacred book to which one can apply critical apparatus without detriment to their own thinking lives, the rest of the course aims to show how lively, momentous, and flexible the text is. I often quote Ivanhoe's remark: "Although the Confucian tradition is formed around a sacred canon and certain central themes, it is not a set of fixed ideas handed down unchanged through time."[19] I emphasize this as the semester progresses to the other Warring States thinkers by rereading parts of the *Analects* that enfold them in the ongoing organic development of Confucian traditions I want students to feel what the Brookses call the "furious integrity" of Confucian thinkers.[20]

My own enthusiasm for this course is very high, but the instructor's enthusiasm only goes so far in making a course successful and appealing to students. What I'm most gratified by is how student enthusiasm remains and even increases as the course develops. Coaxing a return to the *Analects* with each new thinker has given the course itself a furious integrity that students seem to respond to, and, with any luck, they come away with a view of the *Analects* not far off Benjamin Schwartz's vivid description of them: "Like a chiaroscuro painting, or indeed a Chinese landscape painting, highly economical in its use of the brush, a vision may encompass spaces full of unresolved problems and fruitful ambiguities."[21]

NOTES

Portions of this chapter have been taken from two papers I have given at Association of Core Texts and Courses conferences: "Teaching Comparatively While Teaching the Text: Confucius' *Analects* Defamiliarized," Association for Core Texts and Courses, Chicago, April 5; and "Hsun-Tzu in a First Year Seminar," in Brunello, Chiariello, and Lee (eds.), *The Wider World of Core Texts and Courses,* Association of Core Texts and Courses, 2004.

1. Jacques Derrida, *The Ear of the Other: Otobiography, Transference, Translation* (Lincoln: University of Nebraska Press, 1985), p. 35.

2. Fang Zhaohui, "A Critical Reflection on the Systematics of Traditional Chinese Learning," *Philosophy East and West* 52, no. 1 (January 2002): 38.

3. Ibid., p. 40.

4. Fung Yulan quoted from the original Chinese by Fan Zhao-hui, "A Critical Reflection," p. 36. In *A Short History of Chinese Philosophy* (ed. D. Bodde [New York: Free Press, 1976]), Fung says that "Confucianism is no more a religion than, say, than Platonism or Aristotelianism" (p. 1). In fact, he asserts more generally that Chinese thinkers "have not had much concern with religion because they have had so much concern with philosophy" (p. 4).

5. See C. Defoort, "Is There Such a Thing as Chinese Philosophy? Arguments of an Implicit Debate," *Philosophy East and West* 51, no. 3 (July 2001): 401.

6. See Henry Rosemont Jr.'s distinction between what he calls Western and Chinese "concept clusters," in "Why Take Rights Seriously? A Confucian Critique," in L. S. Rouner, ed., *Human Rights and the World's Religions*, Boston University Studies in Philosophy and Religion, vol. 9 (Notre Dame, Ind.: Notre Dame University Press, 1994), pp. 167–82.

7. In an often-quoted epigram from the preface to *The Phenomenology of Spirit*, Hegel states: "What is familiar is not known simply because it is familiar." Familiarity is, he implies further on, deception. See W. Kaufmann, trans. and ed., *Hegel: Texts and Commentary* (Notre Dame, Ind.: University of Notre Dame Press, 1965), p. 48. Saussy also notices the relevance of this passage (H. Saussy, "No Time Like the Present: The Category of Contemporaneity in Chinese Studies," in S. Shankman and S. W. Durrant, eds., *Early China/Ancient Greece: Thinking through Comparisons* [Albany: State University of New York Press, 2002], p. 35).

8. R. Rorty, "The Historiography of Philosophy: Four Genres," in R. Rorty, J. B. Schneewind, and Q. Skinner, *Philosophy in History: Essays on the Historiography of Philosophy* (New York: Cambridge University Press, 1984), p. 57.

9. Derrida has shown how badly we philosophers read our own texts. See, for instance, his "Plato's Pharmacy" in *Dissemination*, trans. B. Johnson (Chicago: University of Chicago Press, 1981).

10. Saussy, "No Time Like the Present."

11. "Philosophy has always insisted upon this: thinking its other. *Its* other." Jacques Derrida, *Margins of Philosophy*, trans. A. Bass (Chicago: University of Chicago Press, 1982), p. x.

12. "Mark you this, Bassanio, The devil can cite Scripture for his purpose." Shakespeare, *The Merchant of Venice*, I. iii. 92ff.

13. S. Salkever and M. Nyland, "Teaching Comparative Political Philosophy: Rationale, Problems, Strategies," unpublished manuscript, 1993, pp. 10–14.

14. B. Van Norden, ed., *Confucius and the Analects: New Essays* (New York: Oxford University Press, 2002), p. 3.

15. Translations from those employed in the volume we use for the course are from P.J. Ivanhoe and B. W. Van Norden, eds., *Readings in Classical Chinese Philosophy* (New York: Seven Bridges Press, 2001).

16. "To read *well*, that is to say, to read slowly, deeply, looking cautiously before and aft, with reservations, with doors left open, with delicate eyes and fingers"

(F. Nietzsche, *Daybreak: Thoughts on the Prejudices of Morality*, trans. R. J. Hollingdale [New York: Cambridge University Press, 1982], p. 5).

17. Inter alia, there is this famous passage from *Dissemination* (p. 36): "If there is nothing outside the text, this implies, with the transformation of the concept of text in general, that the text is no longer the snug, airtight inside of an interiority or an identity-to-itself . . . but rather a different placement of the effects of opening and closing."

18. B. Brooks and T. Brooks, *The Original Analects: Sayings of Confucius and His Successors* (New York: Columbia University Press, 1998), p. vii.

19. P. J. Ivanhoe, "Whose Confucius? Which *Analects*?" in B. Van Norden, ed., *Confucius and the Analects: New Essays* (New York: Oxford University Press, 2002), pp. p. 129.

20. "From first to last, the *Analects* never strays from the furious integrity of Confucius, but it takes it into areas that would have amazed him, transmuting his code of honor into a code of public obligation, and his vertical loyalty into a vision of a reciprocal society, accepting not only of its ruler but of itself" (Brooks and Brooks, *The Original Analects*, p. 197).

21. B. Schwartz, *The World of Thought in Ancient China* (Cambridge, Mass.: Harvard University Press, 1985), p. 62.

REFERENCES

Bloom, H. *The Closing of the American Mind*. New York: Simon and Schuster, 1987.

Brooks, B., and T. Brooks. *The Original Analects: Sayings of Confucius and his successors*. New York: Columbia University Press, 1998.

Defoort, C. "Is There Such a Thing as Chinese Philosophy? Arguments of an Implicit Debate." *Philosophy East and West* 51, no. 3 (July 2001).

Derrida, J. 1981. *Dissemination*, trans. B. Johnson. Chicago: University of Chicago Press.

———. *Margins of Philosophy*, trans. A. Bass. Chicago: University of Chicago Press, 1982.

———. *The Ear of the Other: Otobiography, Transference, Translation*. Lincoln: University of Nebraska Press, 1985.

Fang Zhaohui. "A Critical reflection on the Systematics of Traditional Chinese Learning," *Philosophy East and West* 52, no. 1 (January 2002).

Fung, Yu-Lan. *A Short History of Chinese Philosophy*, ed. D. Bodde. New York: Free Press, 1976.

Ivanhoe, P. J. "Whose Confucius? Which *Analects*?" in B. Van Norden, ed., *Confucius and the Analects: New Essays*. New York: Oxford University Press, 2002, pp. 119–33.

Ivanhoe, P. J., and B. W. Van Norden, eds. *Readings in Classical Chinese Philosophy*. New York: Seven Bridges Press, 2001.

Kaufmann, W., trans. and ed. *Hegel: Texts and Commentary*. Notre Dame, Ind.: University of Notre Dame Press, 1965.

Nietzsche, F. *Daybreak: Thoughts on the Prejudices of Morality*, trans. R. J. Hollingdale. New York: Cambridge University Press, 1982.

Rouner, L. S., ed. *Human Rights and the World's Religions*. Boston University Studies in Philosophy and Religion, vol. 9. Notre Dame, Ind.: Notre Dame University Press, 1994.

Rorty, R. "The Historiography of Philosophy: Four Genres," in R. Rorty, J. B. Schneewind, and Q. Skinner, *Philosophy in History: Essays on the Historiography of Philosophy*. New York: Cambridge University Press, 1984.

Salkever, S., and M. Nylan. "Teaching Comparative Political Philosophy: Rationale, Problems, Strategies." Unpublished manuscript, 1993.

Saussy, H. "No Time Like the Present: The Category of Contemporaneity in Chinese Studies." In S. Shankman and S. W. Durrant, eds., *Early China/Ancient Greece: Thinking through Comparisons*. Albany: State University of New York Press, 2002, pp. 35–54.

Schwartz, B. *The World of Thought in Ancient China*. Cambridge, Mass.: Harvard University Press, 1985.

Van Norden, B., ed. *Confucius and the Analects: New Essays*. New York: Oxford University Press, 2002.

# Teaching Confucianism in Christian Contexts

*Judith A. Berling*

Although there is growing interest in teaching non-Christian faiths in some Christian colleges and seminaries, many institutions opt for teaching religions of the Book (Judaism and Islam) because of their close historical ties to Christianity and the shared (although not uncontended) biblical heritage, or Buddhism because it is one of the great world religions, having a missionary legacy that spread it far beyond its Indian homeland. Compared with Judaism, Islam, and Buddhism, Confucianism can seem rather remote, local (centered in East Asia), and, to put it plainly, not really "religious." In this chapter, I argue that not only are there many incentives for students in Christian contexts to study Confucianism but also the apparent disincentives are not obstacles but opportunities for Christian students to gain a fresh perspective on their tradition.

Why Should Christians Study Confucianism?

In the increasingly globalized world of the twenty-first century, one can no longer imagine that Confucianism is remotely located or isolated in East Asia. For one thing, persons of East Asian background are well represented across the globe, and certainly in North America. The classrooms of Christian colleges and seminaries are well populated with Asian Americans and international students from East Asia. Moreover, a growing number of students not of East

Asian heritage will work, live in, or have extended visits to East Asia or will befriend, work with, or marry persons of East Asian heritage.

Rudyard Kipling had it wrong even in 1889 when he wrote, "Oh, East is East, and West is West, and Never the Twain shall Meet,"[1] but in the twenty-first century, under the impact of globalization, persons, ideas, products, practices, and religions of the "East" are present throughout the "West," and vice versa; East and West are intermixed in a complex mosaic or perhaps like the colored particles that swirl and mix in a kaleidoscope.

The movement and intermixing of people and ideas from the two sides of the Pacific Rim is rendered even more significant by the economic rise of Asian cultures, including several in East Asia: China, Japan, Taiwan, and Korea. Much has been written about the cultural factors in the success of the Asian Tigers, and one factor often cited is the Confucian heritage these cultures share.[2] Whereas Max Weber once extolled the Protestant ethic as a major cultural factor in the rise of the Western industrial world, some scholars and pundits now look to aspects of the Confucian heritage to understand the discipline, commitment, and loyalty that characterizes the East Asian workforce. Educated citizens need to understand the Confucian heritage to critically consider such claims.

For students in Christian contexts, there is yet another factor that recommends the study of Confucianism, namely, the growing importance of Christianity in East Asia and of East Asian Christianity in the global church.[3] Christianity is best established in South Korea, where it is the dominant religion alongside Buddhism. Although minuscule in relation to the entire population, Christianity is steadily growing in the People's Republic of China, both in the cities and in the rural countryside. Even more significant is that East Asian theologians are beginning the task of contextualizing Christian theology, exploring how the Christian message needs to be recast in light of their distinctive cultural values and patterns. Asian and East Asian Christians note that Jesus was an Asian from a West Asian context, not a blond-haired blue-eyed Northern European, as he is sometimes depicted in European and North American church art. Moreover, they are using East Asian concepts, like *dao*, or the sage, to understand and explicate themes in Christian theology, just as Western theologians used Greek and Latin philosophical concepts to help explain Christian theology.[4] These themes come from the Confucian heritage, and they are a significant new resource for Christian theology in the global church. Thus to understand East Asian Christianity and theological developments in the global church, it is necessary to have a basic understanding of Confucianism.

As East Asian Christians are noting, there are indeed rich and suggestive resonances between aspects of Confucian and Christian traditions. Both traditions put strong emphasis on the moral cultivation of character. The lists of virtues may differ, but the meeting point is the importance of ethical living as part of the spiritual path. Both Confucianism and Christianity have profound traditions of "sacred learning," the thoughtful and contemplative study of classics or Scripture to understand, practice, and internalize the core teachings of the tradition. These traditions share the importance of honoring and following a model or models of the spiritual path—Jesus and the saints for Christians and Kongzi and the sages for Confucians. Both articulate an ideal for the community of the faithful: the kingdom of God for Christians and the moral society for Confucians. And both articulate a variety of paths of self-cultivation for practitioners.

Finally, as a practical matter, there is a rich array of books in English on the Confucian traditions: translations of and reflections on classical writings, writings of later Confucian thinkers, novels and short stories to bring the tradition to life for students. There is, in short, no serious practical obstacle to the study of Confucianism in Christian contexts.

That is not to say that the study of Confucianism in Christian contexts is without its challenges. Confucianism profoundly challenges many of the assumptions that Christians bring to the study of religions. The first has to do with whether or in what sense Confucianism is a religion or is religious at all. Because it departs in a number of ways from Western (primarily Protestant) notions of religion, many in the West and in East Asia deny that it is a religion or religious. The second is the Western Christian assumption that belief or doctrine is fundamental and that practice flows from belief. In Confucianism, as in Judaism and a number of other religions, practice is fundamental, and belief flows from practice. The third is the Western Christian notion that religious allegiance must be exclusive: one must choose the true faith and renounce all others. In East Asia, the dominant pattern is religious inclusivity, where people practice and honor a number of religious traditions in different phases of their lives or simultaneously. Fourth is an expectation, particularly in Christian contexts, that other religions are to be studied dialogically, through site visits to the churches (temples, mosques, synagogues) of the other religions, or by inviting representatives for conversation (the local rabbi or imam). In the case of Confucianism, there are no temples to visit, and no clergy to invite. So how does a teacher address the desire for "dialogue?" These challenges of studying Confucianism underscore the otherness of this tradition; Christians cannot simply bring their prior conceptions and ideas and project them onto Confucianism or use them as the selective lens to identify what is relevant for study. The study of Confucianism (and thus its teaching) requires pedagogical strategies to help students accept and negotiate the genuine otherness of the tradition. Thus I

206   TEACHING CONFUCIANISM IN DIALOGUE

discuss the pedagogical principles and strategies before returning to a discussion of these four challenges. Finally, I explore one particularly promising pedagogical approach to the study of Confucianism in Christian contexts.

## Pedagogical Principles for Teaching Confucianism in Christian Contexts

Earlier I proposed a set of reasons for Christians studying Confucianism: (1) the global intermixing of peoples and ideas from East and West, (2) the claim that Confucianism is a significant factor in the rise and flourishing of East Asian economies, (3) the growing numbers of East Asian Christians and increasing importance of East Asian contextual theologies in the global church, and (4) significant and suggestive resonances between Confucianism and Christianity. If these are the reasons for teaching Confucianism to Christians in Christian contexts, the approach to teaching must go beyond simply description and facts. If students are to learn Confucianism to understand their East Asian neighbors and their own experiences in East Asian cultures, to critically consider the proposition that Confucianism is a significant factor in the success of East Asian economies, to appreciate and critically assess the contributions of East Asian contextual theologies to the global church, and to explore resonances between Confucianism and Christianity, their learning of Confucianism needs to be centrally focused on understanding the tradition. Thus, rather than the informational (banking) model of education, in which the teacher devises ways to impart information about Confucianism, I propose a hermeneutical (interpretive/dialogical) model in which the students develop skills for understanding Confucianism.

Paolo Freire famously named and critiqued the banking model in his classic *Pedagogy of the Oppressed*.[5] He argued that traditional education was based on a "banking model," seeing the student as an empty vessel into which the teacher deposits knowledge, so that the student can call on it when needed. John Dewey was also critical of conceptions of knowledge as external to students, as a body of facts they store in a warehouse.[6] Recent pedagogical theorists, such as bell hooks and Maxine Greene,[7] argue that education must empower the students, engaging their imaginations to help them understand and negotiate both the material they study and the world in which they live.

In the field of the study of religion, Gavin Flood has argued for a dialogical and interpretive approach to the study of religions. He cites Mikhail Bakhtin in arguing that our only access to the consciousness of others is dialogical. Bakhtin wrote, "The consciousness of other people cannot be perceived, analyzed, defined as objects or as things—one can only relate to them dialogically. To think about them means to talk with them."[8] Flood sees the study of religion as an interpretive conversation with texts and/or persons. In theological studies, Edward Farley has argued that theological learning is more fundamentally hermeneutic than scientific. What is needed, he writes, "is a shift from theology as a cluster of sciences . . . to theology as historically situated reflection and interpretation. The outcome of that shift is that the structure of theological study or pedagogy is recognized to be determined by basic modes of interpretation rather than by the sciences."[9] If the study of religions and theology is best described as hermeneutic, then the proper teaching of religion and theology develops interpretive capacities in students; the goal is understanding, not an appropriation of facts.

Interpretation, seeking to understand, is an art rather than a science. Interpreters (students) bring to the task their prior views (prejudgments), which have been shaped by their sociocultural locations, life experiences, and prior knowledge. The text to be understood has its own location shaped by its own sociocultural and historical context. These two contexts are separated by a significant gap of difference. The process of interpretation entails a back-and-forth, mutually correcting "dialogue" between interpreters and interpreted in which mutual clarification narrows the gap or distance between them to produce understanding. The gap between the two contexts never completely closes, so that all understanding is partial and incomplete; however imperfect, it is a form of understanding.[10] And that understanding adds to the knowledge and experience of the interpreters, so that they are enriched or changed by the experience of understanding. The teacher of religions seeks to facilitate and nurture this process of understanding.

In a recent book I articulated the process and pedagogical implications of Christians coming to understand other religions.[11] There are pedagogical principles at stake in teaching Confucianism in a Christian context. The learning process is situated between two poles: (1) coming to understand the other religion (Confucianism) as well as possible, as far as is possible on its own terms (though that goal can never be entirely achieved); and (2) reappropriating or reintegrating what is learned of Confucianism into the learners' horizon: What does it mean for their understanding of religion? Of life in general? Of how to relate to others in the world? And—if they are Christians—of Christianity in particular? Too often when Christians learn another religion, the pedagogy is structured around only one of these goals. If the emphasis is on the reappropriation into the learners' contexts, then Confucianism will not be genuinely engaged or understood; the teacher and students will focus on only what accords with students' prior views, so that Confucianism will be presented and understood as a pale reflection of what the students already know. If understanding Confucianism on its own terms is stressed exclusively, the students will find Confucianism alien, strange, and exotic; they will not be able to understand it as a genuine human possibility, a tradition that has shaped and continues to shape lives of persons they can know, respect, and understand. The learning process has to keep these two poles in dynamic tension, moving back and forth between them so that students will be both challenged and enriched by interreligious learning.[12]

The process of students learning Confucianism in a Christian context can be articulated as having five threads, each of which entails certain pedagogical principles. I chose the word *threads* after careful deliberation. It is tempting to say five steps or five phases, but the process is not as neat or linear as those terms would suggest. There is a logical order to the five threads, but the learning process can move back and forth among them. The metaphor of threads suggests separate elements which, when twisted together, form a durable yarn or rope. No thread in isolation is sufficiently strong to carry the learning process, but together they are up to the task.

The first thread is encountering difference. Confucianism is what Wittgenstein called "a form of life," a set of experiences and practices that constitute the world of a community. Confucianism was shaped and honed by the history, conflicts, practices, and values of East Asian cultures; although its adherents and texts are now scattered across the globe, it is still fundamentally shaped by a world very different from that of a Euro-American. To understand Confucianism, students have to encounter that different form of life; they have to imaginatively enter into the worlds of Confucianism through texts, persons, practices, or narratives that stretch them beyond their own familiar territory. Pedagogically, this requires teaching Confucianism by making ample use of its authentic voices: primary writings in translation; guest speakers who represent Confucian viewpoints; novels, stories, or films that invite students into narrative Confucian worlds. It recommends minimal use of textbooks written by non-Confucian authors.

Encountering difference also means engaging some of the distinctive language, ways of thinking, and practices of Confucians. As Clifford Geertz has written, "In each case, I have tried to get at [cross-cultural understanding] not by imagining myself someone else, a rice peasant or a tribal sheikh, and then seeing what I thought, but by searching out and analyzing the symbolic forms—words, images, institutions, behaviors—in terms of which, in each place, people actually represented themselves to themselves and to one another."[13] This principle has at least two pedagogical implications. First, in choosing translations of Asian language texts, one should prefer translations that discuss and illumine the actual language used in the texts, rather than the text in the most facile English without footnotes. A translation can be too readable, so readable that it "loses" the original. Second, there are studies by Western and East Asian scholars that seek profoundly to engage and understand the language and practices of the Confucian texts, illuminating them for English language readers. Two examples are Herbert Fingarette's *The Secular as Sacred* and Hall and Ames's *Thinking through Confucius*.[14]

Finally, encountering difference means that students must recognize the internal diversity, important conflicts, and distinctive points of view within the Confucian tradition. No single text or author, no single guest speaker, should be asked to represent "the Confucian tradition" as a whole. Assignments should represent a variety of voices and points of view; films and novels should be carefully introduced so that students are aware of the location and agendas of directors and authors. When the teaching offers several viewpoints within Confucianism, students realize that they cannot achieve a single authoritative interpretation, and they begin to anticipate diverse points of view within the Confucian tradition.

The second learning thread is that students respond from their own locations. This thread recognizes that in the process of interpretation, learners naturally bring their prejudgments, the interests and views shaped by their own locations and prior experiences. Pedagogically, it recognizes that students will bring interests, selective lenses, and specific questions and concerns shaped by their own backgrounds. This is entirely natural, and teachers can use these interests to engage the students with the material. Initial student interests in and questions about the material may strike the teacher as wide of the mark, or as moving the discussion in the wrong direction. But if students' concerns are too quickly dismissed by the teacher, students can also too quickly dismiss the Confucian material as irrelevant or uninteresting.

Part of the art is to help students find a point of connection with the Confucian situation. I taught Confucianism to college freshmen and sophomores at Indiana University in the late 1970s. The students were at a stage of life when they were asserting their independence from their parents and the mores they had been taught by their elders; Confucian filiality and other values at first seemed to them like the ideology their parents were trying to impose on them. I assigned them to write a letter of advice in the voice of a dying aging parent, passing on their best life wisdom to their children and grandchildren. After struggling with the assignment for a while, they realized that they would not always be youth seeking to define themselves against their elders, but they would become parents and models and mentors for the young people who would come after them, adults with responsibilities for the welfare of the next generation. The assignment opened a door for them to see that Confucianism was not just irrelevant.

The third aspect of learning are threads of conversation, mutually correcting give and take between the students and the voices of the Confucian tradition, the mutually corrective dialogue of the hermeneutical process. The conversational dimension of learning has a number of pedagogical implications. First, if in the second thread it is natural that students raise questions—even negative or critical questions—of Confucian positions from their own perspectives, the conversational thread of learning makes it imperative that Confucian voices talk back, answering the critiques and offering their own different perspectives. Such engagement can be achieved by means of close textual readings, pedagogically designed so that students enter into a sustained dialogue with the texts, perhaps in small groups using well-designed questions about the meaning of the text. I have found it advisable to have students prepare their informal written comments the discussion questions to bring to the group work so that the diversity of student interpretations will be voiced; otherwise the first student to speak or the most verbally facile student may overly dominate the group's discussion. The teacher might also structure students around different Confucian voices, having some students represent one point of view (with their text) and others another (with a different text). The critical point is to structure the assignment so that the texts can "speak back" and resist initial interpretations, leading the students to deeper understandings of Confucian viewpoints. Such dialogue can also take place in a plenary group (if the class is not too large), with the teacher encouraging students to move further into the Confucian meanings.

On the other hand, there also needs to be space for the students to once again talk back to the Confucian viewpoints; to ask "what if?" "what about?" "why not?" "why?" The teacher's job is to help students to see what assumptions or viewpoints lie behind their questions and how their understanding is progressing. Students also need to reflect on why they agree with Confucian ideas (when they do), and why they don't when they do not.

In addition to texts, it is advisable to have students engage genuine Confucian voices, such as those of a guest speaker. Because Confucianism does not have clergy, Confucian speakers would be persons well versed in the tradition and who honor Confucian values. One advantage of guest speakers is that they make visible to the students the dialogical/conversational nature of understanding; students engage in a literal conversation with an actual person. There are two caveats: (1) The class must not ask any one person to represent the entire tradition (a speaker represents *an* authentic voice, not *the* authentic voice of Confucianism), and (2) given the inclusivity of East Asian religiosity, virtually every Confucian will also be a Christian, or a Buddhist, or a Daoist, which can complicate the dialogue by bringing to the conversation ideas and insights that go beyond Confucianism.

Understanding emerges from a sustained mutually correcting conversation, which requires some time. This mandates disciplined selectivity in planning the syllabus. Very often, courses or units on other religions, such as Confucianism, are far too rushed, not allowing the time for the development of understanding by engaging the voices of the tradition in sufficient depth. Coverage of a nearly three-thousand-year tradition is impossible; careful selection is an art. Moreover, given that one of the reasons for studying Confucianism is the presence of East Asian persons in our communities and in the global church, it is important to include some living contemporary voices, a point to which I will return later.

The fourth thread of the learning process is developing relationships or living out understanding. This thread emphasizes that understanding changes one's engagement with the world; it has implications for how one sees and lives. Students can engage this thread hypothetically: now that you have understood $X$ about Confucianism, how will that change your relationships with persons of East Asian backgrounds? How are you better prepared to visit or live in China, Japan, or South Korea? Students can engage this thread experientially: through a visit to a site or a project of service learning. Students can think about how what they have learned about Confucianism enriches or changes their own views. Does it help them to see family relationships in a different way? Do they understand better how learning (or Bible study) can be part of self-cultivation? Do they have a new understanding of the role of liturgy or worship? Do they have a new appreciation of the importance of social courtesies? Any of these techniques can be designed in advance by a teacher, or the appropriate exercise in living out understanding may emerge gradually from the group's engagement with Confucianism; the class might have a discussion to design a "living out" exercise that has emerged from their learning experience.

The final thread of the learning process is internalization. Having engaged in some depth with several Confucian texts or thinkers or in dialogue with a Confucian colleague, students need to reflect on what they have learned about how to learn more about Confucianism. Interpretation across difference is an art, a skill set, which can be adapted in many circumstances.

Having introduced the basic pedagogical approach to and principles involved in teaching Confucianism in a Christian context, I turn to a discussion of four distinctive challenges entailed in teaching Confucianism in Christian contexts.

## Four Challenges

### 1. To What Extent and in What Ways Is Confucianism a Religion?

Many Christians have a hard time recognizing Confucianism as a religion, or even identifying the religious or spiritual dimensions of Confucianism. It does not have many of the attributes Christians associate with religion. There are no ordained clergy; there is no creed; there are no sacraments or formal rites of initiation; there are no Confucian churches; there is no regular communal worship; there is no supreme personal deity. Rather than a religion, Confucianism seems to represent a sort of secular humanism. Confucians emulate wise human models; they study the classics and the humane arts; they seek to cultivate civic, familial, and personal virtues to develop and refine human character. Many fail to see the religious or transcendent dimensions in this humanistic vision.

Many non-Christian East Asians also deny that Confucianism is a religion. They claim it is not a religion but simply an ethical system representing the moral and social practices of Chinese society. In saying this, they are to a large degree repeating what Western missionaries said of Confucianism in the nineteenth century. Part of the problem is that the term religion (*zongjiao* in Chinese) entered the Chinese lexicon only in the nineteenth century, "when it entered through Japanese translations of European works and terminology."[15] There had, of course, been many diverse forms of religious life and practice in Chinese for nearly three millennia, but the term for religion in modern Chinese is based on European understandings of the attributes of religion. Compared to European Christianity, Confucianism did not look much like a religion (*zongjiao*). A second part of the problem is that as Chinese and other East Asians learned more about Western traditions of thought and values, "Confucianism" came to stand for the value core of East Asian cultures and identity rather than a tradition one would choose over another: to be East Asian was to be Confucian. Although there is some merit in both views, they tend to obscure the religious aspects, functions, and dimensions of Confucianism. A number of Chinese scholars and scholars of Confucianism have sought to articulate these religious aspects or dimensions.

Chinese sociologist C. K. Yang went straight to the heart of the definitional problem, arguing that Confucianism represents a distinctive and alternative structural form of religion. Over against "institutional religion" with its theology, rituals, and an independent social organization and leadership, Confucianism represents a sort of "diffused religion." He writes, "The other [form] is diffused religion, with its theology, rituals, and organization intimately merged with the concepts and structures of secular institutions and other aspects of the social order. The beliefs and rituals of diffused religion develop their organizational system as an integral part of the organized social pattern."[16] Confucianism, Yang admits, is intricately embedded in the core of Chinese (and other East Asian) cultures; its theology is social ideology; its "churches" are schools, the family, and other social organizations; its leaders are parents, teachers, and social leaders. It is not separate or distinct as a religious institution, but pervades and gives religious meaning and function to the institutions and practices of society. For Confucianism, as Fingarette famously wrote, the secular is sacred.[17]

Yang's notion of diffused religion is an extremely helpful pedagogical device to challenge students (Christian or otherwise) to think critically about the divisions of secular and sacred in contemporary culture; there has been and continues to be blurring of the boundaries of secular and sacred stemming both from popular culture (the treatment of sports or pop culture heroes as cult figures) and from political leaders who seek to vest various aspects of government and society with "sacred" value. As an overtly diffused religion, Confucianism offers an alternative model for considering the complex interrelationships of religion and society on all levels.

Other scholars have sought to articulate the religious, spiritual, or transcendent dimensions of Confucianism. These efforts can help students in a Christian context begin to see Confucianism as religious. I offer four examples of this effort.

One of the most eminent and eloquent advocates of the transcendent and ethico-religious dimensions of Confucianism is Tu Wei-ming, a representative of the New Confucian movement teaching at Harvard University. The New Confucians, who will be discussed further later, are a group of twentieth- and twenty-first-century Chinese who have articulated a contemporary Confucianism, in dialogue with some Western philosophical traditions as well, as a rich philosophical and spiritual resource not only for East Asians but for the entire human community. Tu has often written eloquently on the transcendent or religious dimensions of Confucianism. I quote one source that demonstrates the tenor of his position:

> Actually, *jen* [co-humanity] is morality, but in Confucianism, especially in the Mencian version, morality is not merely confined to the ethical stage; it also conveys religious significance. Indeed Confucian ethics necessarily extends to the religious realm. . . .
>
> The Confucianists, especially in the Neo-Confucian tradition, therefore, refuse to accept the relevance of a personal God in the

transcendental sense but add a transcendental and religious dimension to the "subjectivity" of *jen* that is both functional and substantial in the self-decision-making process. It is understandable that Confucianism by its very nature does not assume the role of a formal religion, but performs the comparable functions of an ethico-religious system in Chinese society. Therefore, although it is acceptable not to call Confucianism a religion, it is completely unjustified to deny its religiousness.[18]

Tu argues that Confucian ethics "necessarily extends to the religious realm"; that is to say, ethical cultivation has a spiritual and transcendental dimension. Thus, Confucianism may not be formally a religion like other religions, but it is certainly religious.

Rodney Taylor, a scholar of the Confucian tradition, wrote an incisive and useful book, *The Religious Dimensions of Confucianism*. He puts it this way:

Confucianism is an ethical system and humanistic teaching. It is also, however, a tradition that bears a deep and profound sense of the religious, and any interpretation that ignores this quality has missed its quintessential feature. Rather than arguing that East Asian cultures have been largely free of the dominance of religion precisely because Confucianism was the salient form of ideology, one might well argue that East Asian cultures are in part religious because of this dominance. It is time for Confucianism to assume its rightful place amongst the major religious traditions of East Asian cultures and, in turn, the religious traditions of the world.[19]

Taylor goes on to explore major religious themes and spiritual practices of the Confucian tradition.

An excellent extended essay on the classical and Neo-Confucianism components of "The Religious Dimension of Confucianism" is included in John Berthrong's *All under Heaven*,[20] an invaluable resource for teaching Confucianism in Christian contexts.

More recently, Yao Xinzhong, in his influential introduction to Confucianism, reaffirmed that "Confucianism is not purely a secular tradition. It has a profound sense of religiosity and spirituality."[21] His book includes a chapter on ritual and religious practice in Confucianism, including its relationship to other religions in East Asia.

Confucianism was a complex tradition and certainly had important political, social, and educational aspects, but its ethico-religious and spiritual dimensions and functions in East Asian cultures mandate its study as one of the major East Asian religious traditions. The study of this tradition will positively challenge students to think more deeply about the nature and boundaries of religion, and its role in culture and society.

## 2. Doctrine versus Practice

The study of religion in the West, particularly in Christian contexts, tends to assume that one starts to learn another religion by seeking to understand the basic doctrines or creed of the religion, asking "what do Confucians believe?" In the case of Confucianism, as with a number of religions in the world, this is not the most productive starting point. There is no Confucian creed, no succinct statement of belief. Confucianism is most fundamentally a Way (dao), a way of life or practice, a path of self-cultivation. There is of course a worldview, a number of basic concepts or assumptions, that ground the Confucian Way, but one cannot appreciate Confucianism without attending to how the beliefs or concepts of Confucianism are embedded in a way of life, rather than seeing it as a philosophy or theology or even a system of ethics.

Yao Xinzhong's introduction to Confucianism, just introduced, offers an excellent balance and interweaving of practice and belief that conveys well the character of the Confucian tradition.

The centrality of practice and a way of life can also be taught through a careful study of *The Analects of Confucius*, with special attention to the role and importance of ritual.[22] The Neo-Confucian spiritual practice of quiet sitting (*jingzuo*) is explored in *The Confucian Way of Contemplation* by Rodney Taylor.[23]

Any study of Confucianism, especially in a Christian context, should give strong emphasis to practice. This emphasis not only honors the centrality of practice in the Confucian tradition but also offers many opportunities for students to learn aspects of Confucianism that might be beneficial in considering their own lives and practice.

## 3. Inclusive versus Exclusive

One challenge to teaching Confucianism in Christian contexts is the Christian assumption that religious affiliation is exclusive (one must choose the one true faith and spurn all others) with the attendant assumption that religions are distinct and isolated from one another. Both assumptions are obstacles to understanding mainstream East Asian religiosity and the role of Confucianism in East Asian societies. Confucianism is not and never was an isolated religion, but one strand of religious practice, value, and belief among many other religions and folk traditions. The development of Confucianism is the story of its interactions with the rich array of religious ideas and practices around it; Confucianism borrowed from and distinguished itself against the many folk and elite religious traditions of China and other East Asian societies. Moreover, East Asians practiced and participated in a wide range of traditions, sometimes serially (in different phases of life) and sometimes simultaneously (for different and complementary purposes). Instead of opting for one true faith, East Asians took advantage of the broad range of religious practices, ideas, and boons available to them.[24]

East Asian religious inclusivity has at least three pedagogical implications. First, Confucianism must be presented in the context of East Asian religions so that students can understand the immediate factors that have shaped its development. The pluralistic religious context varies according to culture and historical period, so teachers need to consider the broader context of any form of Confucianism that they introduce. Second, Confucian voices (authors or speakers) are almost never "pure" Confucians, but have a complex religious history and a range of religious influences. Not only can no one author or thinker represent the full range of Confucianism, but their articulation of Confucianism almost always carries echoes and resonances of (and resistance to) other religious influences and ideas. These resonances need to be acknowledged in the teaching of Confucianism. Third, when teaching Confucianism in Christian contexts, it is important to consider that virtually all Christians of East Asian background also carry the Confucian heritage to some degree; some have embraced Confucianism as part of their East Asian identity and seek to reconcile it with their Christian beliefs. They see no fundamental conflict between these parts of their selves. Others affirm the exclusivist claims of Christianity and resist embracing Confucianism but nonetheless retain certain values or attitudes as part of their cultural identity. For East Asians, Confucian-Christian dialogue is often and primarily intrapersonal—their attempts to understand and reconcile various strands of their identity.[25]

## 4. Dialogue with Contemporary Confucianism

As I have discussed, the process of coming to understand Confucianism as another religion is a hermeunetical process that is by its very nature conversational or dialogical. Students enter into a sustained, mutually correcting dialogue with texts, thinkers, or actual persons. Students in Christian contexts bring to this hermeneutical conversation an appetite for some sort of religious dialogue; they want to engage Confucians in conversations on issues that are important to them; they want to test and try to understand Confucianism as a religious possibility, and then articulate their own critical response. Another way to put this point is that in Christian contexts the interest in understanding other religions is to understand living faiths, what those religions mean (or have meant) to actual believers, and particularly what they mean to believers today.

The Confucian classics (the writings of Kongzi, Mengzi, and Xunzi) can be very pedagogically effective for introducing basic Confucian values, issues, and practices, but concentrating on the classics alone does not provide a contemporary voice of living Confucianism and carries the danger of "antiquating" the Confucian tradition, rendering it a quaint remnant of ancient times, dramatically and safely removed from the students in time, space, and cultural setting. I am not arguing against the classics; in fact, in the next section I suggest one highly effective pedagogical strategy for teaching the Confucian classics. I am arguing for including some more contemporary Confucian voices so that students understand that they are engaging a living tradition.

The contemporary voice of Confucianism is well represented by the New Confucians, a group of Confucian scholars also trained in Western philosophy, who have sought to revive and rearticulate the Confucian vision in the contemporary world. The New Confucians include thinkers with diverse agendas, although several of them signed a common manifesto in 1957.[26] Despite their diverse views, they all used tools and ideas gained from study of Western philosophy to identify and develop what they considered the key points of the Confucian tradition relevant to the modern world. The original group is usually considered to include Feng Youlan (Fung Yu-lan), Xu Fuguan (Hsü Fu-kuan), Mou Zongsan (Mou Tsung-san), and Qian Mu (Ch'ien Mu). In the next generation, often living and teaching in the West, are Liu Shuxian (Liu Shu-hsien), Cheng Zhongying (Cheng Chung-ying), Julia Ching, Du Weiming (Tu Wei-ming), Antonio Cua, Yu Yingshi (Yü Ying-shih), and Cai Renhou (Ts'ai Jen-hou), among others.[27] Unfortunately, not many of the primary writings of the original generation are available in English, but there are resources to provide significant contemporary voices.[28]

The New Confucian best published in English is without a doubt Du Weiming (Tu Wei-ming). I have already discussed several of his essays from *Humanity and Self-Cultivation*.[29] For teaching purposes, an outstanding resource is his wonderful essay, essentially a Confucian theological reading of the Confucian classic, "The Doctrine of the Mean."[30] This little book offers a contemporary philosophical and religious reflection on a Confucian classic that was central both to classical Confucianism and in the development of the Neo-Confucian vision. It offers students a sense of how the philosophical and religious vision evolved out of a close reading of the classics.

John Berthrong published an essay on the Confucian religious thought of Tu Weiming and of Mou Tsung-san (Mou Zongsan), another of the major New Confucians, in his *All under Heaven*. This work allows students to appreciate two very different interpretations on the religious implications of the Confucian tradition by two preeminent modern Confucians.[31] He follows this essay with a discussion of resonances between New Confucianism and process philosophy/theology, a subject he develops further in a forthcoming book.[32]

Another way to engage students in the living Confucian tradition is to study its engagement with contemporary issues. An excellent resource for such engagement is the volume on Confucianism and ecology in the Religions of the World and Ecology Series.[33] This volume includes two essays by Tu Wei-ming, one by Cheng Chung-ying, and others by eminent specialists in Chinese, Japanese, and Korean Confucianism, among them Robert Neville and John Berthrong, who consider themselves "Boston Confucians," that is to say, Western Christians who are also profoundly shaped by the Confucian tradition.

Including contemporary voices of Confucianism speaking to issues of concern to contemporary students facilitates the mutually correcting conversation that leads to understanding, including the reflexive movement of students reintegrating what they have learned into their understanding of life, religion, and even Christianity. They begin to see new possibilities for relationship and engagement with others and also begin to see their prior views and tradition in a fresh light.

The four challenges posed by Confucianism (its very different religiosity, the primacy of practice over doctrine, its inclusive approach to religious practice and affiliation, and its distinctive voice on contemporary issues) are all, at base, pedagogical opportunities. Confucianism by its distinctiveness stretches students into new and unfamiliar territory, inviting them to critically consider basic assumptions that have never before been challenged. Confucianism, by its engagement with contemporary issues, engages students in a global dialogue on issues of meaning, value, and justice in the contemporary world.

Learning Confucianism through Confucian Pedagogy

To this point, I have considered the pedagogical challenges, implications, and opportunities entailed in the nature and substance of the Confucian tradition. However, one of the great opportunities of teaching Confucianism, particularly in Christian contexts, is that the pedagogical practices and traditions of Confucianism are themselves a wonderful window onto the values of the tradition, values of great potential benefit for students in Christian contexts. Confucians perceived learning (in particular the study of the classics) as a way of moral cultivation, a path to sagehood, a sacred endeavor. The Confucian way of learning texts can be adopted or adapted to the classroom and considered in relationship to the *lectio divina* tradition of Christian sacred reading.[34]

Confucian learning of a text involved six steps:

## 1. Reading the Text Closely and Carefully, with Appropriate Commentaries

As is the case with the Christian biblical tradition, Chinese texts have come down to the present in a long commentarial tradition. Contemporary readers read the text "back through" a line of commentaries that comprise their community of interpretation. Thus, in reading the text, students not only engage the text but also are socialized into the views of the community. This is one reason why Tu Wei-ming's *Centrality and Commonality* is such a valuable resource; it is a contemporary translation and reading of the text by a contemporary interpreter of the tradition, who reads that text in a particular commentarial line.

## 2. Copying the Text

Copying texts in Chinese calligraphy using brush and ink was not only a mode of learning but a discipline of aesthetic and spiritual cultivation, a method of character formation. It can be helpful to have Western students learn some Chinese calligraphy (at least a few characters), either with a felt pen or with a Chinese brush and ink, to get a sense of what this practice entailed for Chinese learners. They can be invited to consider this practice in relation to the Christian monks who copied and illuminated biblical texts, reflecting on what "texts" meant in cultures where mass printing (not to say photocopying and faxing) were unavailable.

Copying is also a method for memorizing texts. Students could be assigned or invited to copy a chosen text in English daily, while maintaining a contemplative frame of mind, as a means of fixing their attention on the text and fixing the text in their minds.

## 3. Memorizing and Reciting the Text

In the premodern era, Confucian students learned texts by memorizing and reciting them; some forms of Confucian and Buddhist education in East Asia continue this practice. The Chinese word *nien* means to recite, to think, to remember. Recitation literally embodies the text, using the tongue and vocal chords to reproduce the text by means of the body and to hold the thought (recited sounds) of the text in the mind. Recitation and memorization thus makes the text part of one's internal landscape. This is one reason that traditional Chinese writings were full of allusions to classical texts without any references; such texts had been integrated into the mental landscape of the writers. Like copying, memorization is not meant to be simply a mechanical task but an internalization or absorption of the text.

## 4. Putting the Text into Practice

Confucian learning was never merely amassing information but was for the sake of and informed by practice. Confucian texts were guides to living, and they needed to be "understood" by putting them into practice. This point was made most famously by Neo-Confucian Wang Yangming: "Suppose we say that so-and-so knows filial piety and so-and-so knows brotherly respect. They must have actually practiced filial piety and brotherly respect before they can be said to know them. It will not do to say that they know filial piety and brotherly respect simply because they know them in words. Or take one's knowledge of pain. Only after one has experienced pain can one know pain. The same is true of cold or hunger. How can knowledge and action be separated?"[35]

Once the text has been memorized, the student tests or develops his or her understanding by putting it into practice. Putting learning into practice is the foundation of moral self-cultivation and of the establishment of a moral society. This vision is articulated in the Confucian classic "The Great Learning":

> The ancients who wished to manifest their clear character to the world would first bring order to their states. Those who wished to bring order to their states would first regulate their families. Those who wished to regulate their families would first cultivate their personal lives. Those who wished to cultivate their personal lives would first rectify their minds. Those who wished to rectify their minds would first make their wills sincere. Those who wished to make their wills sincere would first extend their knowledge. The extension of knowledge consists in the investigation of things. When things are investigated, knowledge is extended; when knowledge is extended, the will becomes sincere; when the will is sincere, the mind is rectified; when the mind is rectified, the personal life is cultivated; when the personal life is cultivated, the family will be regulated;

when the family is regulated, the state will be in order; and when the state is in order, there will be peace throughout the world. From the Son of Heaven down to the common people, all must regard cultivation of the personal life as the root or foundation.[36]

## 5. Reflection on What Is Learned in Practice

After students have put the text into practice, they reflect on what was actually learned, trying to gain a fuller understanding of the text.

## 6. Dialogue with a Teacher or Fellow Learners

Having learned the text and tested/developed it in practice, students now talk with a teacher or fellow students about what they have learned and receive feedback from others' understanding and internalization of the text.

For Western students learning a Confucian text, this could be followed by reflection and conversation about whether and in what ways the learning of the text is applicable to their own experiences and worldview.

The Confucian way of learning texts engages the students deeply in an intellectual, experiential, and reflective/interpretive encounter with the text and the tradition behind it. Such learning can also deepen the students' sense of how to learn, practice, and critically reappropriate their own tradition in a more thoughtful and intentional way. The Confucian model can be adapted as the individual and collective practice of a Christian community of interpretation.

In addition to using these methods to study a Confucian text or texts, students can be invited to also use the methods on a Western or biblical text, testing whether the pedagogical method would enhance their theological learning. Or at yet another level, the exercise can be extended to a comparative reflection on Confucian modes of learning for Confucian texts, and lectio divina for Christian sacred texts. The possibilities are very rich indeed.

## Conclusion

In this chapter, I argued that there are significant reasons for teaching Confucianism in Christian contexts and that the nature of these reasons requires a dialogical approach to teaching that develops students skills for understanding Confucianism.

I articulated a set of pedagogical principles to help students develop an understanding of another religion. Fundamental is maintaining a balance between the two poles of the learning process: (1) understanding Confucianism well and accurately in its own distinctive language and voice, and (2) critically reappropriating that understanding in light of the students' understanding of life in general, or religion, and of their own tradition in particular. Then I articulated the five threads of the hermeneutical learning process: (1) encountering difference, (2) responding from the students' location, (3) mutual give-and-take of conversation, (4) living out understanding, and (5) internalizing the learning process.

I addressed four ways that Confucianism is challenging to Christian learners because it challenges assumptions about religion: (1) the very different nature of Confucian "religiosity," (2) the primacy of practice over belief, (3) the inclusivity of Confucian religiosity and practice, and (4) the distinctive ways Confucians engage contemporary issues.

Finally, I explored a particularly promising approach to teaching Confucianism in Christian contexts, using Confucian pedagogical approaches to learning classical texts as self-cultivation. This approach, I suggested, can be adapted for students to study Chinese texts or both Chinese and Western texts. It can also be used in comparison and contrast with the Christian pedagogy of *lectio divina*.

Confucianism can be taught effectively and well in Christian contexts to the significant benefit of the students.

NOTES

1. Rudyard Kipling, *The Ballad of East and West* (1889). Actually, the stanza continues, "There is neither East nor West, border, nor breed nor birth / When two strong men stand face to face, though they come from the ends of the earth." The rest of the stanza is seldom quoted. However, even the full stanza demonstrates that Kipling had no conception of the permeability, interconnectedness, and global spread of cultures.

2. See, for instance, Peter L. Berger and Hsin-huang Michael Hsiao, eds., *In Search of an East Asian Development Model* (Brunswick, N.J.: Transaction Books, 1988).

3. A U.S. House of Representatives study of religious demography and religious freedom in East Asia yielded the following statistics. As of 2003, 53.3 million Christians in the People's Republic of China, 540,000 in Hong Kong, 787, 814 in Taiwan, 1.143 million in Japan, 11,711,066 in South Korea, and 600,000 in Singapore. The number of East Asian Christians has grown in the past ten years, particularly in the People's Republic of China. Available online at www http://foreignaffairs.house.gov/archives/109/20429.pdf, accessed 5 June 2007.

4. For instance, see Heup Young Kim, *Christ and the Dao* (Hong Kong: Christian Conference of Asia, 2003) and Joseph Loya, Wanli Ho, and Chang-shin Jih, *The Tao of Jesus—An Experiment in Interfaith Understanding* (New York: Paulist Press, 1998).

5. Paolo Freire, *Pedagogy of the Oppressed* (New York: Herder and Herder, 1970).

6. John Dewey, *Democracy and Education* (New York: Free Press, 1916).

7. bell hooks, *Teaching to Transgress: Education as the Practice of Freedom* (New York: Routledge, 1994); Maxine Green, *Releasing the Imagination: Essays on Education, The Arts, and Social Change* (San Francisco: Jossey-Bass, 1995).

8. Mikhail Bakhtin, *Problems of Dostoyevsky's Poetics* (Minneapolis: University of Minnesota Press, 1984), p. 68, cited in Gavin Flood, *Beyond Phenomenology: Rethinking the Study of Religion* (London: Cassell, 1999), p. 111.

9. Edward Farley, *The Fragility of Knowledge: Theological Education in the Church and the University* (Philadelphia: Fortress Press, 1988), p. 128.

10. To students this hermeneutical process can sound fairly abstract. I have sometimes explained it using the example of the challenge of men and women trying to understand each other's views of the world, given their very different socializations and their different biological constitutions. Although we can never completely close the gender gap, sustained and mutually corrective conversations can lead to significant insights and better (although always imperfect) mutual understanding.

11. Judith A. Berling, *Understanding Other Religious Worlds: A Guide for Interreligious Understanding* (Maryknoll, N.Y.: Orbis Books, 2004). See particularly chapter 5 on the process of interreligious learning and chapter 6 on classroom learning.

12. Interreligious learning or education is a relatively new field in the United States, but it is well established in Europe because several countries mandate interreligious learning in public secondary education. I attended a conference on Interreligious Learning at University of Leuven, Belgium, January 5–15, 2005. A conference volume was published in January 2007. For a volume by a leading European authority, see Hans-Georg Ziebertz, *Religious Education in a Plural Western Society: Problems and Challenges* (Munster: Lit Verlag, 2003).

13. Clifford Geertz, *Local Knowledge: Further Essays in Interpretive Anthropology*, 2nd ed. (New York: Basic Books, 2000), p. 58.

14. Herbert Fingarette, *Confucius—The Secular as Sacred* (New York: Harper and Row, 1972), and David L. Hall and Roger T. Ames, *Thinking through Confucius* (Albany: State University of New York Press, 1987).

15. Hans Küng and Julia Ching, *Christianity and Chinese Religions* (New York: Doubleday, 1989), p. 63.

16. C. K. Yang, *Religion in Chinese Society: A Study of Contemporary Social Functions of Religion and Some of their Historical Factors* (Berkeley: University of California Press, 1967), p. 20.

17. Fingarette, Confucius.

18. Tu Wei-ming, *Humanity and Self-Cultivation: Essays in Confucian Thought* (Berkeley, Calif.: Asian Humanities Press, 1979), pp. 8–9.

19. Rodney L. Taylor, *The Religious Dimensions of Confucianism* (Albany: State University of New York Press, 1990), p. 2.

20. John L. Berthrong, *All under Heaven: Transforming Paradigms in Confucian-Christian Dialogue* (Albany: State University of New York Press, 1994), pp. 69–101.

21. Xinzhong Yao, *An Introduction to Confucianism* (Cambridge: Cambridge University Press, 2000), p. 155.

22. See D. C. Lau, *Confucius, The Analects* (Middlesex: Penguin Books, 1979); Hall and Ames, *Thinking through Confucius*; and Tu, *Humanity and Self-Cultivation*, "Part One: Classical Confucian Ideas."

23. Rodney Taylor, *The Confucian Way of Contemplation* (Columbia: University of South Carolina Press, 1988).

24. On the patterns of inclusive religious participation, see Judith A. Berling, *A Pilgrim in Chinese Culture: Negotiating Religious Diversity* (Maryknoll, N.Y.: Orbis Books, 1997) and Valerie Hansen, *Changing Gods in Medieval China 1127–1276* (Princeton, N.J.: Princeton University Press, 1990).

25. For some examples of Confucian-Christian dialogue by authors who are both Confucian and Christian, see *Ching Feng: A Journal of Christianity and Chinese Religion and Culture* 1, no. 1 (Spring 2000), special issue on Confucian Christian dialogue.

26. Chang Hao, "New Confucianism and the Intellectual Crisis of Contemporary China," in Charlotte Furth, ed., *The Limits of Change: Essays on Conservative Alternatives in Republican China* (Cambridge, Mass.: Harvard University Press, 1976).

27. Berthrong, *All under Heaven*, p. 37.

28. On the New Confucians, see John Makeham, ed., *New Confucianism, A Critical Examination* (Houndmills: Palgrave Macmillan, 2003); Liu Shu-hsien, *Essentials of Contemporary Neo-Confucian Philosophy* (Westport, Conn.: Praeger, 2003); Cheng Chung-ying and Nicholas Bunnin, eds., *Contemporary Chinese Philosophy* (Malden, Mass.: Blackwell, 2002).

29. See Tu, *Humanity and Self-Cultivation*.

30. Tu Wei-ming, *Centrality and Commonality: An Essay on Confucian Religiousness* (Albany: State University of New York Press, 1989).

31. Berthrong, *All under Heaven*, pp. 103–31.

32. John L. Berthrong, *Expanding Processes* (Albany: State University of New York Press, submitted).

33. Mary Evelyn Tucker and John Berthrong, eds., *Confucianism and Ecology: The Interrelations of Heaven, Earth, and Humans* (Cambridge, Mass.: Harvard Center for the Study of World Religions, 1998).

34. See Michael Casey, *Sacred Reading: The Ancient Art of Lectio Divina* (Liguori, Mo.: Triumph Books, 1996).

35. Wang Yang-ming, *Instructions for Practical Living*, p. 1:5b–8a, cited in Wing-tsit Chan, *A Source Book in Chinese Philosophy* (Princeton, N.J.: Princeton University Press, 1963), p. 669.

36. "The Great Learning," trans. in Chan, *Source Book of Chinese Philosophy*, pp. 86–87.

# Index

*Accounts of Exemplary Women* (*Lienü zhuan* 列女傳), 41, 45, 46–47
Adorno, Theodor, 190
Ames, Roger, 175, 209
*Analects* (*Lunyu* 論語), 5, 27–29, 31, 33–35, 36–37, 40, 48, 63, 137, 142, 163, 176, 187–198, 215
   1:9, 196
   3:8, 32–33, 34
   3:26, 29
   4:25, 5
   6:3, 35
   10:3, 29
   10:7, 29
   10:9, 29
   12:1, 195
   15:5, 196
   17:2, 197
ancestors. *See* filiality
Aristotle, 193
Augustine, 192
Austin, John, 176

Bakhtin, Mikhail, 206–207
Berger, Peter, 177
Berthrong, John, 175, 214, 218
Bloom, Allan, 192–194

Bo Mou, 176
Brooks, E. Bruce and A. Taeko, 195, 198
Buddhism, 5, 6, 8, 10–11, 12, 13–14, 15, 61, 108, 109, 112–116, 123, 125, 130–131, 146, 158, 162, 163–165, 167, 172, 174, 203, 204, 211, 219
Bultmann, Rudolf, 190

Cai Renhou (Ts'ai Jen-hou), 217
centeredness (*zhong* 中 [*chung*]), 12, 13
Chan Wing-tsit, 158, 174
Chang, Carsun, 161
Chang Hao, 174–175
change, principle of (*yi* 易 [*i*]), 12, 13, 65
chastity (*zhen* 貞 [*chen*]), 48, 51
*cheng* 誠 (*ch'eng*). *See* sincerity
Cheng Hao 程顥 (Ch'eng Hao), 11, 122–123, 127, 130–139, 142, 146, 164, 173
Cheng Yi 程頤 (Ch'eng I), 11, 62, 109, 111, 123, 127, 130–139, 142–143, 146, 164, 173
Cheng Zhongying (Cheng Chung-ying), 217–218

# INDEX

Ching, Julia, 7, 217
Chong Kim-chong, 176
*Chunqiu* 春秋. See *Spring and Autumn Annals*
Christianity, 4–6, 7, 15, 16, 55, 73, 75, 108, 161–162, 167, 203–222
*Classic of Changes* (*Yijing* 易經 [*I-ching*]), 34, 55, 59, 61–75, 117, 124–127, 137, 144
*Classic of Odes* (*Shijing* 詩經 [*Shih-ching*]), 27, 31–34, 35, 37, 117, 137, 144
Confucianism
   and Buddhism, 11, 12, 13–14, 61, 112–116, 123, 130–131, 146, 158, 163–165, 167, 172, 174, 211
   and Christianity, 4–6, 16, 73, 75, 161–162, 167, 203–222
   and Daoism, 10, 12, 13–14, 63, 112–114, 116–117, 123, 130–131, 146, 163–165, 195–196, 211
   and economic success, 5, 177–179, 204
   and Platonism, 161–162, 170, 174
   and the term *Ru* 儒, 4, 40, 41, 50, 86
   and the modern West, 5, 7, 14, 16, 47, 157–158, 162, 165–172, 180
   and women, 14, 45–47
   as Chinese government ideology, 8–9, 10, 41, 63, 107, 118–119, 120–123, 141, 145–146, 157
   "epochs" of, 9–14, 15, 160–161
   in Boston, 175, 218
   in Japan, 11, 14, 16, 159, 165, 172–174, 211, 218
   in Korea, 5, 6, 11, 14, 16, 159, 211, 218
   in Singapore, 5, 159, 176
   in Taiwan, 158–159, 166
   in Vietnam, 14
   "Neo-," 9, 11–14, 15, 42, 55–75, 107–147, 159, 163, 172–174, 217, 220
   "New," 5, 14, 159–180, 213–214, 217–218
   philosophical dimensions of, 169–176, 179–180, 187–198
   religious dimensions of, 3–9, 49–50, 59, 73–75, 101–104, 147, 163–164, 181 n. 12, 212–218
Confucius
   as historical figure, 9–10, 11, 15, 27–30, 32–33, 35–37, 40, 67, 69, 85, 112, 115, 138, 144, 160, 161, 163–164, 166, 172, 176, 187–198, 217
   Chinese name of, 4
   cult of, 58–59
   origin of Latinized name, 4
*Confucius Discusses the Odes* (*Kongzi shilun* 孔子詩論), 32, 34
Cua, Antonio S., 176, 187–188, 217

*Da Dai Liji* 大戴禮記. See *Elder Dai's Record of Ritual*
Dai Zhen 戴震 (Tai Chen), 13
*dao* 道 (*tao*). See Way
*Daodejing* 道德經 (*Tao-te-ching*). See *Laozi*
Daoism, 5, 8, 10, 12, 13–14, 15, 63, 69, 112–114, 116–117, 123–125, 130–131, 146, 163–165, 195–196, 211
*daoxue* 道學 (*tao-hsüeh*). See Confucianism, Neo-
*Daxue* 大學 (*Ta-hsüeh*). See *Great Learning*
*de* 德 (*te*). See virtue
de Bary, Theodore, 174–175
Derrida, Jacques, 188, 190, 193, 194, 197
Descartes, René, 172, 175–176
Dewey, John, 206
divination, 55–75
*Doctrine of the Mean* (*Zhongyong* 中庸 [*Chung-yung*]), 8, 63, 66, 137, 142, 144, 164, 217
Dong Zhongshu 董仲舒 (Tung Chung-shu), 10

Ebrey, Patricia, 60
*Elder Dai's Record of Ritual* (*DaDai Liji* 大戴禮記), 28–30
emotion [*qing* 情 [*ch'ing*]), 13
Epictetus, 198
*Ershisi xiao* 二十四孝. See *Twenty-Four Filial Exemplars*

Evidential Learning (*hanxue* 漢學 [*han-hsüeh*]), 13

faithfulness (*xin* 信 [*hsin*]), 8, 86
*Family Rituals* (*Jia li* 家禮 [*Chia-li*]), 61
Fang Zhaohui, 189
Farley, Edward, 207
Feng Youlan 馮友蘭 (Fung Yu-lan), 159, 171–172, 174, 189, 217
filiality (*xiao* 孝 [*hsiao*]), 6, 29, 41–44, 48, 51, 57, 97, 209–210
Fingarette, Herbert, 59, 74, 176, 209, 213
Five Classics (*Wujing* 五經), 62–63, 139
Five Dynasties period, 117–118
*Five Kinds of Action* (*Wuxing* 五行), 34, 36
Flood, Gavin, 206–207
Four Books (*Sishu* 四書), 63, 137, 139, 142
Freire, Paolo, 206

gentleman (*junzi* 君子 [*chün-tzu*]), 34
Geertz, Clifford, 208
*Great Learning* (*Daxue* 大學 [*Ta-hsüeh*]), 63, 74, 108, 116, 124, 137, 142–143, 166–167, 220
Greene, Maxine, 206

Hall, David, 175, 209
Han 漢 dynasty, 8, 10, 29, 30, 41, 63, 85, 112, 114, 163
Han Fei 韓非, 4
Han Yu 韓愈, 11, 111–118, 123, 127–128, 130, 134, 138, 146–147
*hanxue* 漢學 (*han-hsüeh*). *See* Evidential Learning
harmony (*he* 和 [*ho*]), 12, 13
*he* 和 (*ho*). *See* harmony
heart-mind (*xin* 心 [*hsin*]), 8, 13, 35, 65, 89–90, 92, 95–96, 100, 143–144
Heaven (*Tian* 天), 5, 49–50, 74–75, 89, 101–104, 132, 163–164, 166–167
Hegel, Georg Wilhelm Friedrich, 162, 167–168, 174
Heidegger, Martin, 188
hooks, bell, 206

Hu Shi 胡適 (Hu Shih), 30–31, 158, 169–171, 175, 189
Huang Zongxi 黃宗羲 (Huang Tsung-hsi), 13
human nature (*xing* 性 [*hsing*]), 13, 70, 86–95, 132, 197
humanness (*ren* 仁 [*jen*]), 8, 41, 48, 69, 74, 86, 164, 194, 213–214
Hume, David, 178
Huntington, Samuel, 180
Husserl, Edmund, 187

Islam, 5, 7, 14, 203
Itō Jinsai 伊藤仁斎, 172–174

Jaspers, Karl, 175
*Jia li* 家禮 [*Chia-li*]). *See Family Rituals*
Jia Yi 賈誼 (Chia I), 30
*Jinsi lu* 近思錄. *See Reflections on Things at Hand*
Judaism, 5, 7, 15, 55, 203
*junzi* 君子 (*chün-tzu*). *See* gentleman

Kant, Immanuel, 162, 170, 172, 174
King, Ambrose, 177
Kipling, Rudyard, 204
Kongzi 孔子. *See* Confucius
*Kongzi shilun* 孔子詩論. *See Confucius Discusses the Odes*

Lacan, Jacques-Marie-Émile, 190
*Laozi* 老子 (*Lao-tzu*), 112, 113–114, 192
Legge, James, 3, 73
Leibniz, Gottfried Wilhelm, 192
Levenson, Joseph, 175
*li* 禮. *See* ritual
Liang Shumin 梁漱溟, 158.
*Liji* 禮記 (*Li-chi*). *See Records of Ritual*
*li* 理. *See* principle
*Lienü zhuan* 列女傳. *See Accounts of Exemplary Women*
*lixue* 理學 (*li-hsüeh*). *See* Zhu Xi (Chu Hsi)
Li Ao 李翺, 11
Lin Shuen-fu, 141

Liu Xiang 劉向 (Liu Hsiang), 45, 47
Liu Zongyuan 柳宗元 (Liu Tsung-yuan), 11
loyalty (*zhong* 忠 [*chung*]), 48, 51, 163
Lu Xun 魯迅 (Lu Hsün), 43–44, 107
*Lunyu* 論語. See *Analects*

Marxism, 4–6, 190
May Fourth Movement, 107–108, 157–158, 165, 169
Mencius (*Mengzi* 孟子 [*Meng-tzu*]) [text], 10, 11, 15, 35, 40, 45–46, 62, 63, 69, 74, 85–104, 111, 127, 130, 134, 137, 139, 143, 160, 161, 164, 176, 195, 217
   2A2, 90, 96
   2A6, 90, 95
   2B13, 101
   3A4, 92
   3A5, 92
   3B9, 89
   4B19, 93
   4B26, 95
   6A2, 86, 95
   6A7, 89, 90, 91, 92, 95
   6A8–15, 92
   6A8, 89, 91
   6A14, 92, 93
   6A15, 93
   6B15, 101
   7A1, 66, 70, 101
   7A3, 101
   7A4, 101
   7B14, 74
   7B24, 92
Mengzi 孟子 (Meng-tzu) [person]. See *Mencius*
Min Ziqian 閔子騫 (Min Tzu-ch'ien), 41
mind. See heart-mind
Ming 明 dynasty, 11–12, 13, 61, 98, 159, 163–164
Mou Zongsan 牟宗三 (Mou Tsung-san), 108, 158–162, 164–168, 172, 174, 177, 217–218

Mozi 墨子 (Mo-tzu), 112, 189, 192, 195, 196

nature. See human nature
Neo-Confucianism. See Confucianism, Neo-Confucianism
Neville, Robert, 175, 218
Nietzsche, Friedrich, 197, 198
Nylan, Michael, 32, 188, 193

Ogyū Sorai 荻生徂徠, 172–174
oracle bones, 57–59
*Original Way, The* (*Yuan dao* 元道), 111–118, 123, 127, 130, 137

Plato, 161–162, 170, 174, 189, 191, 192, 193, 194
Plotinus, 192
Pound, Ezra, 32
principle (li 理), 12, 13, 70, 131–136, 144, 147, 161

qi 氣 (*ch'i*). See vital energy
Qian Mu 錢穆, 7, 159, 217
Qin 秦 (Ch'in) dynasty, 10, 44, 112
Qing 清 (Ch'ing) dynasty, 13, 61, 165
*qing* 情 (*ch'ing*). See emotion

*Records of the Grand Historian* (*Shiji* 史記 [*Shih-chi*]), 45
*Records of Ritual* (*Liji* 禮記 [*Li-chi*]), 30, 36, 60, 63, 137, 144
*Reflections on Things at Hand* (*Jinsi lu* 近思錄), 142, 145
religion, definitions of, 7, 73, 181 n. 12, 205, 212–215
ren 仁 (*jen*). See humanness
Ricci, Matteo, 193
righteousness (*yi* 義 [*i*]), 8, 41, 48, 74, 86, 163
ritual (li 禮), 6, 8, 28–31, 36–37, 41, 48, 55–75, 85–86, 93–94, 97, 163
Rorty, Richard, 175, 190
Ryle, Gilbert, 176
Ru 儒. See Confucianism

sacrifice, 6, 28–29, 55–62
sages (shengren 聖人), 65, 69, 72–73, 74, 93, 97, 100, 108, 139
Salkever, Stephen, 188, 193
Sartre, Jean-Paul, 187
Saussy, Haun, 193
Schwartz, Benjamin, 174–175, 198
Shang 商 dynasty, 55–57, 59, 115, 163
Shao Yong 邵雍, 11, 63
shen 神. See spirit(s)
shengren 聖人. See sages
Shiji 史記 (Shih-chi). See Records of the Grand Historian
Shijing 詩經 (Shih-ching). See Classic of Odes
Shun Kwong-loi, 176
Sima Guang 司馬光 (Ssu-ma Kuang), 62, 121, 123
Sima Qian 司馬遷 (Ssu-ma Ch'ien), 45
sincerity (cheng 誠 [ch'eng]), 12, 13, 66, 69
Sishu 四書. See Four Books
Smith, Wilfred Cantwell, 3
Sombart, Werner, 178–179
Song 宋 dynasty, 8, 10, 11–12, 13, 15, 16, 55, 60–75, 109, 118–147, 159, 163–164
spirit(s) (shen 神), 12, 13, 36, 65, 67, 69, 70, 102
Spring and Autumn Annals (Chunqiu 春秋), 4, 12, 65, 117, 137
Streng, Frederick, 73
Su Shi 蘇軾 (Su Shih), 121–123
Sui 隋 dynasty, 114

Tang 唐 dynasty, 11, 109–117, 130, 146
Tang Junyi 唐君毅 (T'ang Chün-i), 158–162, 172
Taoism. See Daoism
Taylor, Rodney, 7, 214, 215
Tian 天. See Heaven
Tu Wei-ming, 7, 8, 9, 14, 147, 160–161, 177, 213–214, 217–219
Twenty-Four Filial Exemplars (Ershisi xiao 二十四孝), 40–51

Van Norden, Bryan, 194
virtue (de 德 [te]), 35–36, 61, 95–101, 113–114
vital energy (qi 氣 [ch'i]), 12, 13, 35–36, 62, 65, 95–97, 131, 135–136, 143–144, 147, 164

Wang Anshi 王安石 (Wang An-shih), 119–120
Wang Bi 王弼 (Wang Pi), 10
Wang Fuzhi 王夫之 (Wang Fu-chih), 13
Wang Yangming 王陽明, 12, 13, 75, 98, 160–161, 165, 220
Way (dao 道 [tao]), 7, 12–3, 67, 71, 87, 89, 98, 103, 113–114, 132, 142, 160–161, 174, 215
Weber, Max, 5, 169, 176–179, 204
Western Inscription (Ximing 西銘 [Hsi-ming]), 127–129, 132
Whitehead, Alfred North, 175
wisdom (zhi 智 [chih]), 8, 86
Wittgenstein, Ludwig, 187
Wujing 五經. See Five Classics
Wuxing 五行. See Five Kinds of Action

Ximing 西銘 (Hsi-ming). See Western Inscription
xiao 孝 (hsiao). See filiality
xin 心 (hsin). See heart-mind
xing 性 (hsing). See human nature
xinxue 心學 (hsin-hsüeh). See Wang Yangming
xin 信 (hsin). See faithfulness
Xiong Shili 熊十力 (Hsiung Shih-li), 158–159, 166–168
Xu Fuguan 徐复观 (Hsu Fu-kwan), 158, 161, 164, 217
Xun Yue 荀悅 (Hsün Yueh), 10
Xunzi 荀子 (Hsün-tzu), 10, 11, 15, 30, 35, 40, 69, 85–104, 134, 187, 196, 217

Yan Hui 顏回 (Yen Hui), 35, 37, 40, 41
Yang, C. K., 7, 212–213
Yang Xiong 揚雄 (Yang Hsiong), 10
Yang Zhu 楊朱 (Yang Chu), 88–89, 112
Yao, Xinzhong, 214, 215

*yi* 義 *(i). See* righteousness
*yi* 易 *(i). See* change, principle of
*Yijing* 易經 *(I-ching). See Classic of Changes*
Yu, Ying-shih 余英时, 159, 162, 174–175, 217
*Yuan dao* 元道. *See Original Way, The*
Yuan 元 dynasty, 11–12, 61

Zengzi 曾子 (Tseng-tzu), 41, 196
Zhang Zai 張載 (Chang Tsai), 11, 12, 123–124, 127–130, 132, 142, 146, 164–165
*zhen* 貞 *(chen). See* chastity
*zhi* 智 *(chih). See* wisdom
*zhong* 中 *(chung). See* centeredness
*zhong* 忠 *(chung). See* loyalty

*Zhongyong* 中庸 *(Chung-yung). See Doctrine of the Mean*
Zhou 周 dynasty, 4, 5, 11–12, 15, 36, 59, 64, 69, 89, 112, 115, 119, 163–164, 195
Zhou Dunyi 周敦頤 (Chou Tun-i), 11, 62, 63, 123–129, 138, 142, 146, 164–165
*Zhouyi* 周易. *See Classic of Changes*
Zhu Xi 朱熹 (Chu Hsi), 7, 11–12, 16, 42, 55, 62–75, 109, 127, 141–147, 164–165, 172–175
*Zhuangzi* 莊子 *(Chuang-tzu)*, 136, 188, 190, 192, 196
Zisi 子思 (Tzu-ssu), 144
Zixia 子夏 (Tzu-hsia), 33–34, 41
Ziyou 子游 (Tzu-yu), 41